W9-CQO-558

the death of Buffy THE VAMPIRE SLAYER™

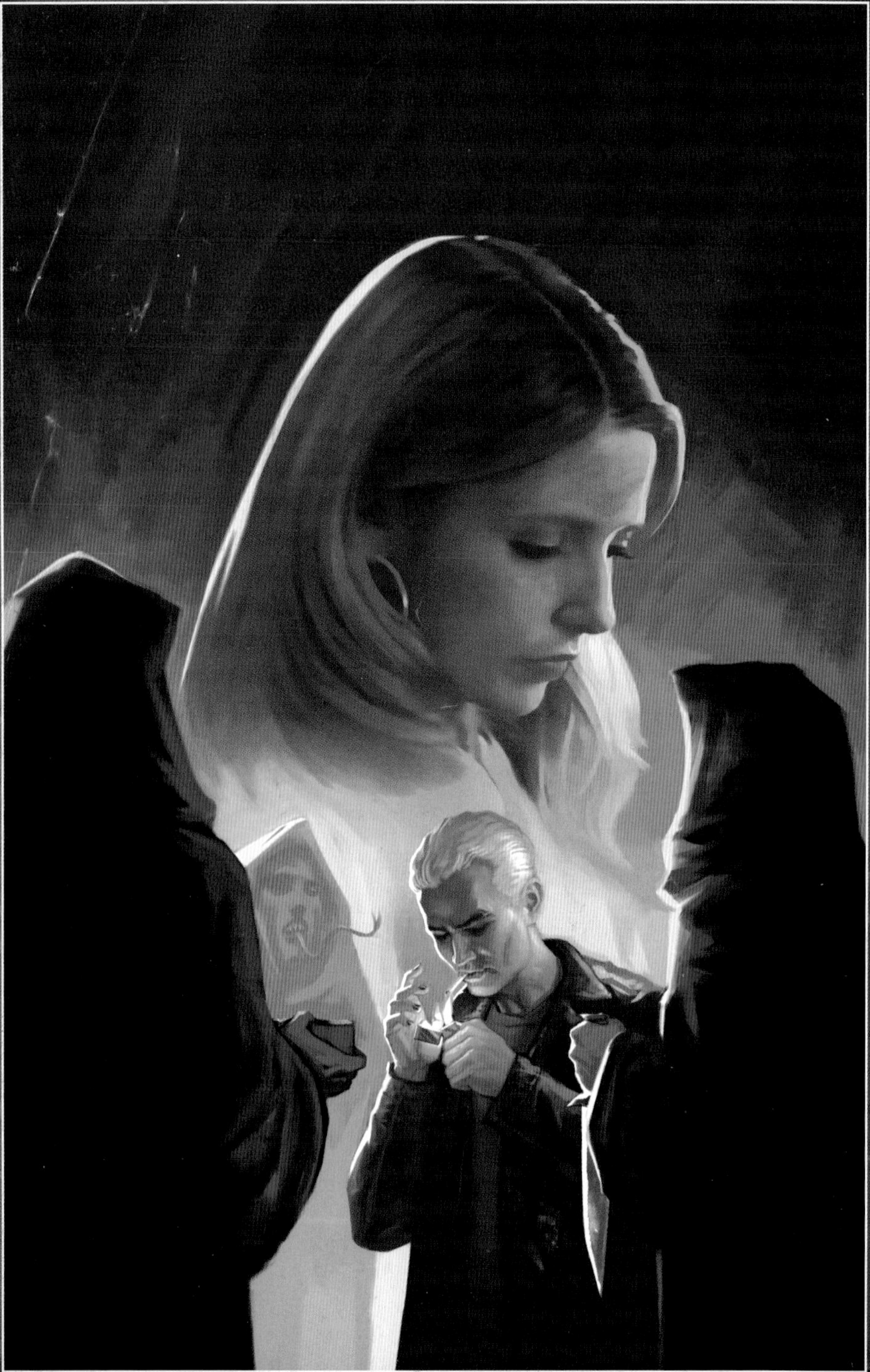

PAUL LEE *and* BRIAN HORTON

Buffy the Vampire Slayer™

the death of Buffy

based on the television series created by
JOSS WHEDON

writers **TOM FASSBENDER & JIM PASCOE,**
and **FABIAN NICIEZA**

penciller **CLIFF RICHARDS**

inkers **JOE PIMENTEL & WILL CONRAD**

colorist **DAVE MCCAIG**

letterer **CLEM ROBINS**

cover art **PAUL LEE & BRIAN HORTON**

This story takes place after Buffy the Vampire Slayer's fifth season.

Pacific Grove Public Library

Y

publisher
MIKE RICHARDSON

editor
SCOTT ALLIE
with MICHAEL CARRIGLITTO

designer
LANI SCHREIBSTEIN

art director
MARK COX

special thanks to
DEBBIE OLSHAN AT FOX LICENSING
AND DAVID CAMPITI AT GLASS HOUSE GRAPHICS

Buffy the Vampire Slayer™: The Death of Buffy. Published by Dark Horse Comics, Inc., 10956 SE Main Street, Milwaukie, OR, 97222. Buffy the Vampire Slayer™ & © 2002 Twentieth Century Fox Film Corporation. All rights reserved. TM designates a trademark of Twentieth Century Fox Film Corporation. The stories, institutions, and characters in this publication are fictional. Any resemblance to actual persons, living or dead, events, institutions, or locales, without satiric intent, is purely coincidental. No portion of this book may be reproduced, by any means, without express written permission from the copyright holder. Dark Horse Comics® and the Dark Horse logo are trademarks of Dark Horse Comics, Inc., registered in various categories and countries. All rights reserved.

PUBLISHED BY
DARK HORSE COMICS, INC.
10956 SE MAIN STREET
MILWAUKIE, OR 97222

FIRST EDITION
AUGUST 2002
ISBN: 1 - 56971 - 748 - 6

1 3 5 7 9 10 8 6 4 2

PRINTED IN CHINA

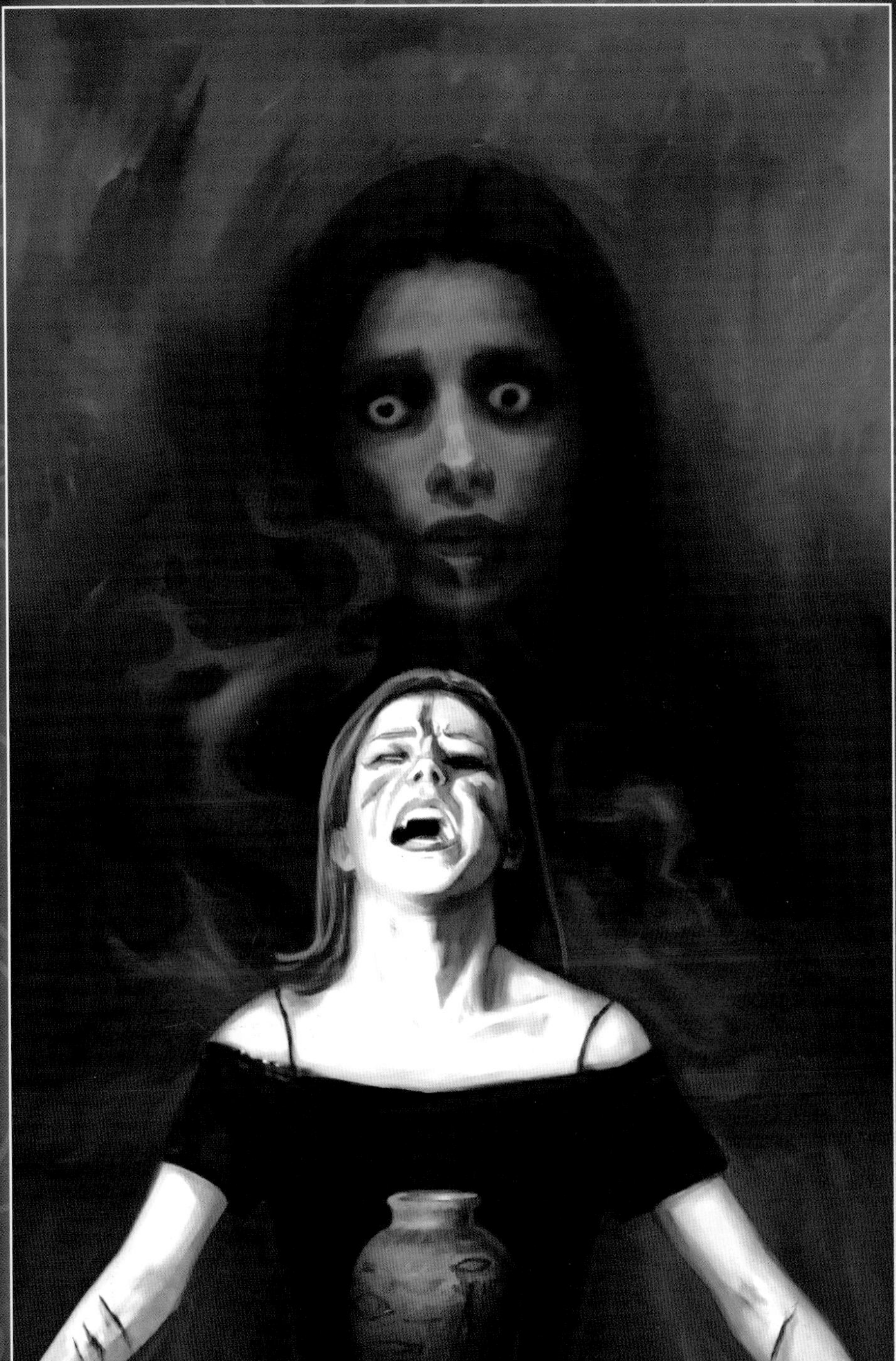

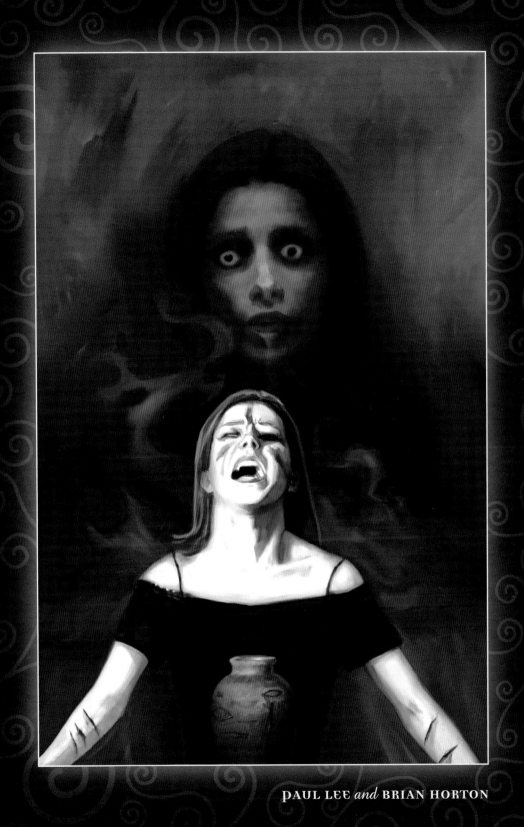

PAUL LEE *and* BRIAN HORTON

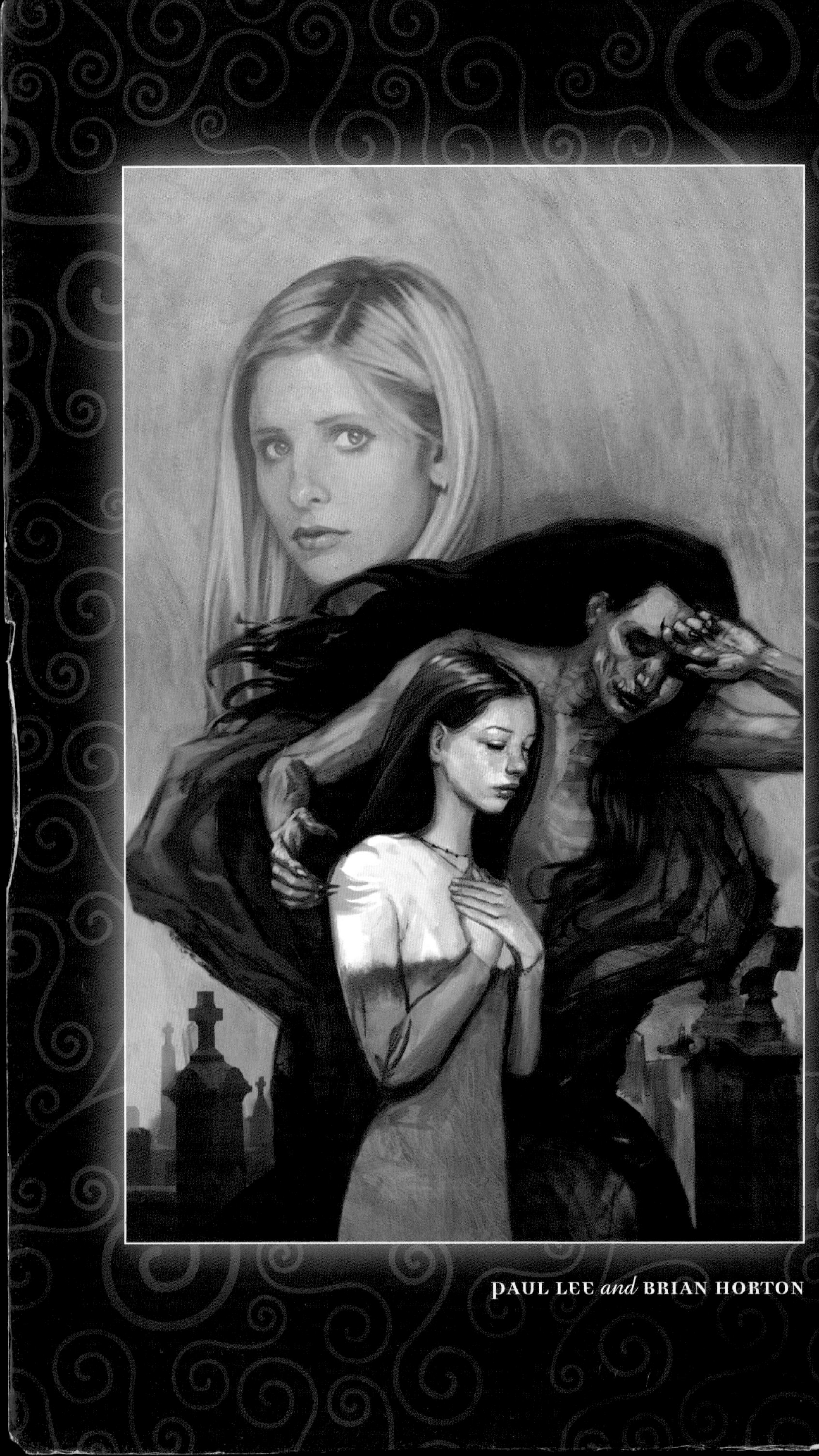

PAUL LEE *and* BRIAN HORTON

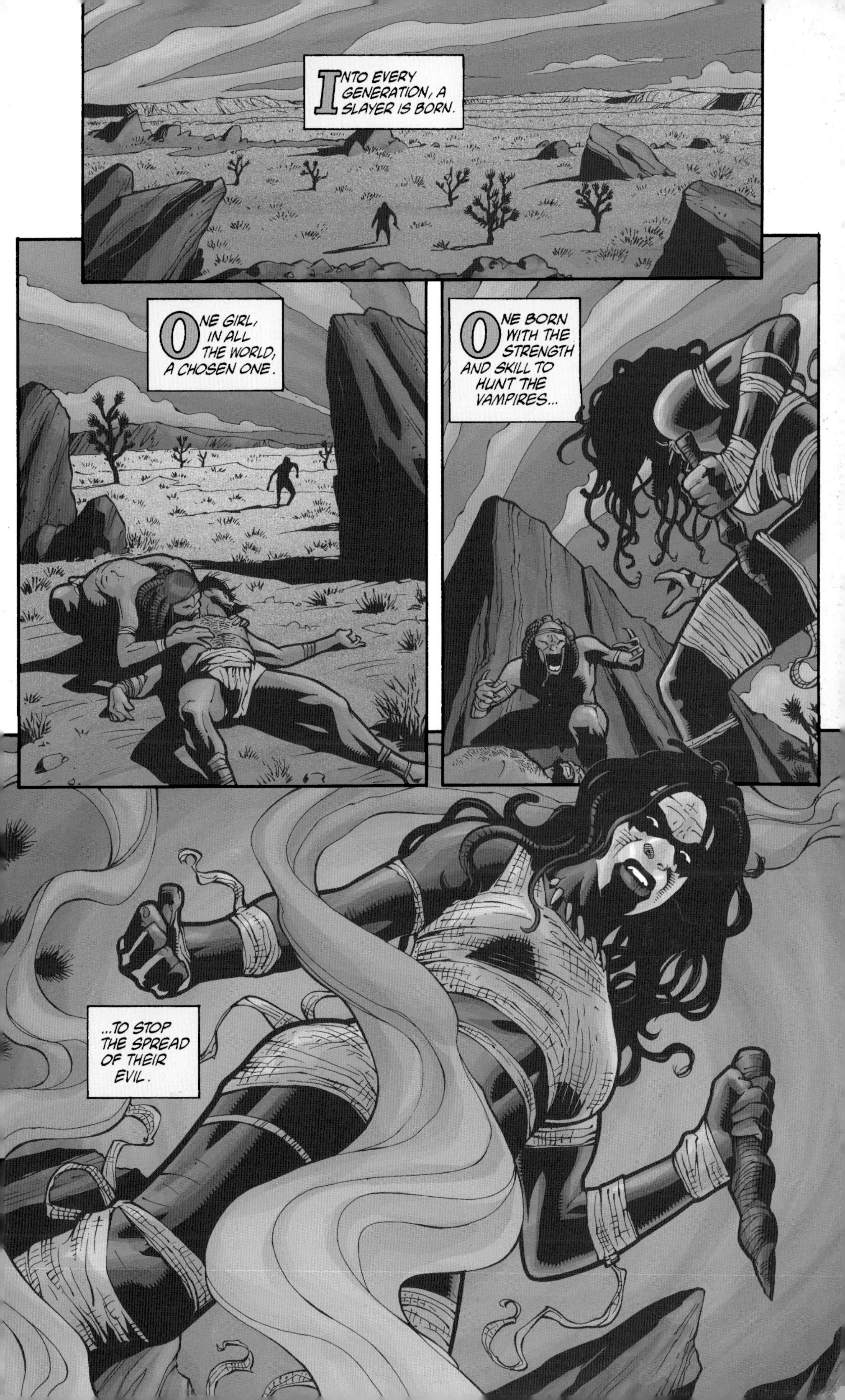
INTO EVERY GENERATION, A SLAYER IS BORN.
ONE GIRL, IN ALL THE WORLD, A CHOSEN ONE.
ONE BORN WITH THE STRENGTH AND SKILL TO HUNT THE VAMPIRES...
...TO STOP THE SPREAD OF THEIR EVIL.

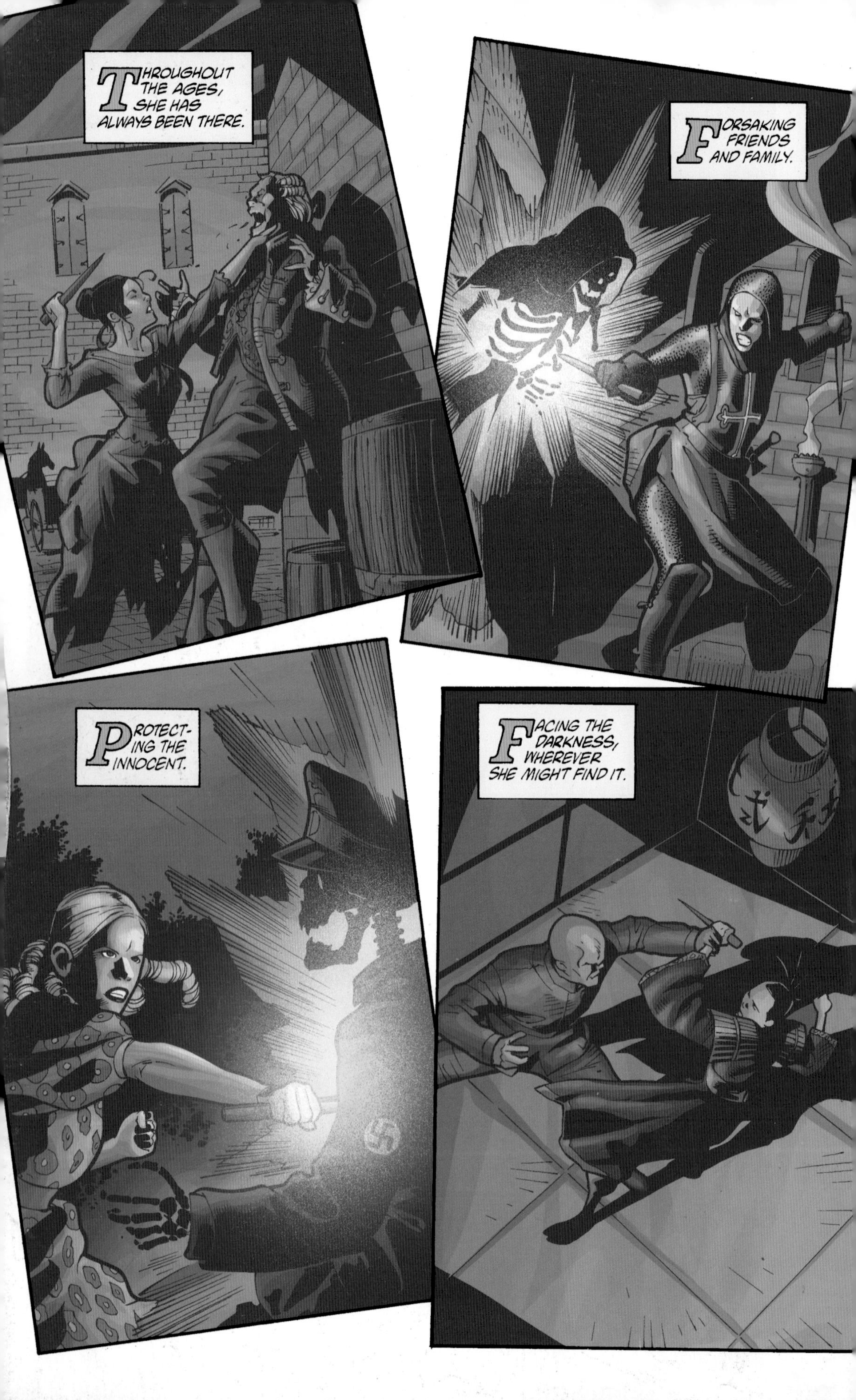
THROUGHOUT THE AGES, SHE HAS ALWAYS BEEN THERE.
FORSAKING FRIENDS AND FAMILY.
PROTECTING THE INNOCENT.
FACING THE DARKNESS, WHEREVER SHE MIGHT FIND IT.

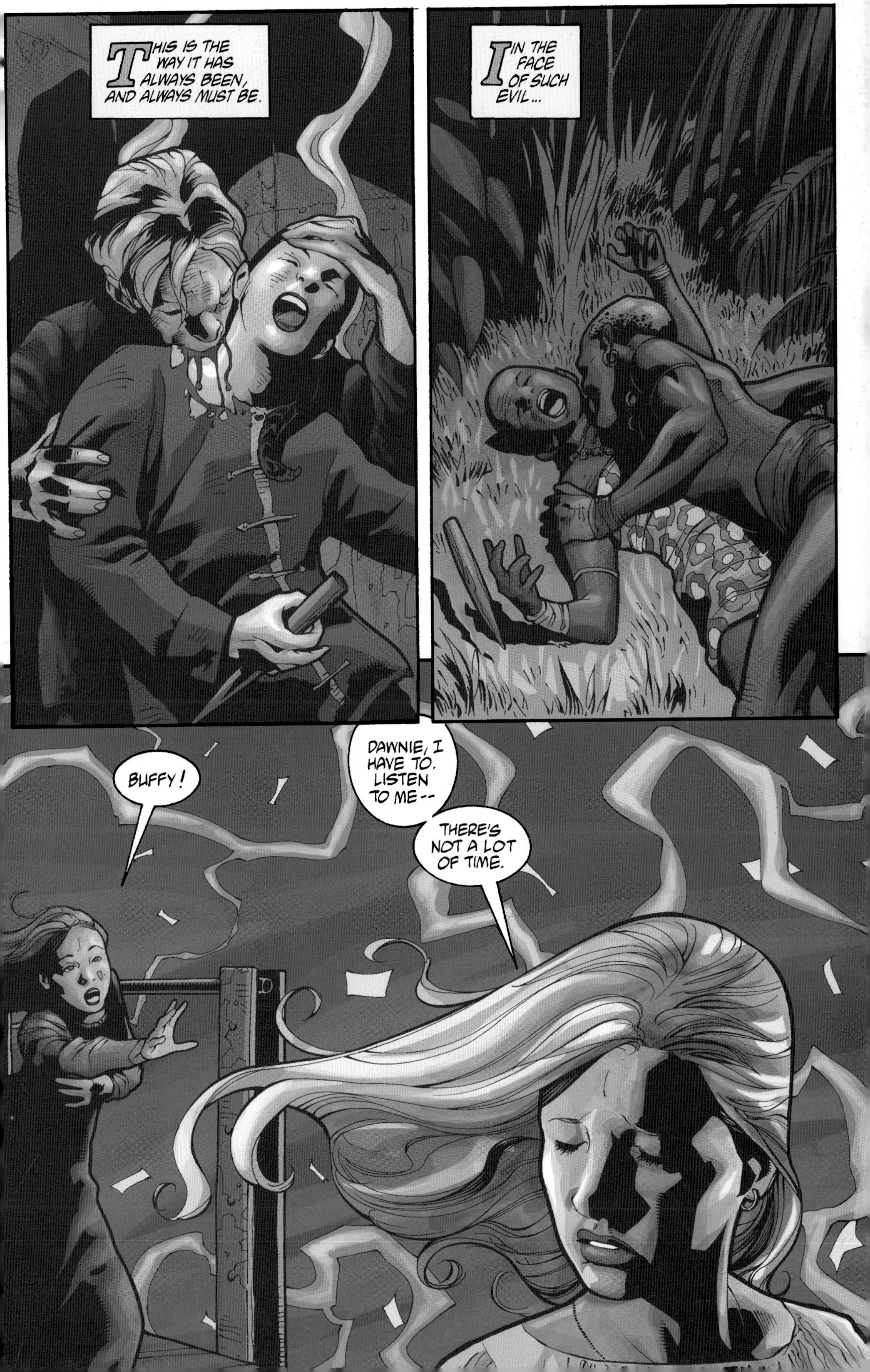
THIS IS THE WAY IT HAS ALWAYS BEEN, AND ALWAYS MUST BE.
IN THE FACE OF SUCH EVIL...
BUFFY!
DAWNIE, I HAVE TO. LISTEN TO ME--
THERE'S NOT A LOT OF TIME.

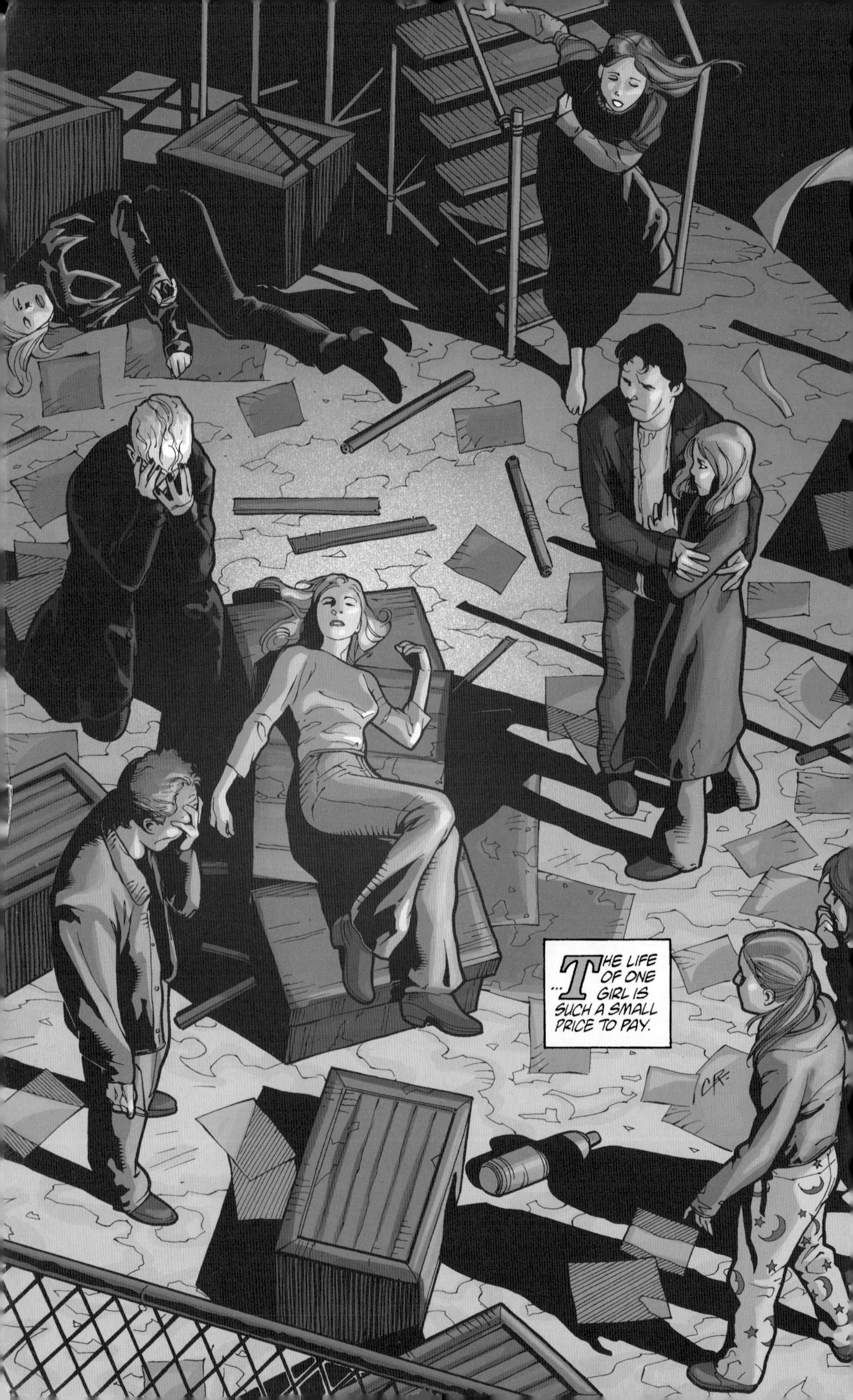
...THE LIFE OF ONE GIRL IS SUCH A SMALL PRICE TO PAY.
CR

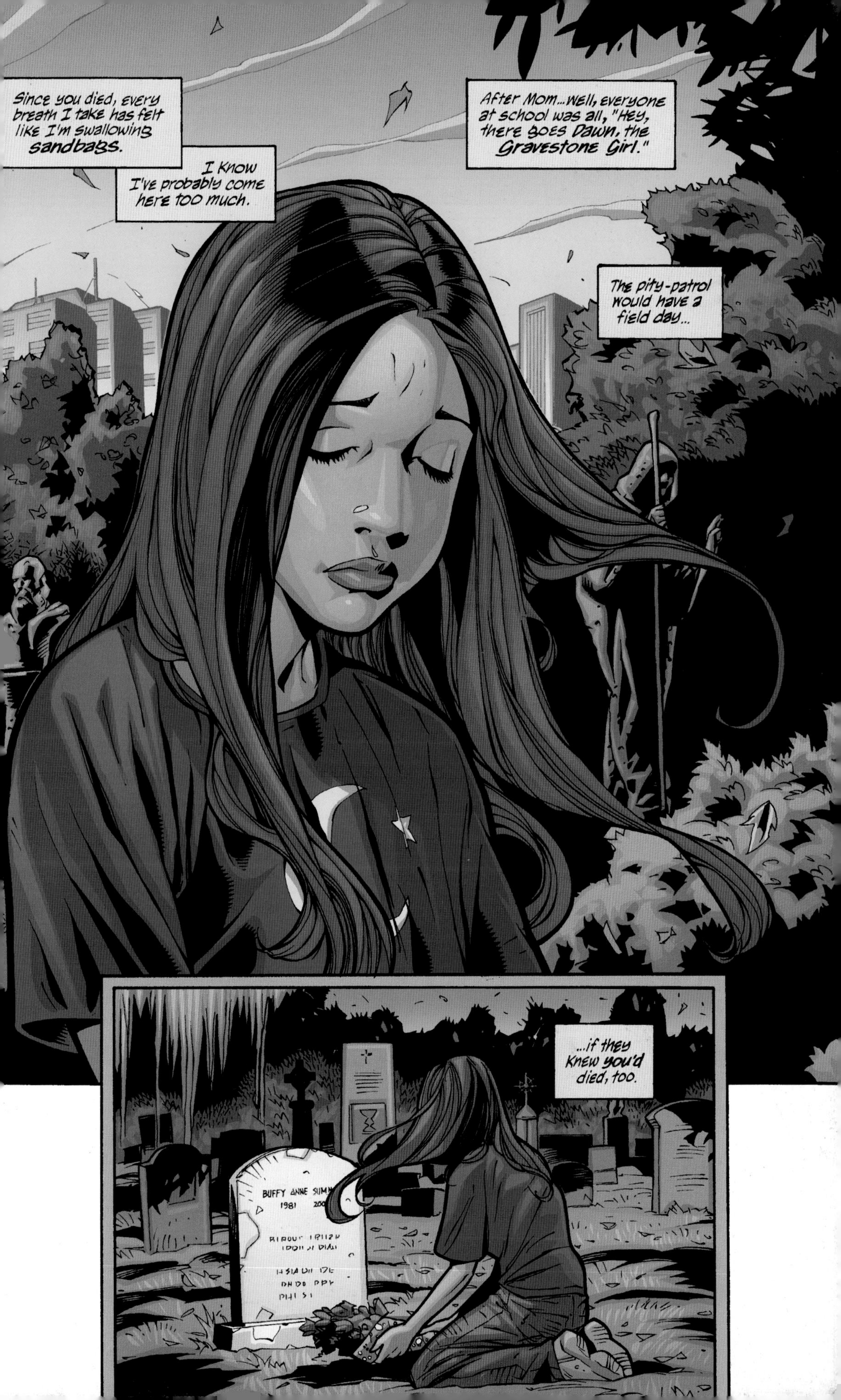
Since you died, every breath I take has felt like I'm swallowing sandbags.
I know I've probably come here too much.
After Mom...well, everyone at school was all, "Hey, there goes Dawn, the Gravestone Girl."
The pity-patrol would have a field day...
...if they knew you'd died, too.

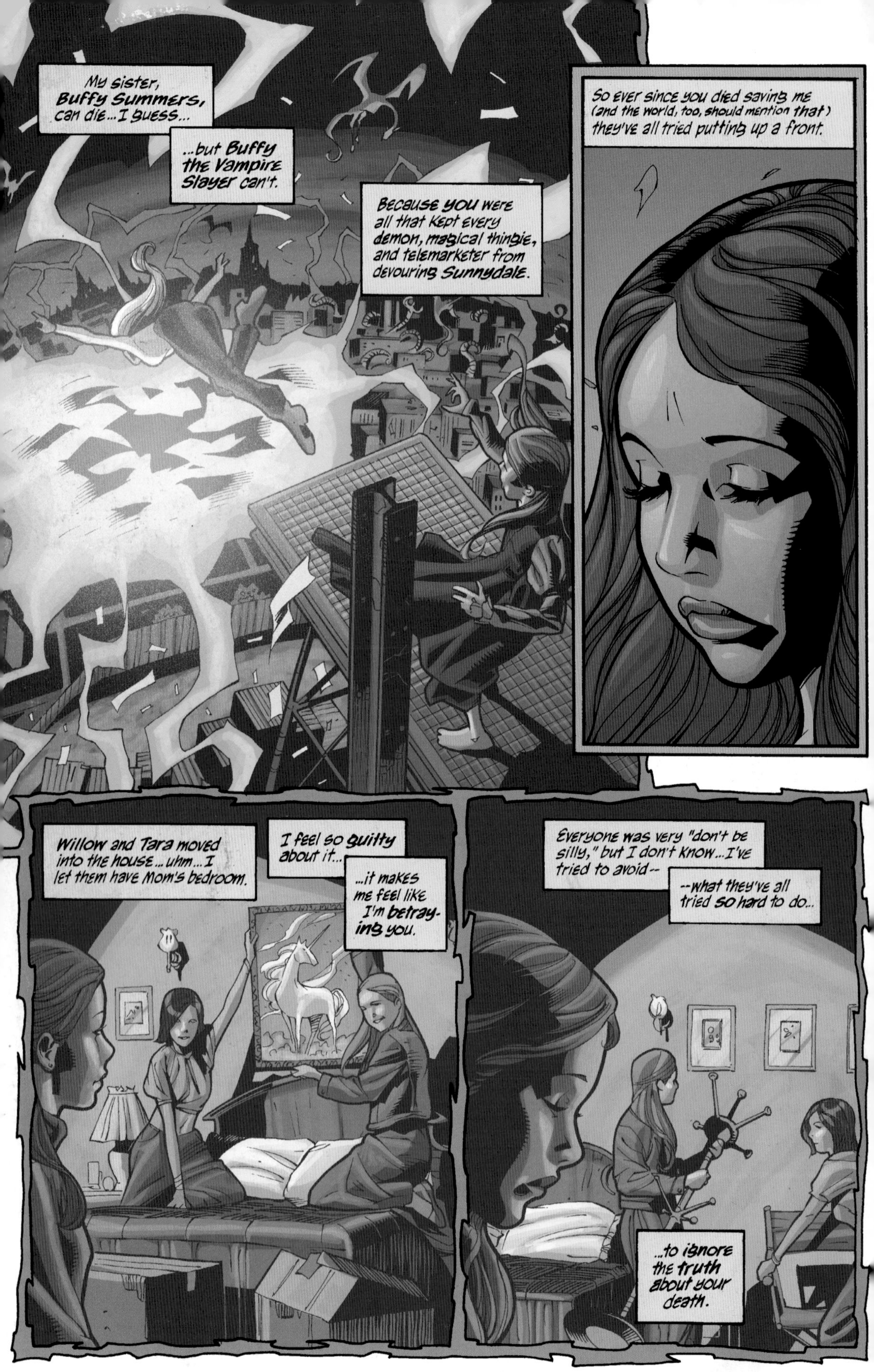

My sister, Buffy Summers, can die... I guess...
...but Buffy the Vampire Slayer can't.
Because you were all that kept every demon, magical thingie, and telemarketer from devouring Sunnydale.
So ever since you died saving me (and the world, too, should mention that) they've all tried putting up a front.
Willow and Tara moved into the house... uhm... I let them have Mom's bedroom.
I feel so guilty about it...
...it makes me feel like I'm betraying you.
Everyone was very "don't be silly," but I don't know... I've tried to avoid--
--what they've all tried so hard to do...
...to ignore the truth about your death.

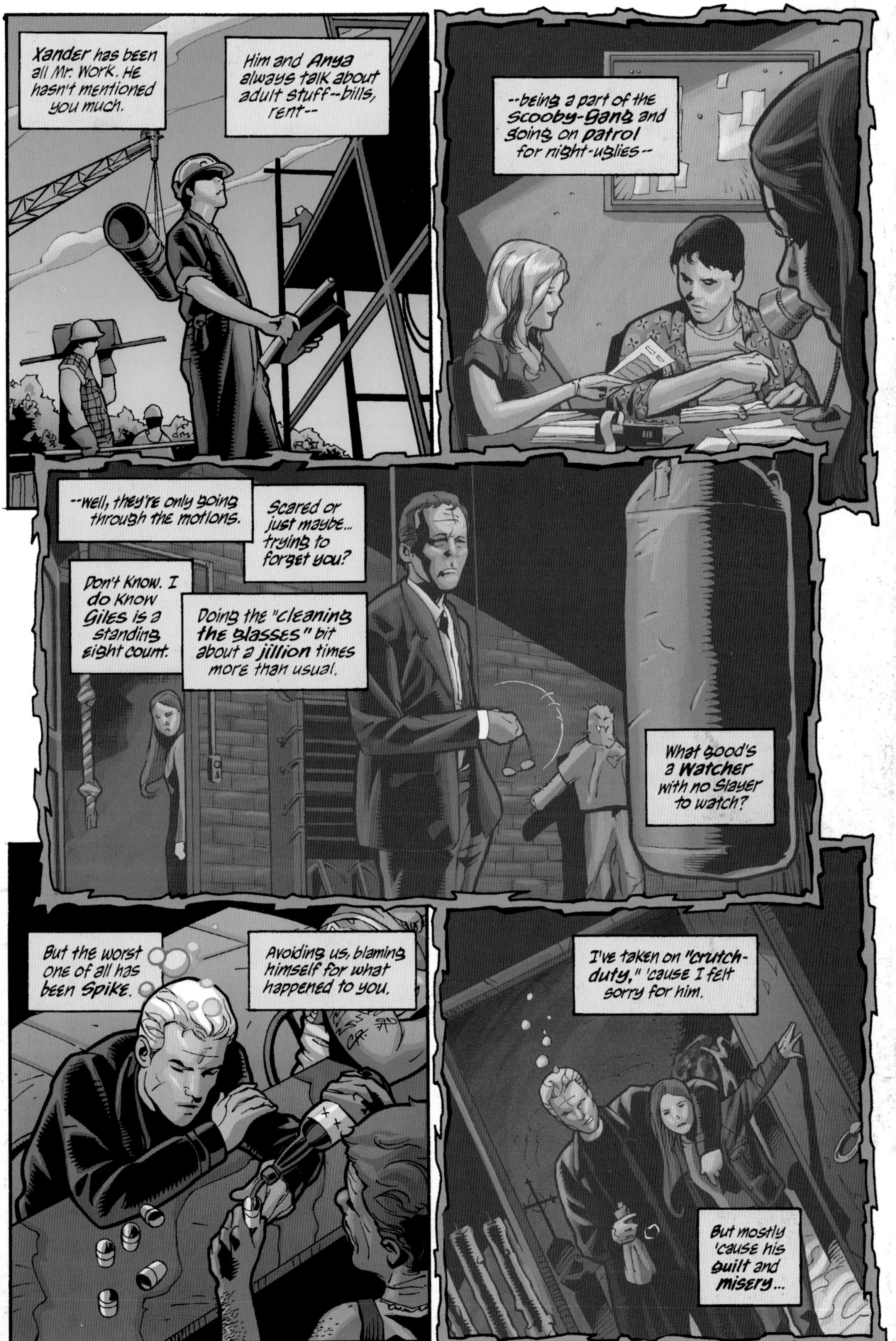
Xander has been all Mr. Work. He hasn't mentioned you much.
Him and Anya always talk about adult stuff--bills, rent--
--being a part of the Scooby-Gang and going on patrol for night-uglies--
--well, they're only going through the motions.
Scared or just maybe... trying to forget you?
Don't know. I do know Giles is a standing eight count.
Doing the "cleaning the glasses" bit about a jillion times more than usual.
What good's a Watcher with no Slayer to watch?
But the worst one of all has been Spike.
Avoiding us, blaming himself for what happened to you.
I've taken on "crutch-duty," 'cause I felt sorry for him.
But mostly 'cause his guilt and misery...

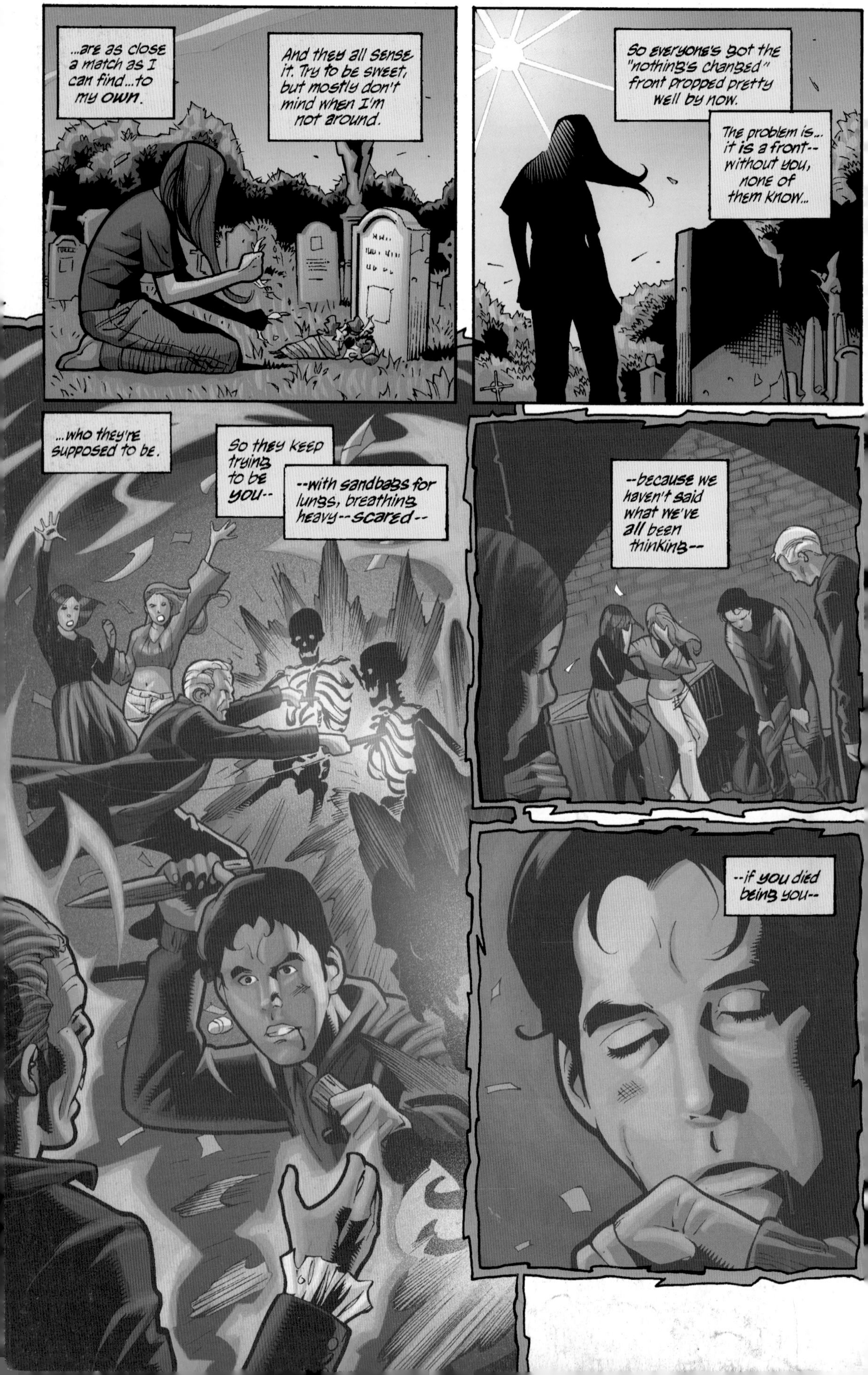
...are as close a match as I can find...to my own.
And they all sense it. Try to be sweet, but mostly don't mind when I'm not around.
So everyone's got the "nothing's changed" front propped pretty well by now.
The problem is... it is a front-- without you, none of them know...
...who they're supposed to be.
So they keep trying to be you--
--with sandbags for lungs, breathing heavy--scared--
--because we haven't said what we've all been thinking--
--if you died being you--

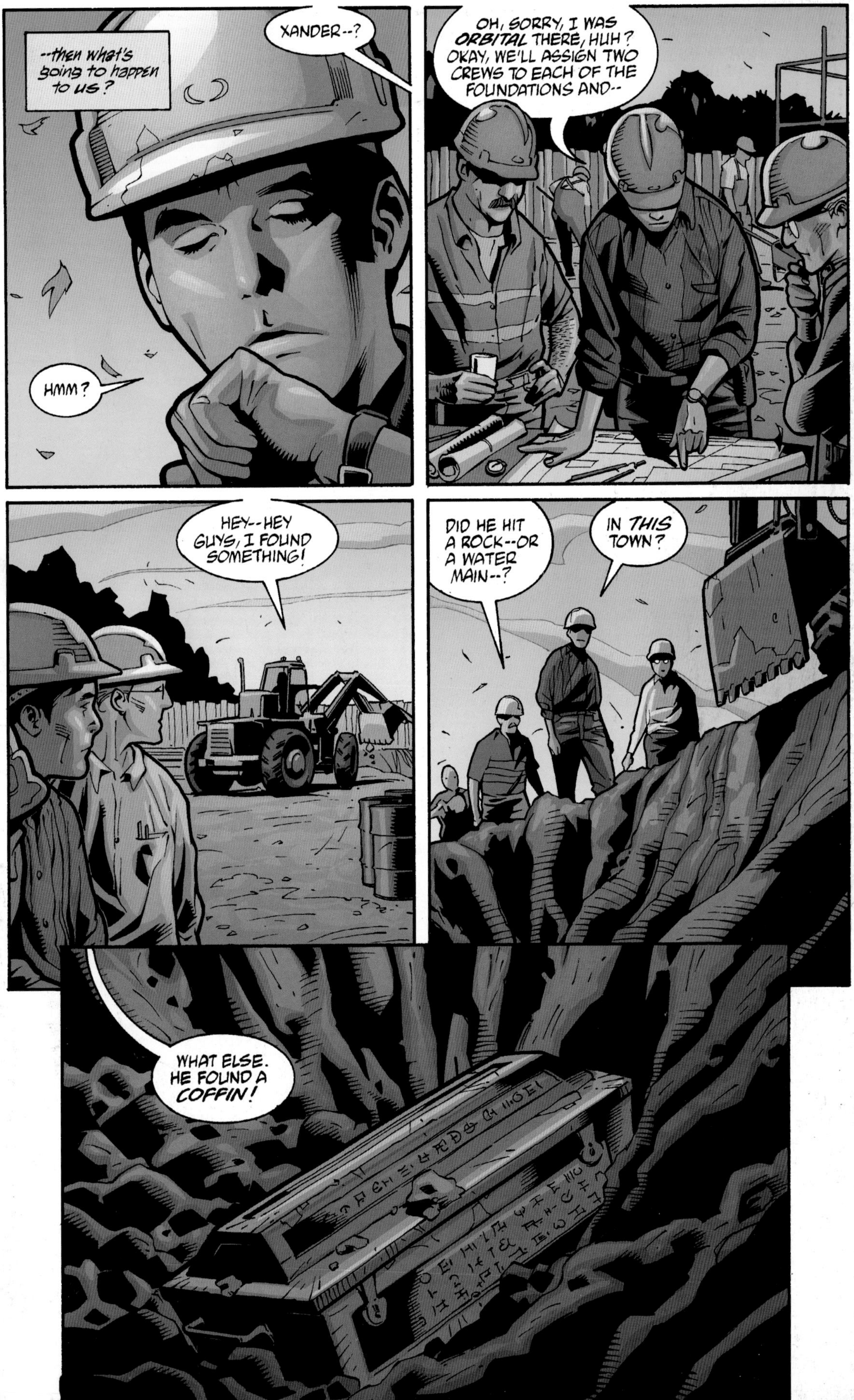
--then what's going to happen to us?
XANDER--?
HMM?
OH, SORRY, I WAS ORBITAL THERE, HUH? OKAY, WE'LL ASSIGN TWO CREWS TO EACH OF THE FOUNDATIONS AND--
HEY--HEY GUYS, I FOUND SOMETHING!
DID HE HIT A ROCK--OR A WATER MAIN--?
IN THIS TOWN?
WHAT ELSE. HE FOUND A COFFIN!

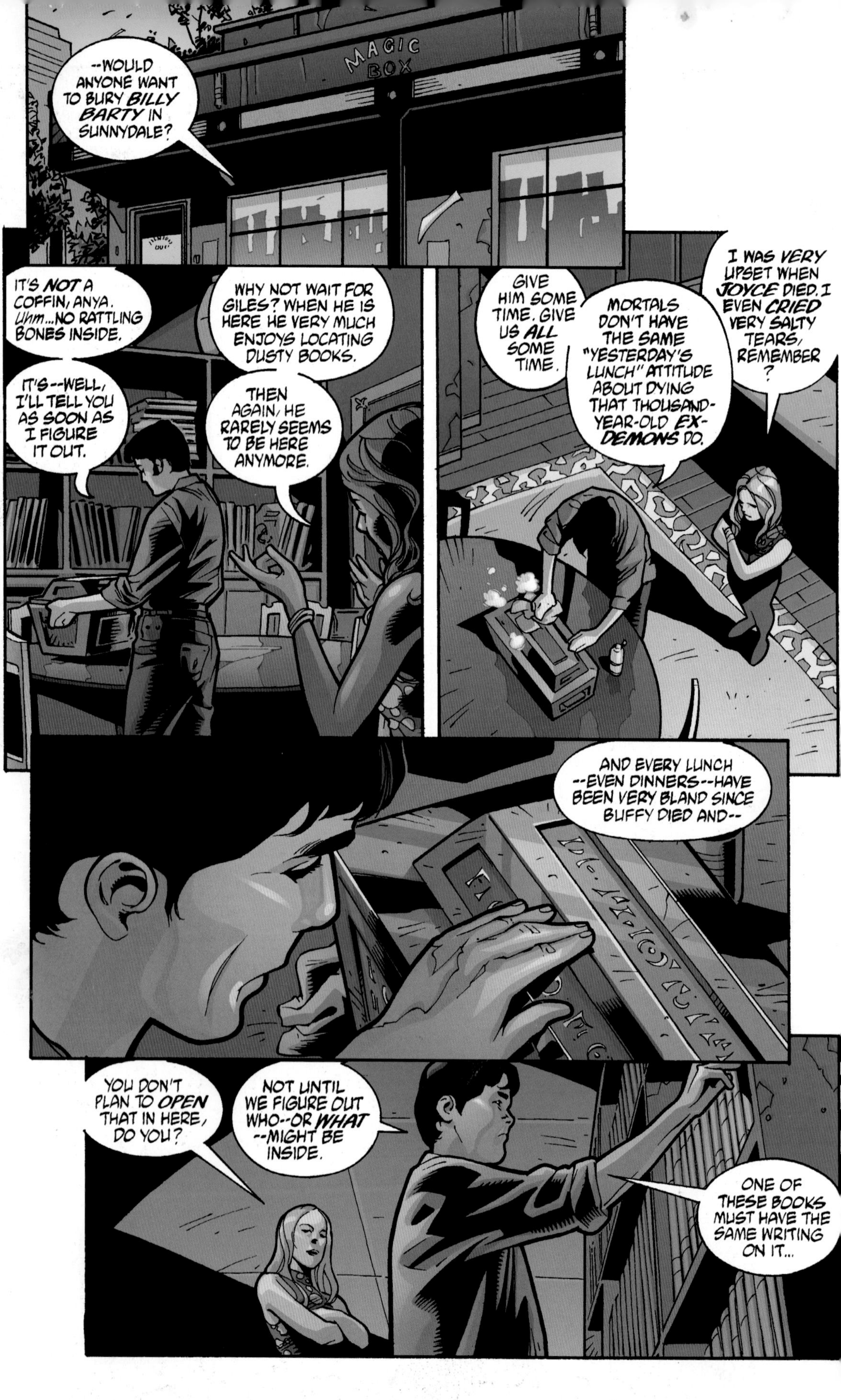
MAGIC BOX
--WOULD ANYONE WANT TO BURY BILLY BARTY IN SUNNYDALE?
IT'S NOT A COFFIN, ANYA. Uhm...NO RATTLING BONES INSIDE.
IT'S--WELL, I'LL TELL YOU AS SOON AS I FIGURE IT OUT.
WHY NOT WAIT FOR GILES? WHEN HE IS HERE HE VERY MUCH ENJOYS LOCATING DUSTY BOOKS.
THEN AGAIN, HE RARELY SEEMS TO BE HERE ANYMORE.
GIVE HIM SOME TIME. GIVE US ALL SOME TIME.
MORTALS DON'T HAVE THE SAME "YESTERDAY'S LUNCH" ATTITUDE ABOUT DYING THAT THOUSAND-YEAR-OLD EX-DEMONS DO.
I WAS VERY UPSET WHEN JOYCE DIED. I EVEN CRIED VERY SALTY TEARS, REMEMBER?
AND EVERY LUNCH --EVEN DINNERS--HAVE BEEN VERY BLAND SINCE BUFFY DIED AND--
YOU DON'T PLAN TO OPEN THAT IN HERE, DO YOU?
NOT UNTIL WE FIGURE OUT WHO--OR WHAT --MIGHT BE INSIDE.
ONE OF THESE BOOKS MUST HAVE THE SAME WRITING ON IT...

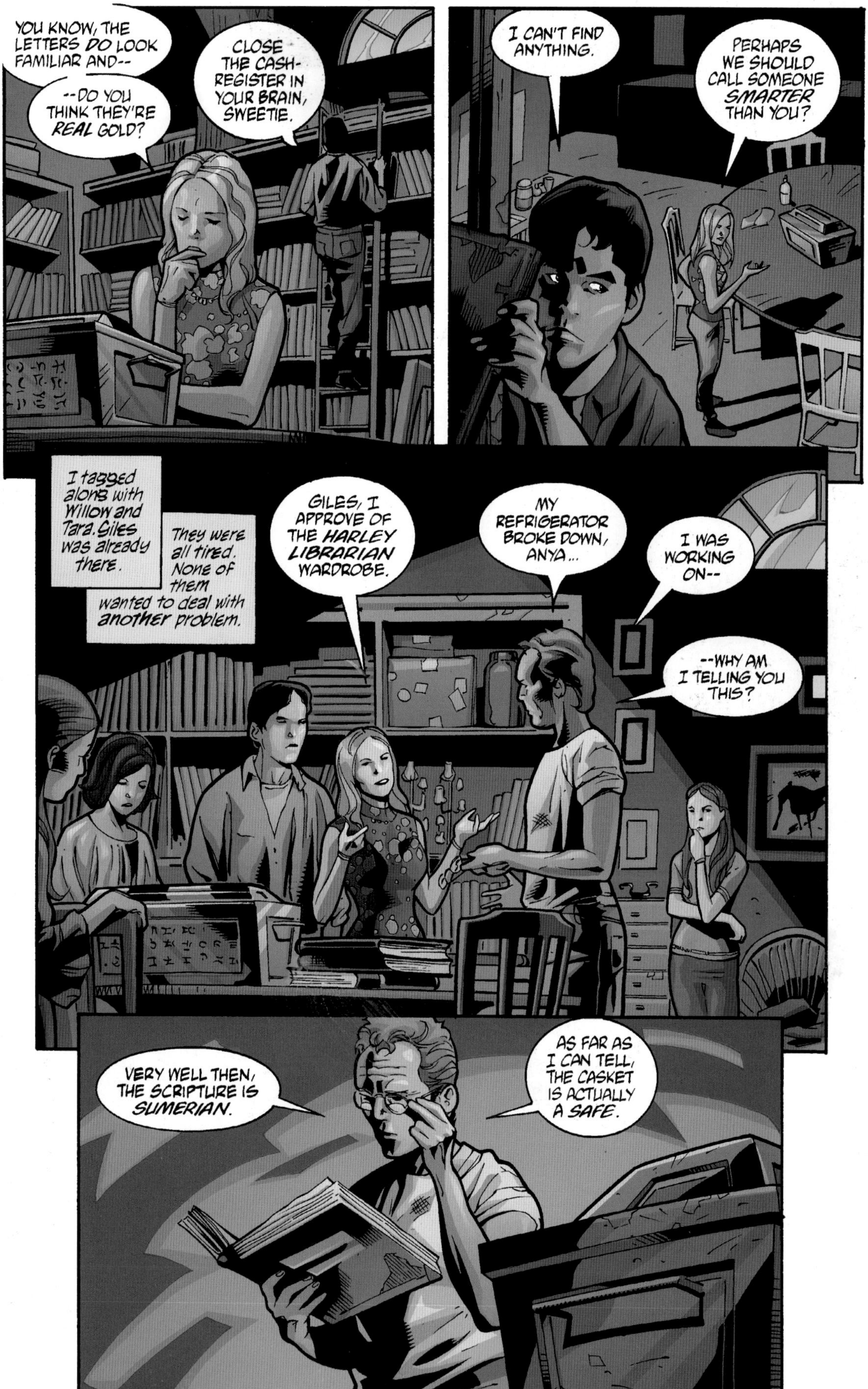
YOU KNOW, THE LETTERS DO LOOK FAMILIAR AND--
--DO YOU THINK THEY'RE REAL GOLD?
CLOSE THE CASH-REGISTER IN YOUR BRAIN, SWEETIE.
I CAN'T FIND ANYTHING.
PERHAPS WE SHOULD CALL SOMEONE SMARTER THAN YOU?
I tagged along with Willow and Tara. Giles was already there.
They were all tired. None of them wanted to deal with another problem.
GILES, I APPROVE OF THE HARLEY LIBRARIAN WARDROBE.
MY REFRIGERATOR BROKE DOWN, ANYA...
I WAS WORKING ON--
--WHY AM I TELLING YOU THIS?
VERY WELL THEN, THE SCRIPTURE IS SUMERIAN.
AS FAR AS I CAN TELL, THE CASKET IS ACTUALLY A SAFE.

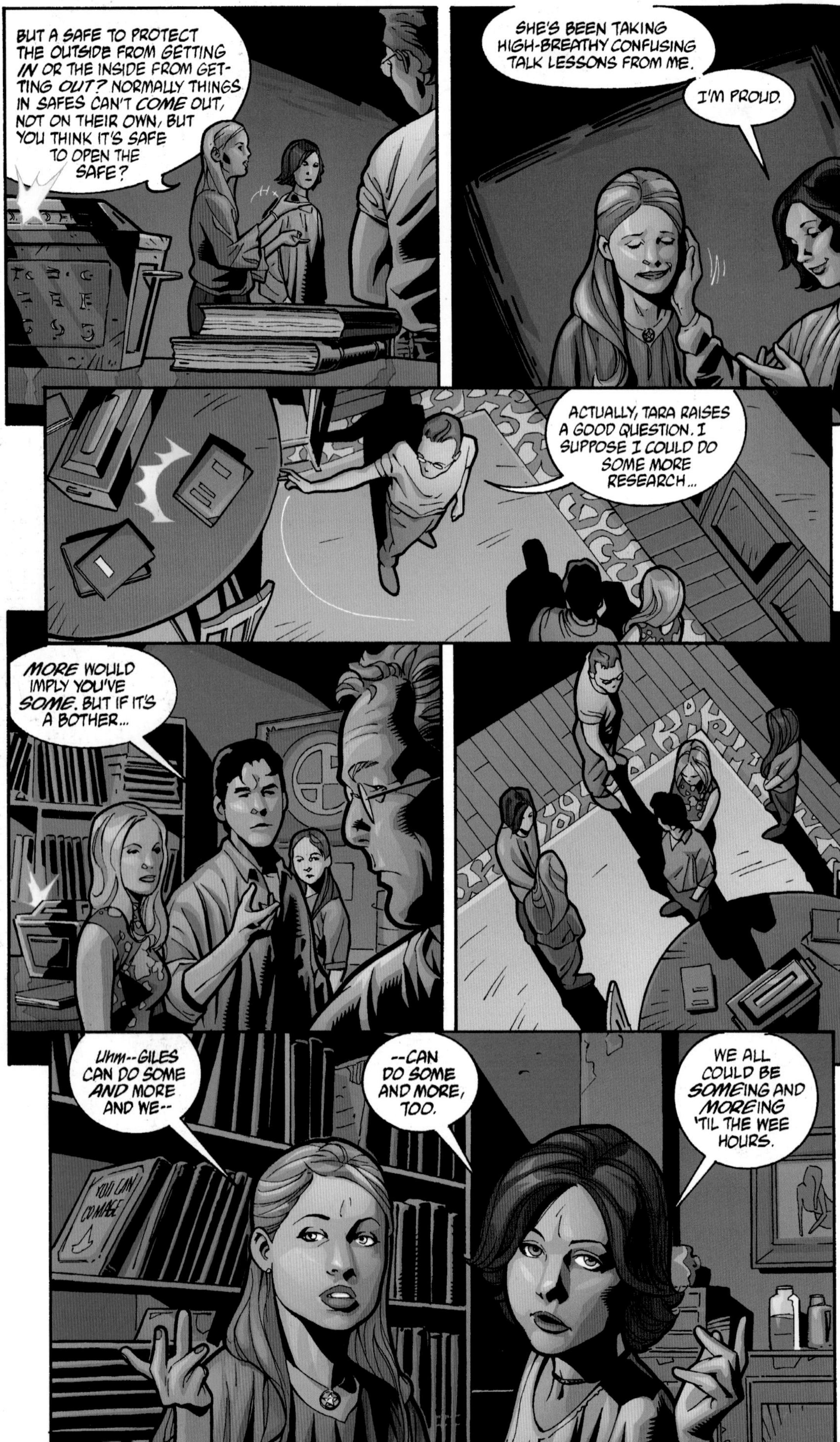
BUT A SAFE TO PROTECT THE OUTSIDE FROM GETTING IN OR THE INSIDE FROM GETTING OUT? NORMALLY THINGS IN SAFES CAN'T COME OUT, NOT ON THEIR OWN, BUT YOU THINK IT'S SAFE TO OPEN THE SAFE?
SHE'S BEEN TAKING HIGH-BREATHY CONFUSING TALK LESSONS FROM ME.
I'M PROUD.
ACTUALLY, TARA RAISES A GOOD QUESTION. I SUPPOSE I COULD DO SOME MORE RESEARCH...
MORE WOULD IMPLY YOU'VE SOME. BUT IF IT'S A BOTHER...
Uhm--GILES CAN DO SOME AND MORE AND WE--
--CAN DO SOME AND MORE, TOO.
WE ALL COULD BE SOMEING AND MOREING 'TIL THE WEE HOURS.

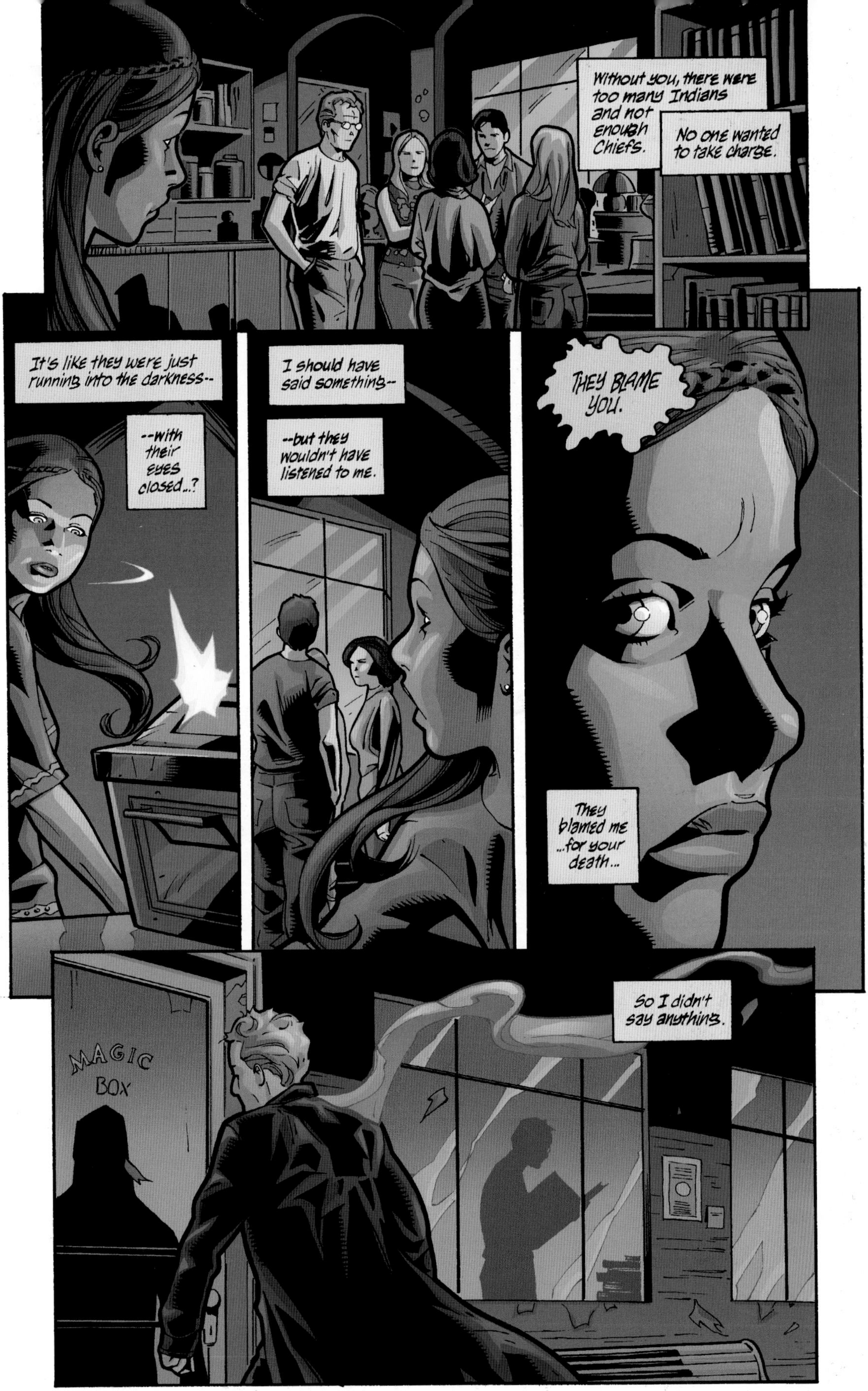

Without you, there were too many Indians and not enough Chiefs.
No one wanted to take charge.
It's like they were just running into the darkness--
--with their eyes closed...?
I should have said something--
--but they wouldn't have listened to me.
THEY BLAME YOU.
They blamed me ...for your death...
MAGIC BOX
So I didn't say anything.

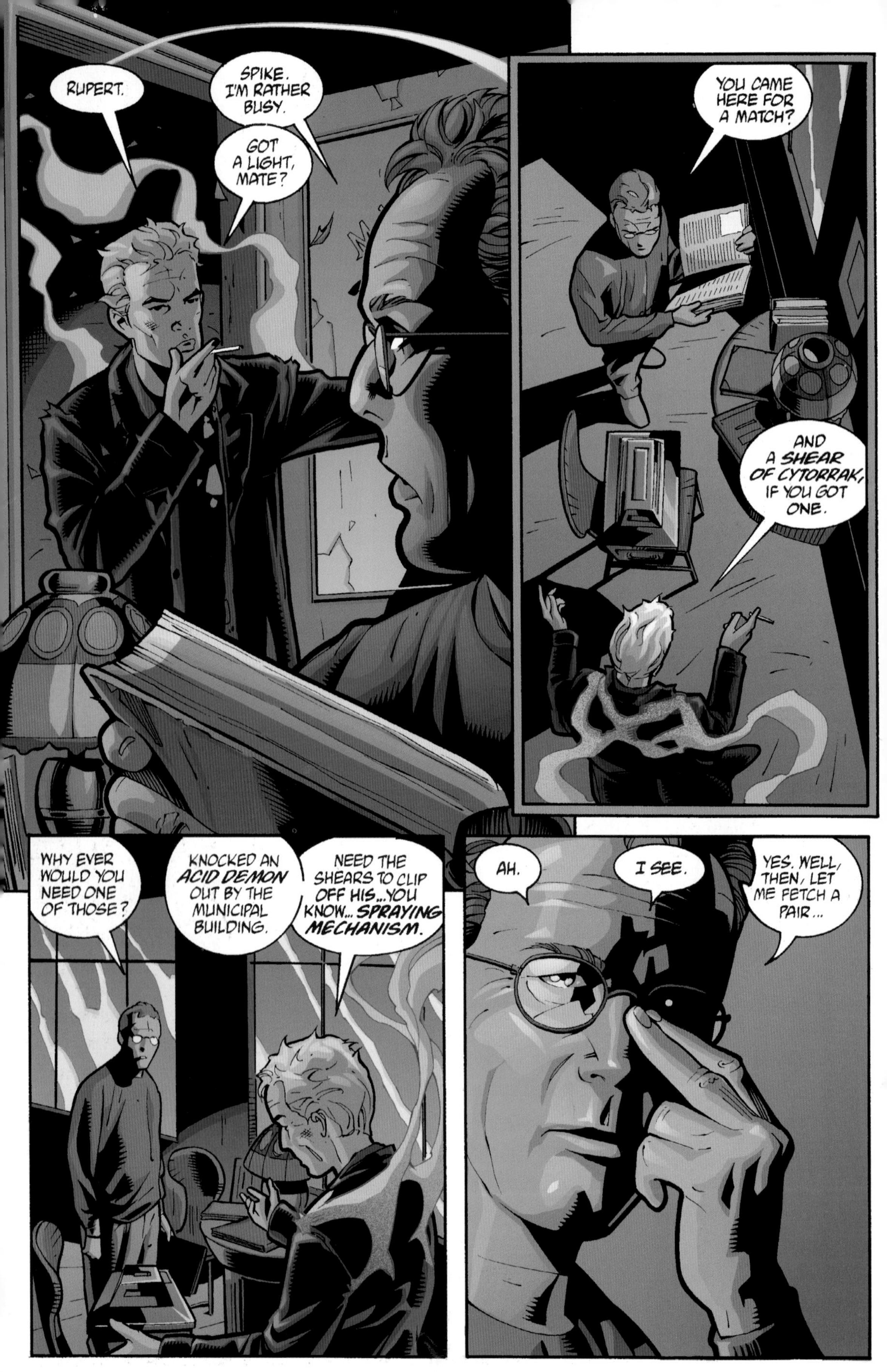
RUPERT.
SPIKE. I'M RATHER BUSY.
GOT A LIGHT, MATE?
YOU CAME HERE FOR A MATCH?
AND A **SHEAR OF CYTORRAK,** IF YOU GOT ONE.
WHY EVER WOULD YOU NEED ONE OF THOSE?
KNOCKED AN **ACID DEMON** OUT BY THE MUNICIPAL BUILDING.
NEED THE SHEARS TO CLIP OFF HIS... YOU KNOW... **SPRAYING MECHANISM.**
AH.
I SEE.
YES. WELL, THEN, LET ME FETCH A PAIR...

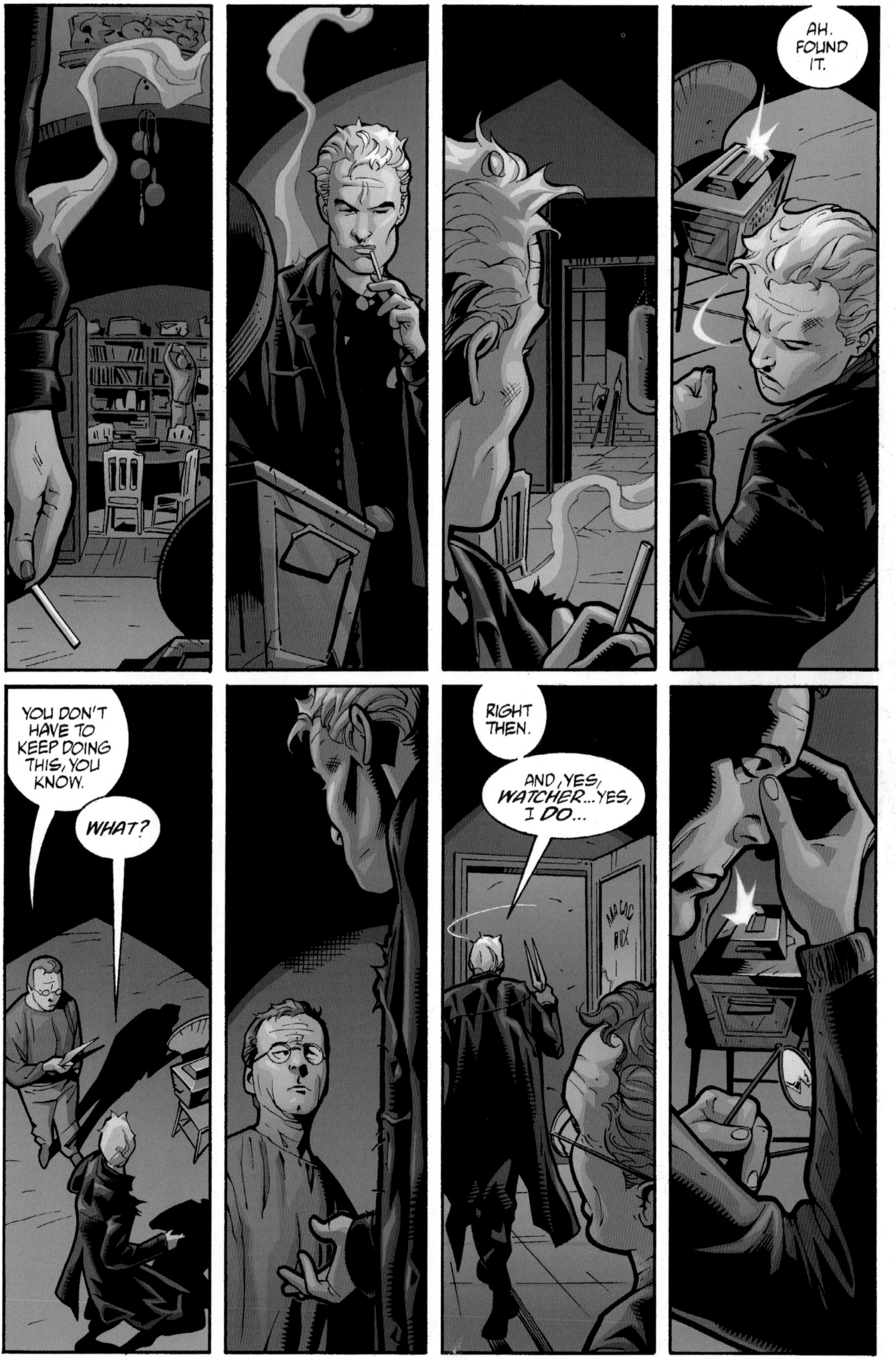
AH. FOUND IT.
YOU DON'T HAVE TO KEEP DOING THIS, YOU KNOW.
WHAT?
RIGHT THEN.
AND, YES, WATCHER...YES, I DO...

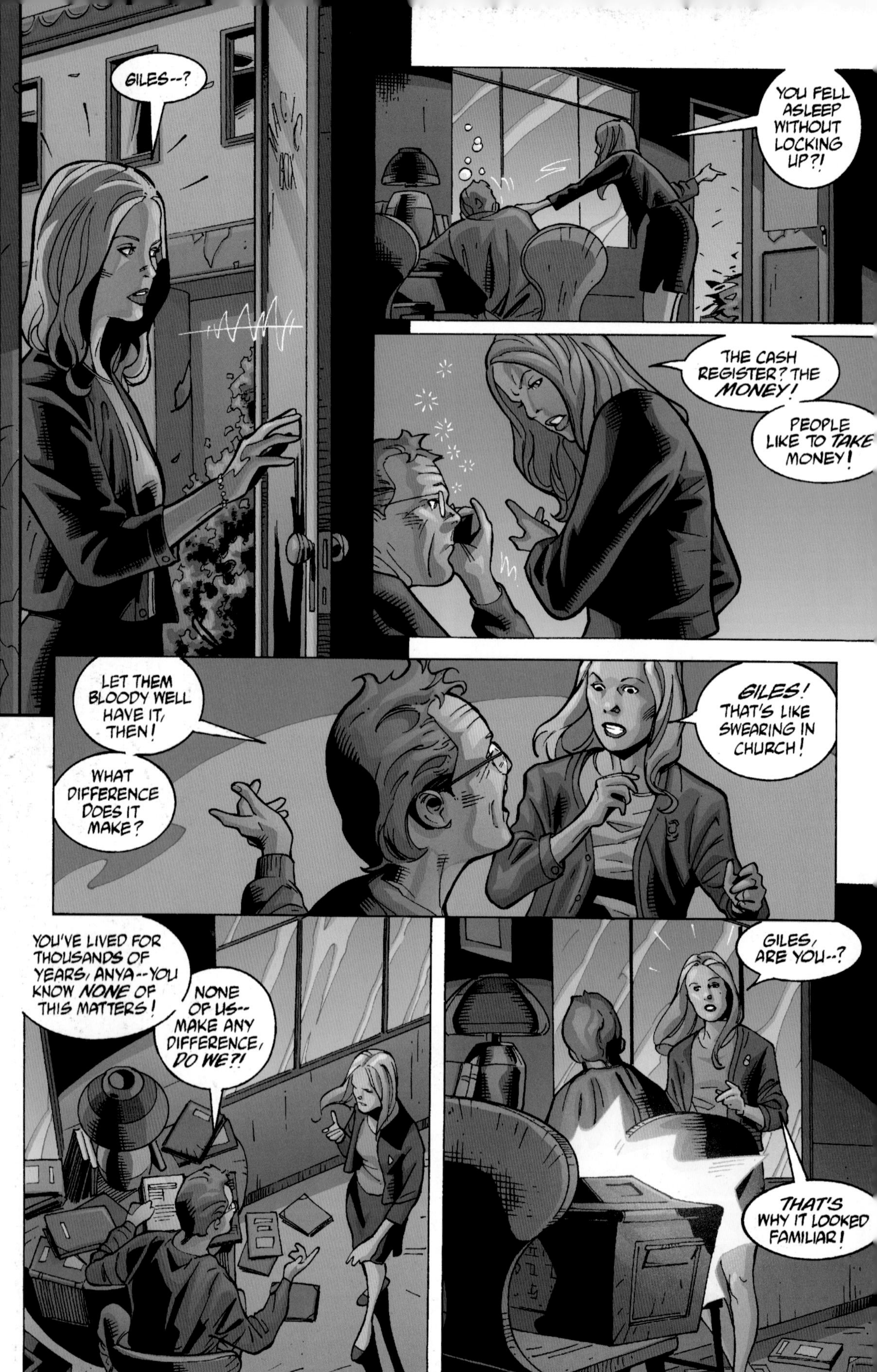
GILES--?
YOU FELL ASLEEP WITHOUT LOCKING UP?!
THE CASH REGISTER? THE MONEY!
PEOPLE LIKE TO TAKE MONEY!
LET THEM BLOODY WELL HAVE IT, THEN!
WHAT DIFFERENCE DOES IT MAKE?
GILES! THAT'S LIKE SWEARING IN CHURCH!
YOU'VE LIVED FOR THOUSANDS OF YEARS, ANYA--YOU KNOW NONE OF THIS MATTERS!
NONE OF US-- MAKE ANY DIFFERENCE, DO WE?!
GILES, ARE YOU--?
THAT'S WHY IT LOOKED FAMILIAR!

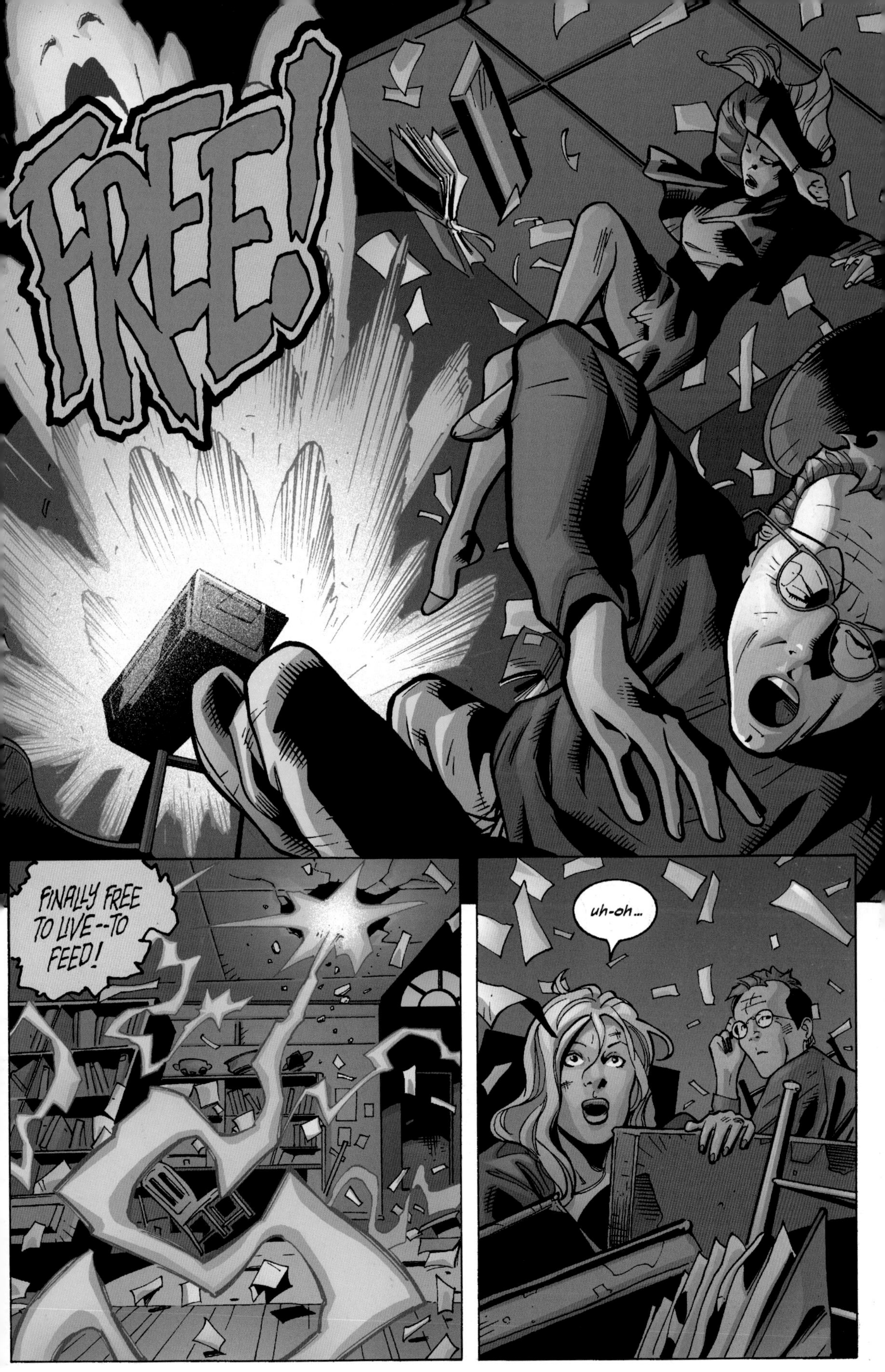
FREE!
FINALLY FREE TO LIVE--TO FEED!
uh-oh...

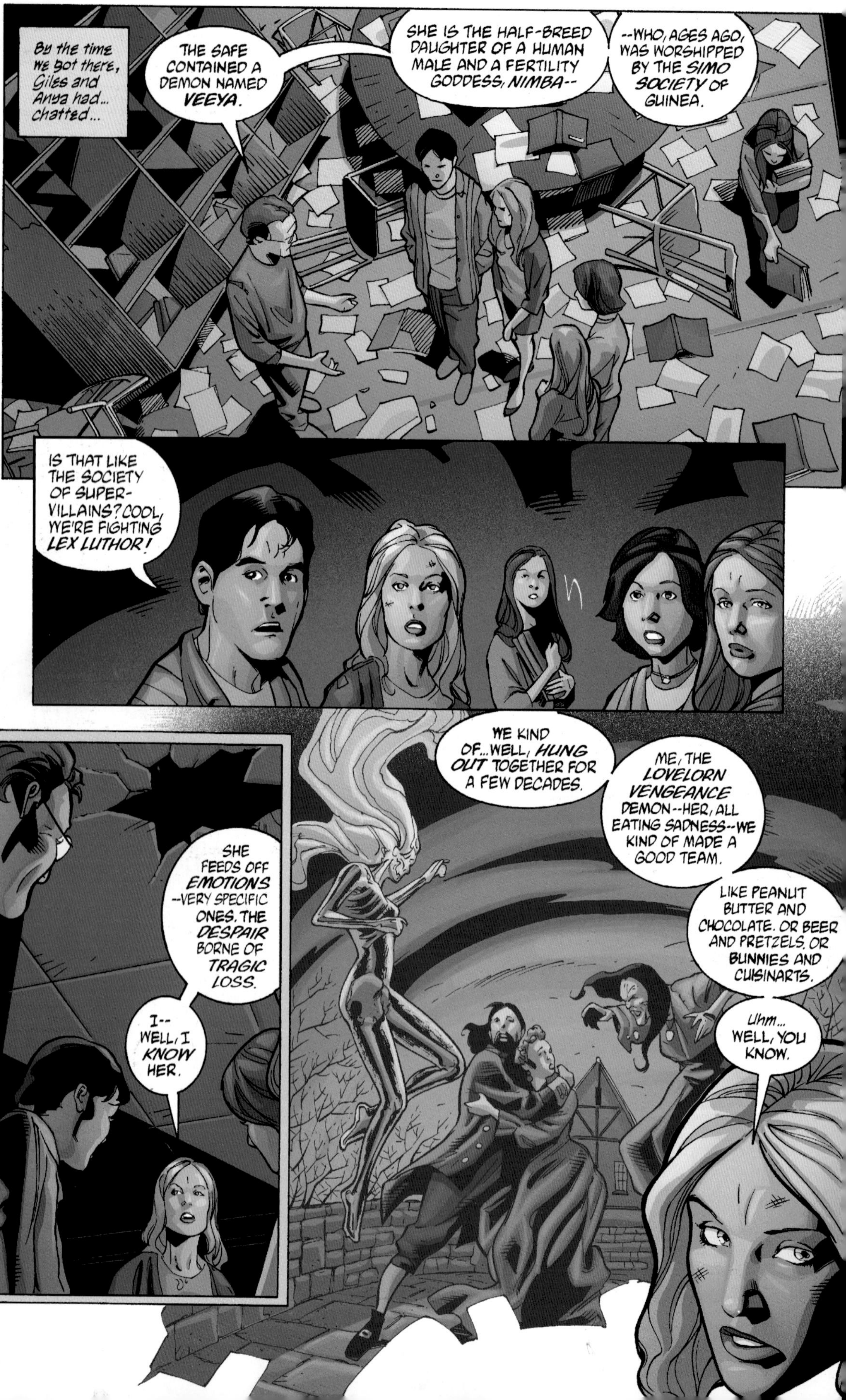

By the time we got there, Giles and Anya had... chatted...
THE SAFE CONTAINED A DEMON NAMED VEEYA.
SHE IS THE HALF-BREED DAUGHTER OF A HUMAN MALE AND A FERTILITY GODDESS, NIMBA--
--WHO, AGES AGO, WAS WORSHIPPED BY THE SIMO SOCIETY OF GUINEA.
IS THAT LIKE THE SOCIETY OF SUPER-VILLAINS? COOL, WE'RE FIGHTING LEX LUTHOR!
SHE FEEDS OFF EMOTIONS --VERY SPECIFIC ONES. THE DESPAIR BORNE OF TRAGIC LOSS.
I-- WELL, I KNOW HER.
WE KIND OF... WELL, HUNG OUT TOGETHER FOR A FEW DECADES.
ME, THE LOVELORN VENGEANCE DEMON--HER, ALL EATING SADNESS--WE KIND OF MADE A GOOD TEAM.
LIKE PEANUT BUTTER AND CHOCOLATE. OR BEER AND PRETZELS. OR BUNNIES AND CUISINARTS.
Uhm... WELL, YOU KNOW.

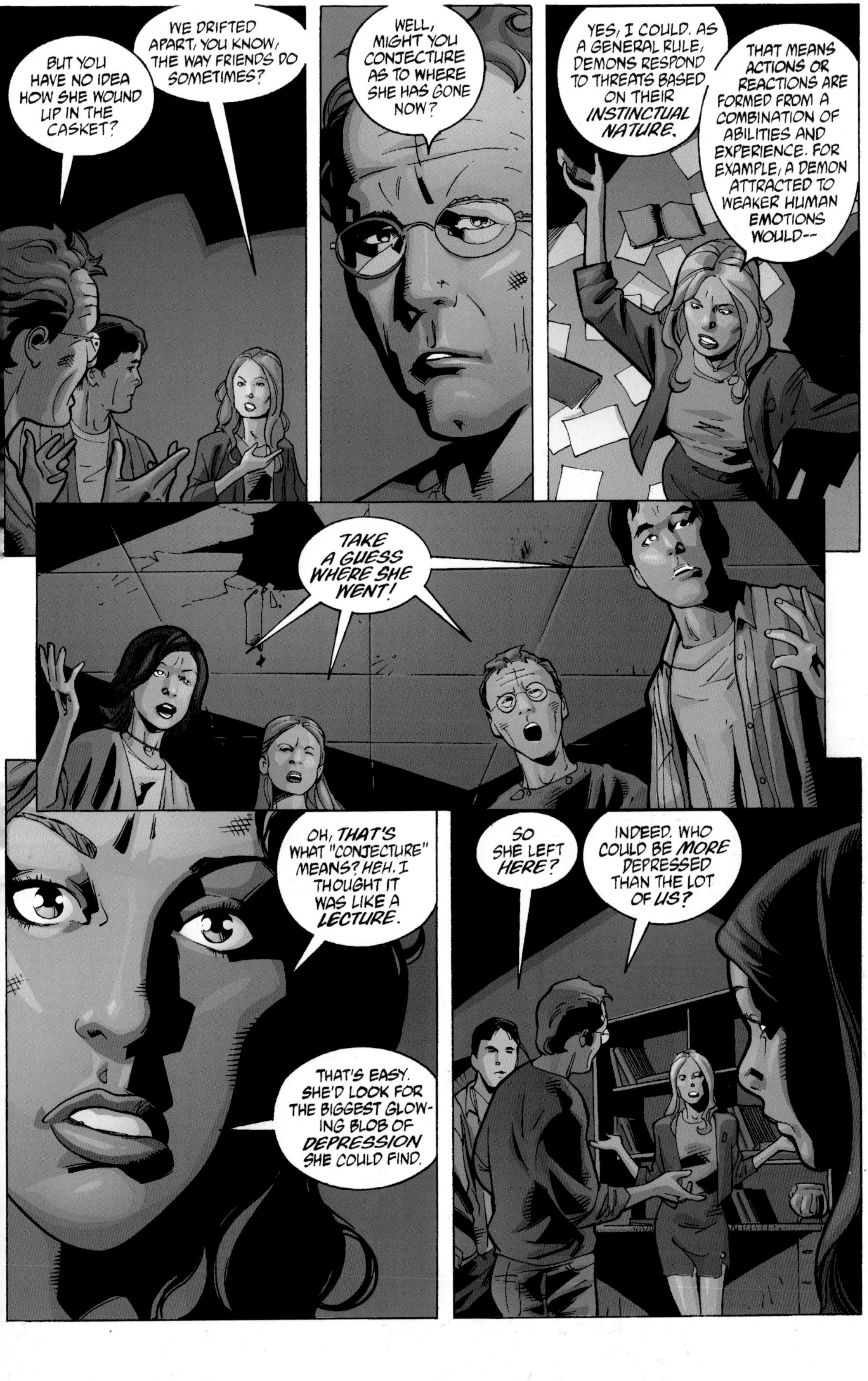
BUT YOU HAVE NO IDEA HOW SHE WOUND UP IN THE CASKET?
WE DRIFTED APART, YOU KNOW, THE WAY FRIENDS DO SOMETIMES?
WELL, MIGHT YOU CONJECTURE AS TO WHERE SHE HAS GONE NOW?
YES, I COULD. AS A GENERAL RULE, DEMONS RESPOND TO THREATS BASED ON THEIR INSTINCTUAL NATURE.
THAT MEANS ACTIONS OR REACTIONS ARE FORMED FROM A COMBINATION OF ABILITIES AND EXPERIENCE. FOR EXAMPLE, A DEMON ATTRACTED TO WEAKER HUMAN EMOTIONS WOULD--
TAKE A GUESS WHERE SHE WENT!
OH, THAT'S WHAT "CONJECTURE" MEANS? HEH. I THOUGHT IT WAS LIKE A LECTURE.
THAT'S EASY. SHE'D LOOK FOR THE BIGGEST GLOWING BLOB OF DEPRESSION SHE COULD FIND.
SO SHE LEFT HERE?
INDEED. WHO COULD BE MORE DEPRESSED THAN THE LOT OF US?

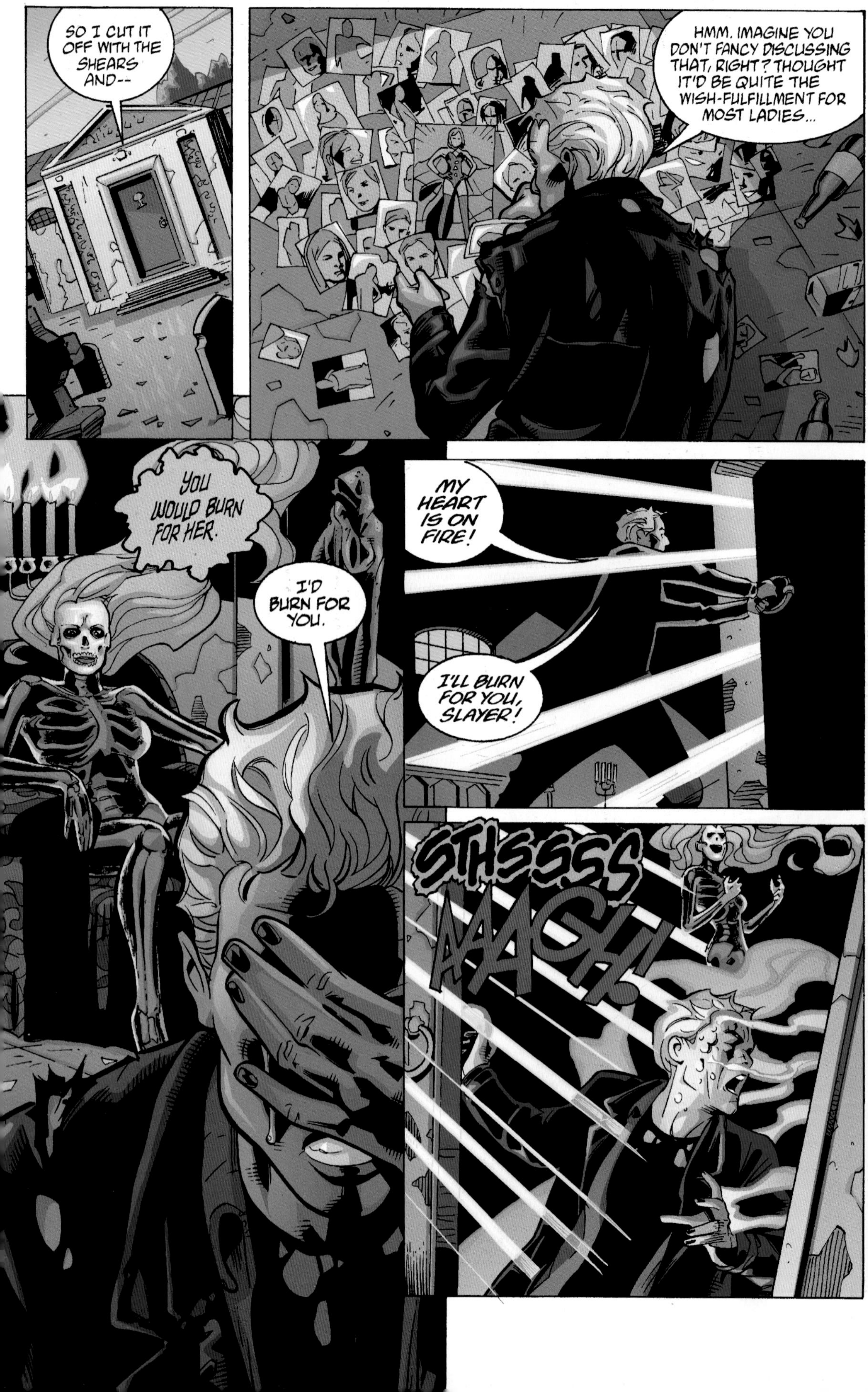
SO I CUT IT OFF WITH THE SHEARS AND--
HMM. IMAGINE YOU DON'T FANCY DISCUSSING THAT, RIGHT? THOUGHT IT'D BE QUITE THE WISH-FULFILLMENT FOR MOST LADIES...
YOU WOULD BURN FOR HER.
I'D BURN FOR YOU.
MY HEART IS ON FIRE!
I'LL BURN FOR YOU, SLAYER!
STHSSSS
AAAGH!

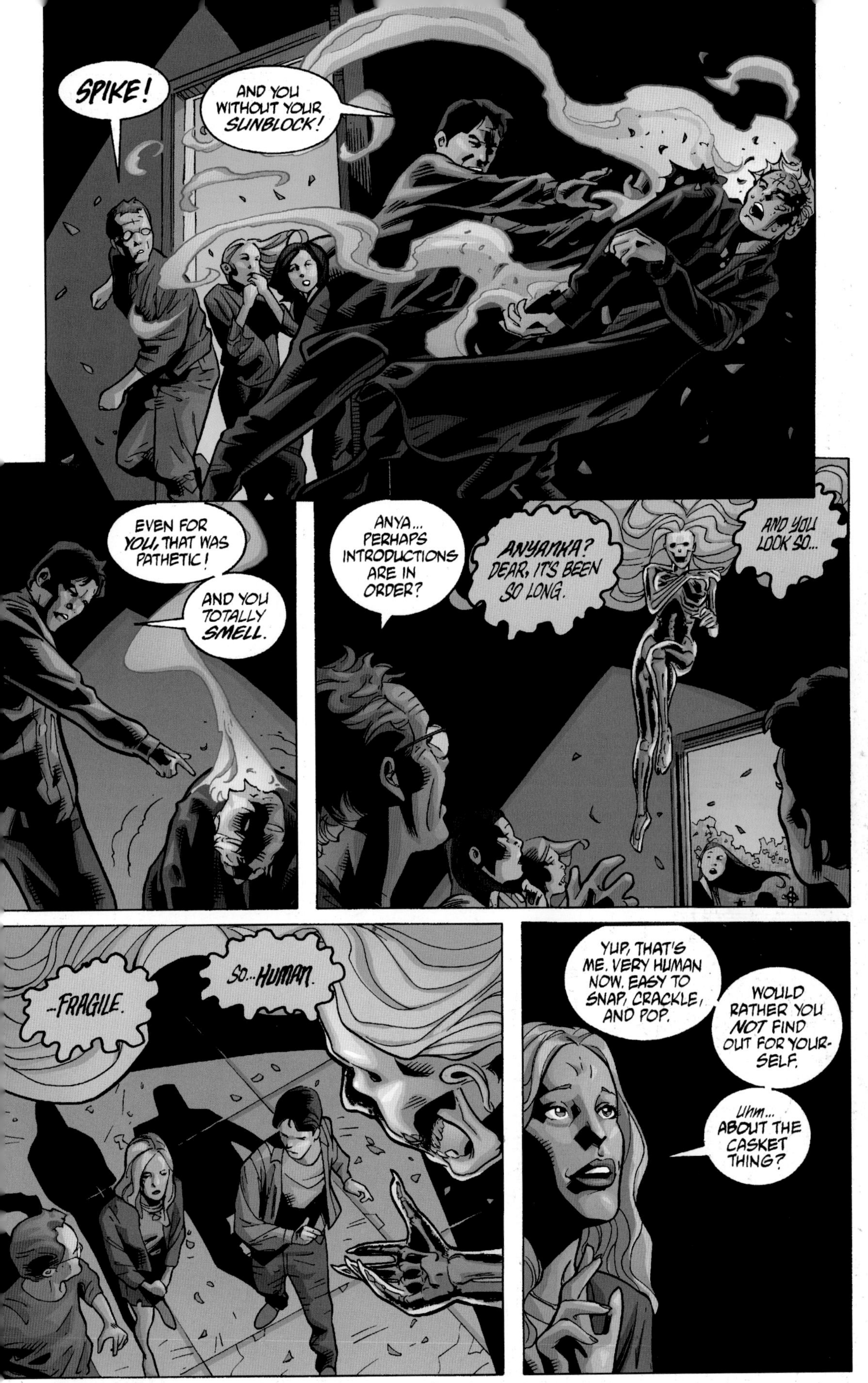
SPIKE!
AND YOU WITHOUT YOUR SUNBLOCK!
EVEN FOR YOU, THAT WAS PATHETIC!
AND YOU TOTALLY SMELL.
ANYA... PERHAPS INTRODUCTIONS ARE IN ORDER?
ANYANKA? DEAR, IT'S BEEN SO LONG.
AND YOU LOOK SO...
--FRAGILE.
SO...HUMAN.
YUP, THAT'S ME. VERY HUMAN NOW. EASY TO SNAP, CRACKLE, AND POP.
WOULD RATHER YOU NOT FIND OUT FOR YOURSELF.
UHM... ABOUT THE CASKET THING?

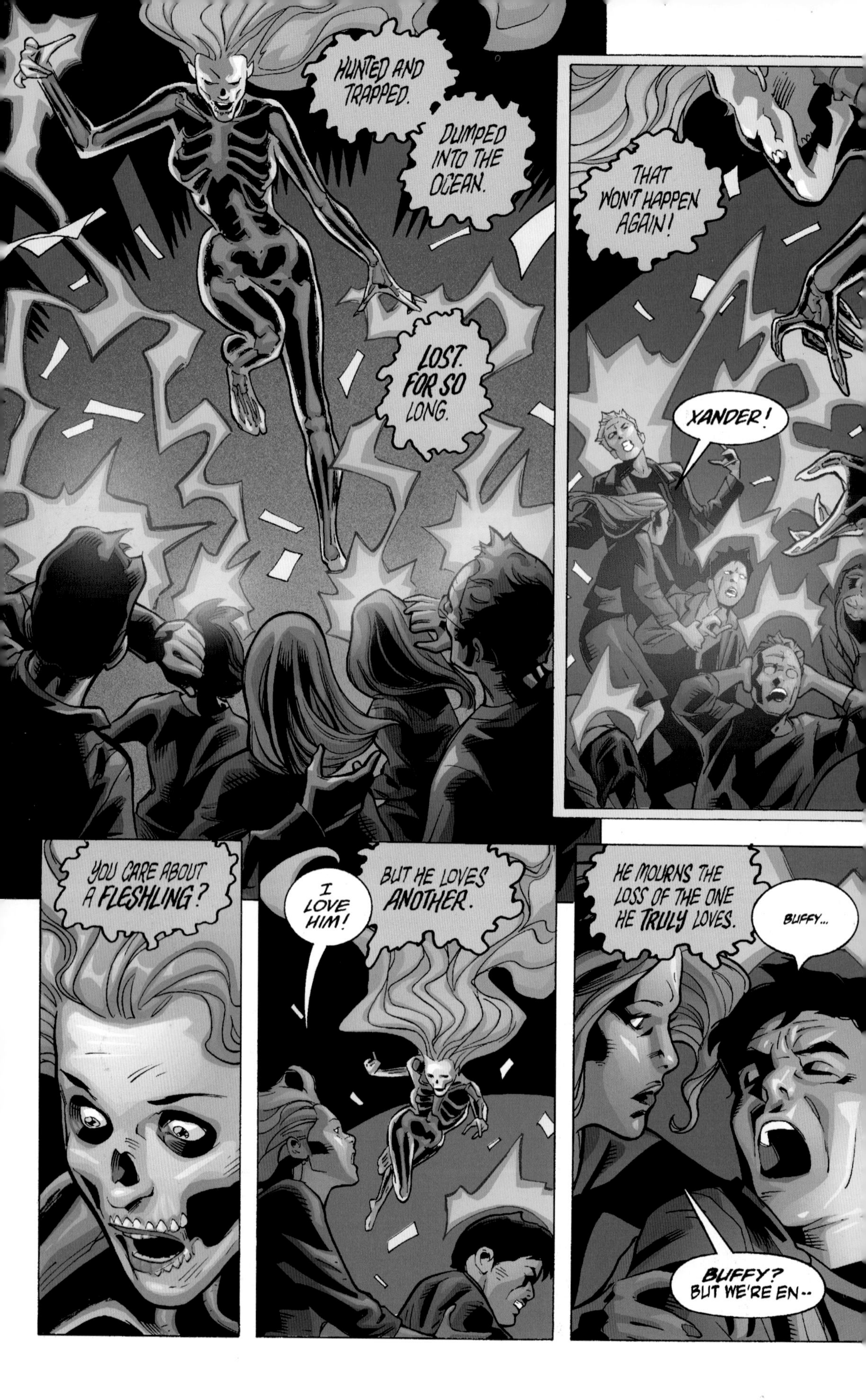
HUNTED AND TRAPPED.
DUMPED INTO THE OCEAN.
LOST. FOR SO LONG.
THAT WON'T HAPPEN AGAIN!
XANDER!
YOU CARE ABOUT A FLESHLING?
I LOVE HIM!
BUT HE LOVES ANOTHER.
HE MOURNS THE LOSS OF THE ONE HE TRULY LOVES.
BUFFY...
BUFFY? BUT WE'RE EN--

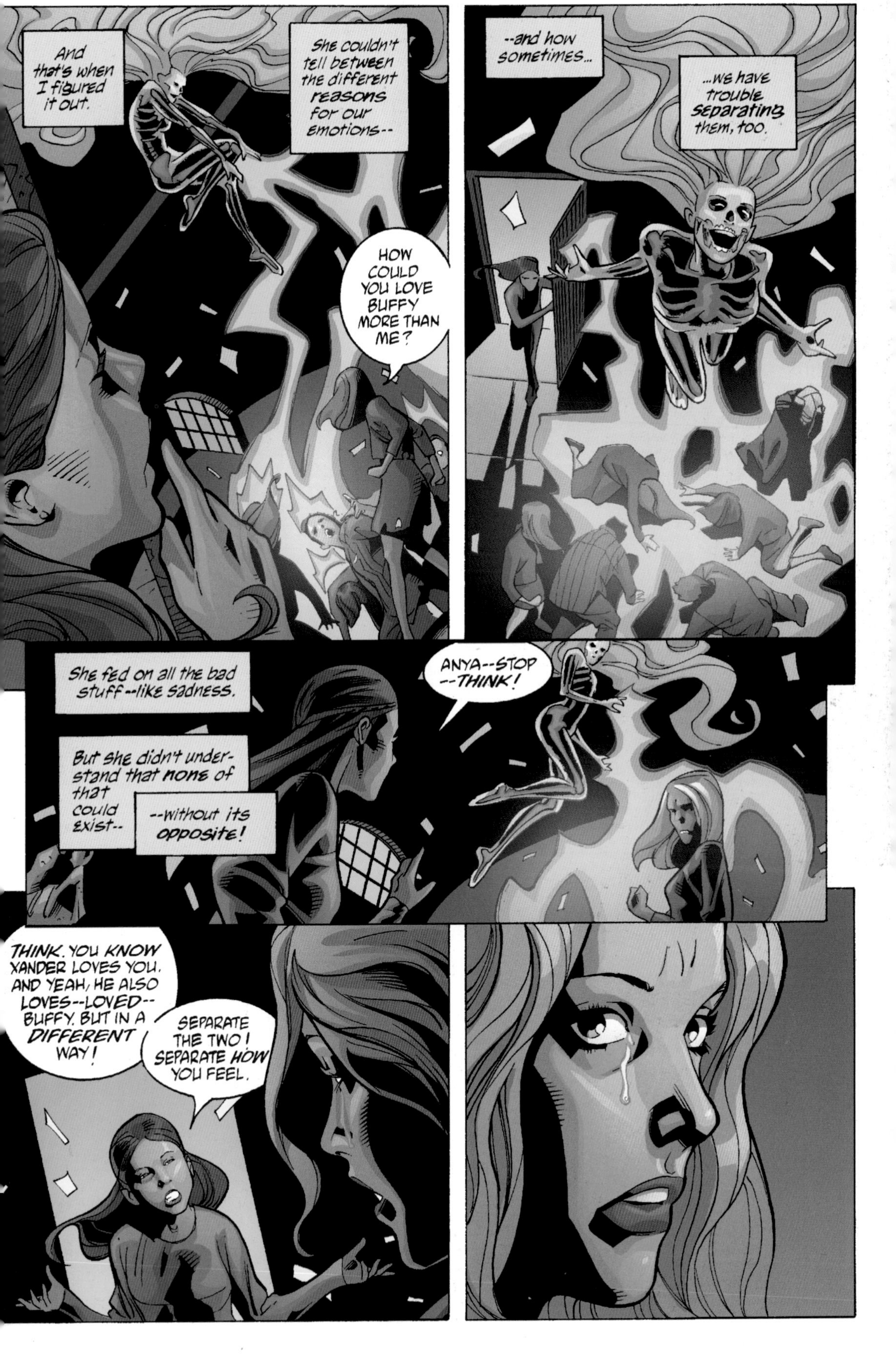

And that's when I figured it out.
She couldn't tell between the different reasons for our emotions--
HOW COULD YOU LOVE BUFFY MORE THAN ME?
--and how sometimes...
...we have trouble separating them, too.
She fed on all the bad stuff--like sadness.
But she didn't understand that none of that could exist--
--without its opposite!
ANYA--STOP --THINK!
THINK. YOU KNOW XANDER LOVES YOU. AND YEAH, HE ALSO LOVES--LOVED--BUFFY. BUT IN A DIFFERENT WAY!
SEPARATE THE TWO! SEPARATE HOW YOU FEEL.

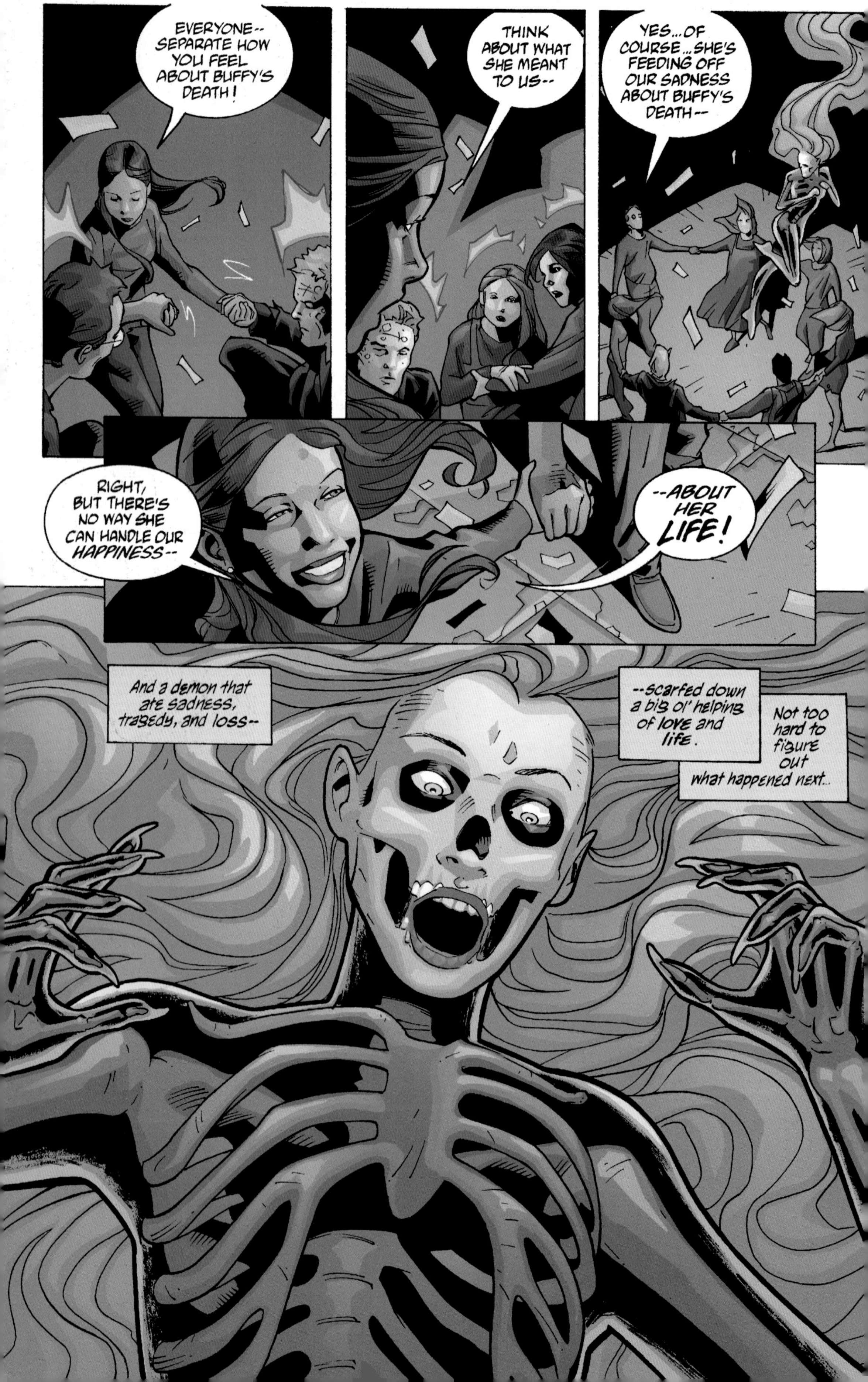
EVERYONE--
SEPARATE HOW YOU FEEL ABOUT BUFFY'S DEATH!
THINK ABOUT WHAT SHE MEANT TO US--
YES...OF COURSE...SHE'S FEEDING OFF OUR SADNESS ABOUT BUFFY'S DEATH--
RIGHT, BUT THERE'S NO WAY SHE CAN HANDLE OUR HAPPINESS--
--ABOUT HER LIFE!
And a demon that ate sadness, tragedy, and loss--
--scarfed down a big ol' helping of love and life.
Not too hard to figure out what happened next...

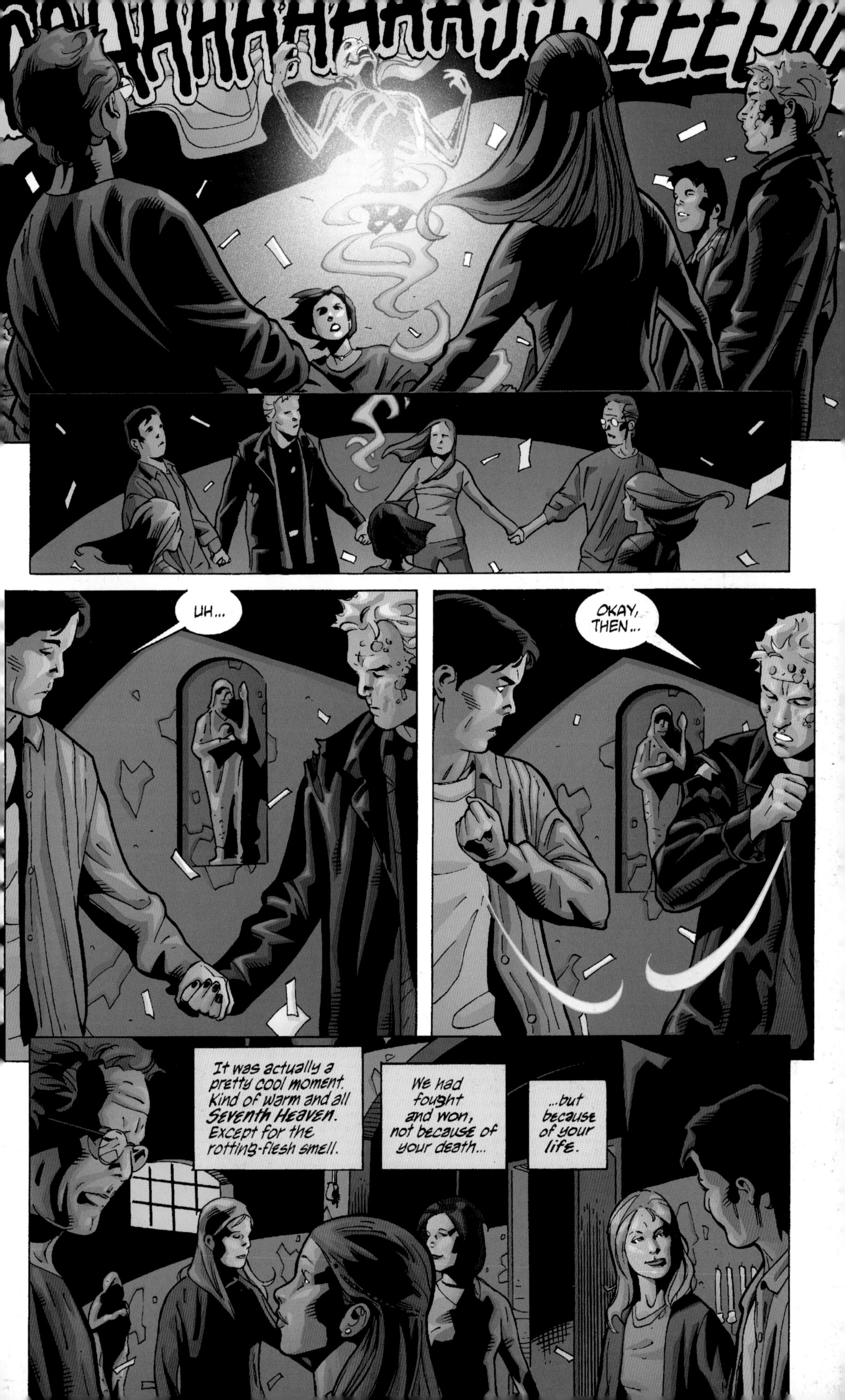
UH...
OKAY, THEN...
It was actually a pretty cool moment. Kind of warm and all Seventh Heaven. Except for the rotting-flesh smell.
We had fought and won, not because of your death...
...but because of your life.

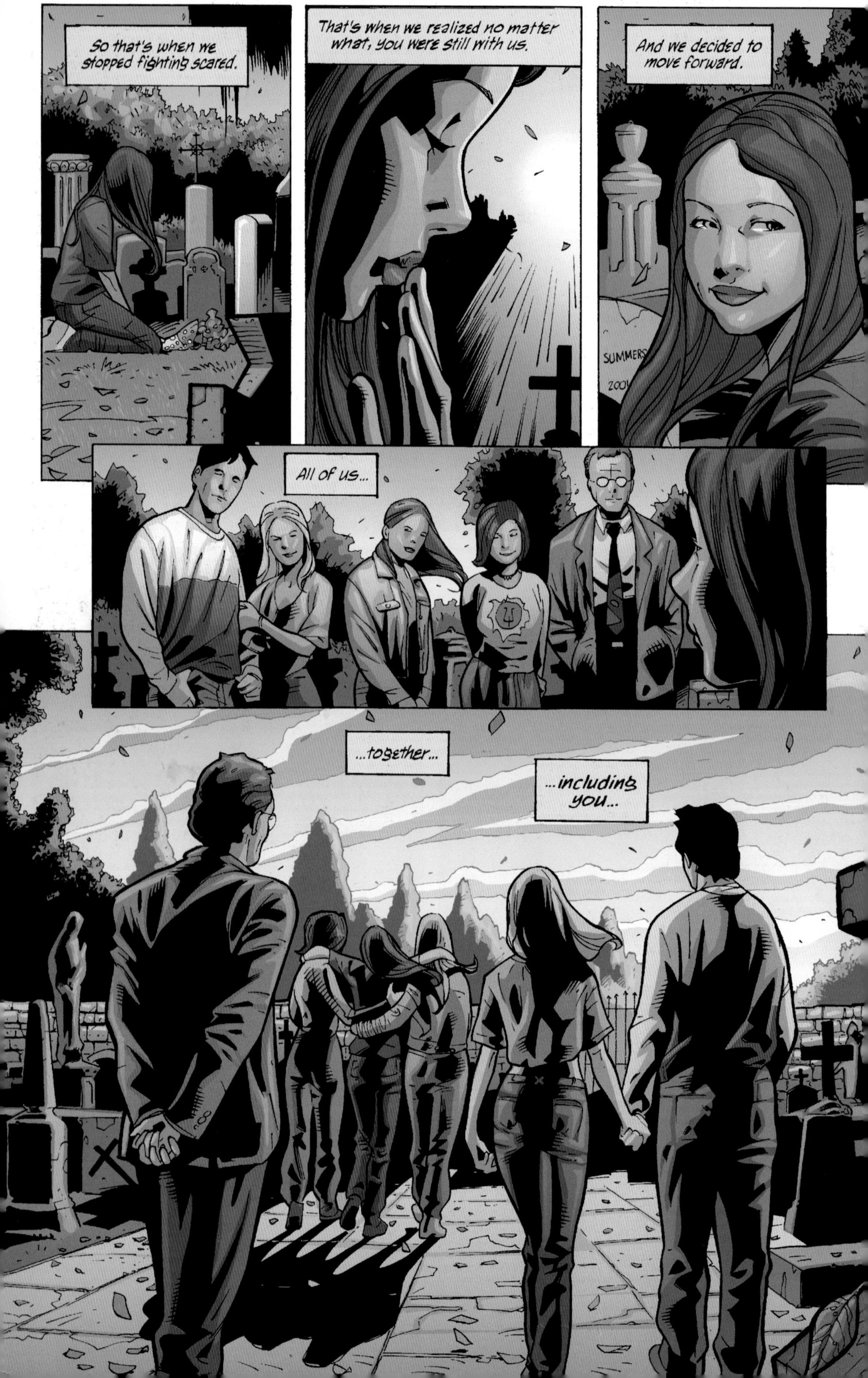
So that's when we stopped fighting scared.
That's when we realized no matter what, you were still with us.
And we decided to move forward.
SUMMERS
All of us...
...together...
...including you...

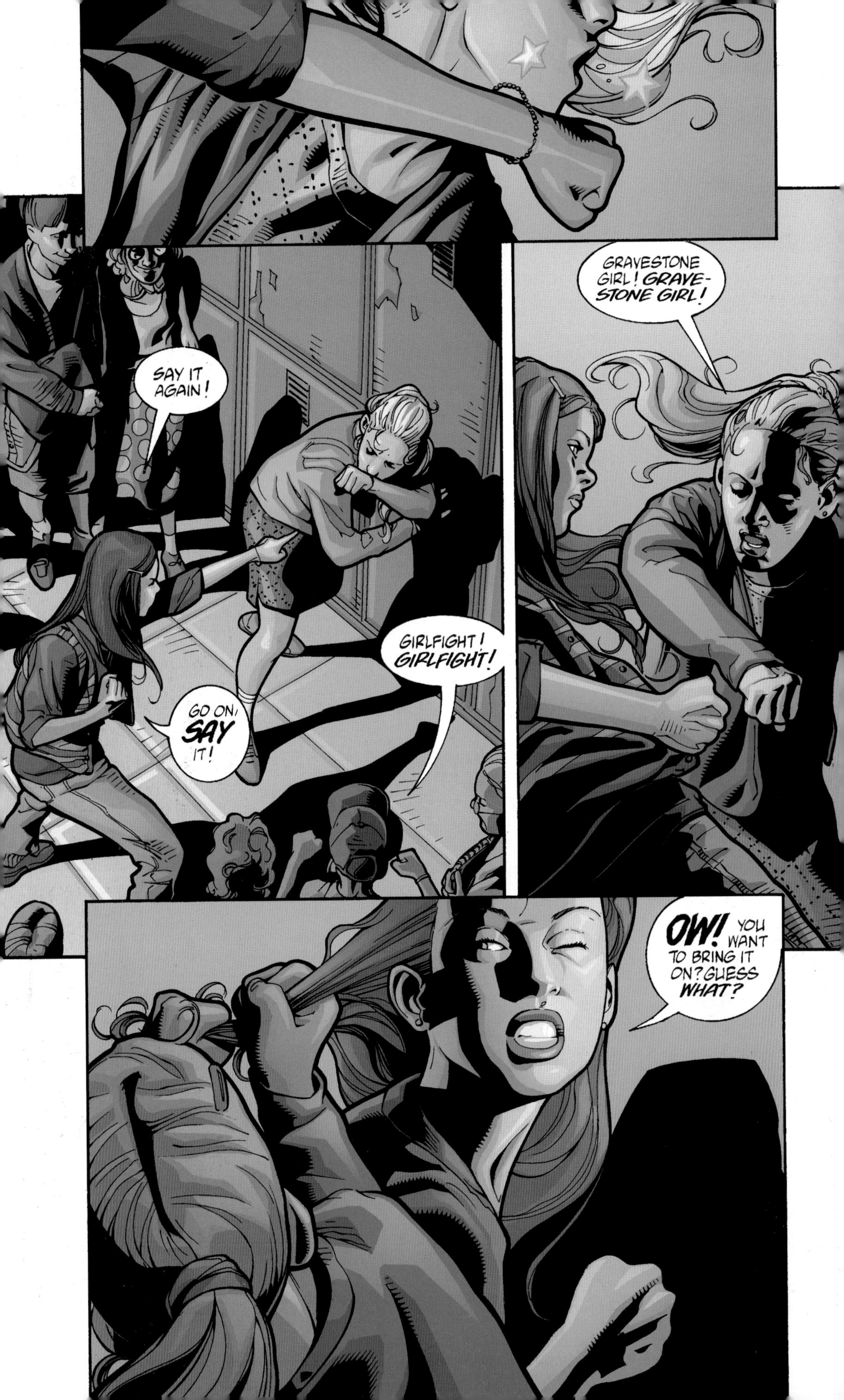
SAY IT AGAIN!
GO ON, SAY IT!
GIRLFIGHT! GIRLFIGHT!
GRAVESTONE GIRL! GRAVE-STONE GIRL!
OW! YOU WANT TO BRING IT ON? GUESS WHAT?

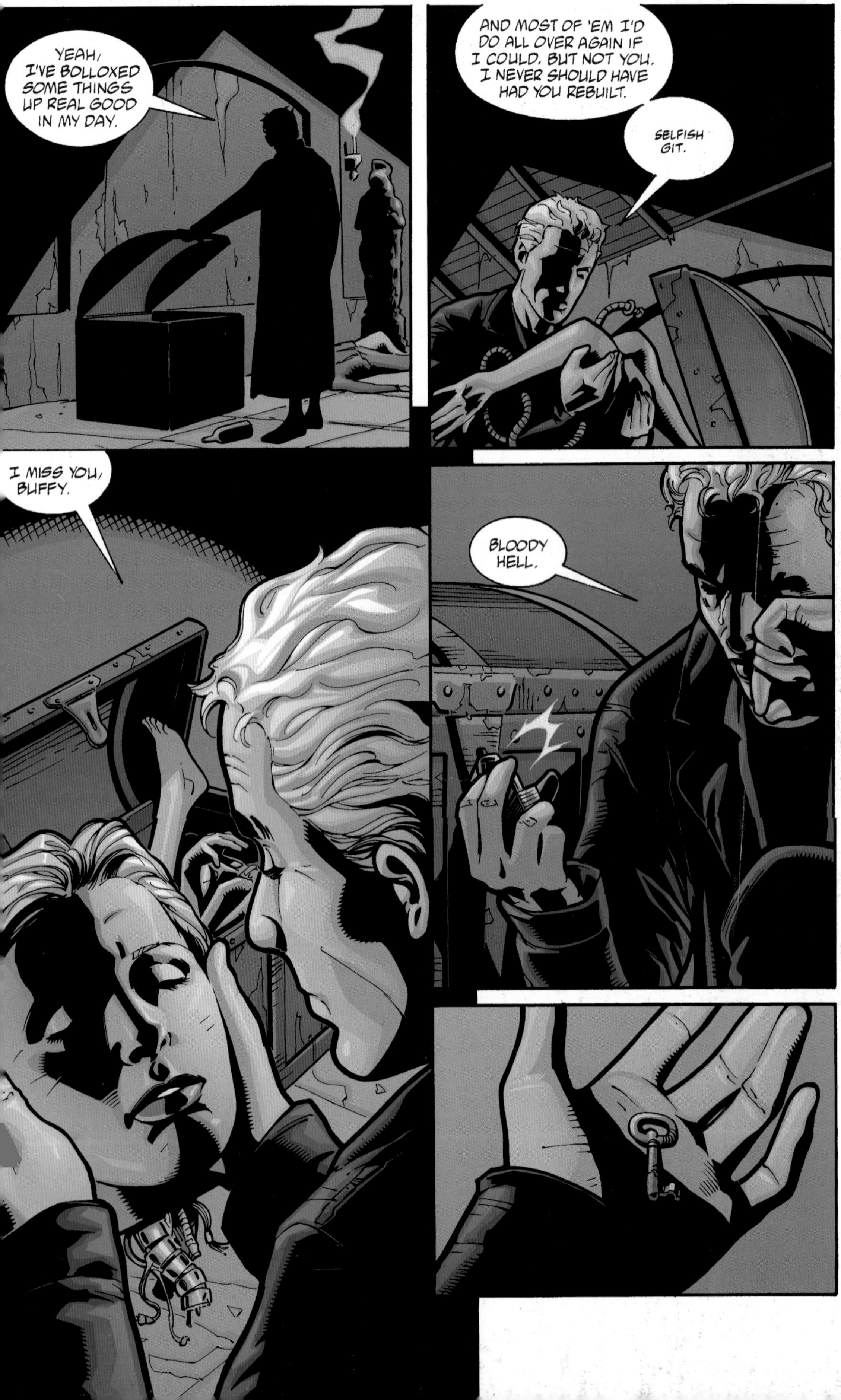
YEAH, I'VE BOLLOXED SOME THINGS UP REAL GOOD IN MY DAY.
AND MOST OF 'EM I'D DO ALL OVER AGAIN IF I COULD. BUT NOT YOU. I NEVER SHOULD HAVE HAD YOU REBUILT.
SELFISH GIT.
I MISS YOU, BUFFY.
BLOODY HELL.

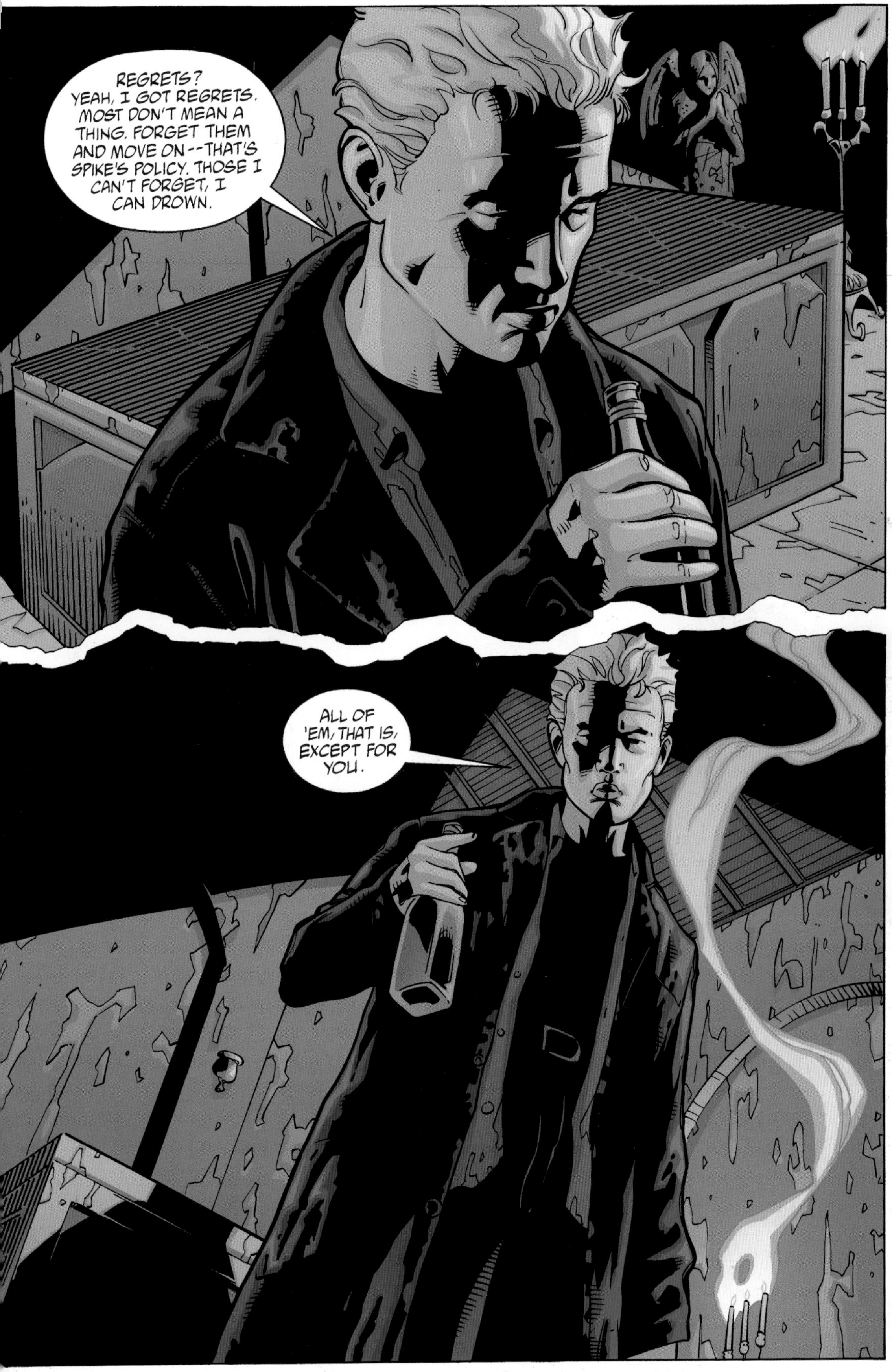
REGRETS? YEAH, I GOT REGRETS. MOST DON'T MEAN A THING. FORGET THEM AND MOVE ON--THAT'S SPIKE'S POLICY. THOSE I CAN'T FORGET, I CAN DROWN.
ALL OF 'EM, THAT IS, EXCEPT FOR YOU.

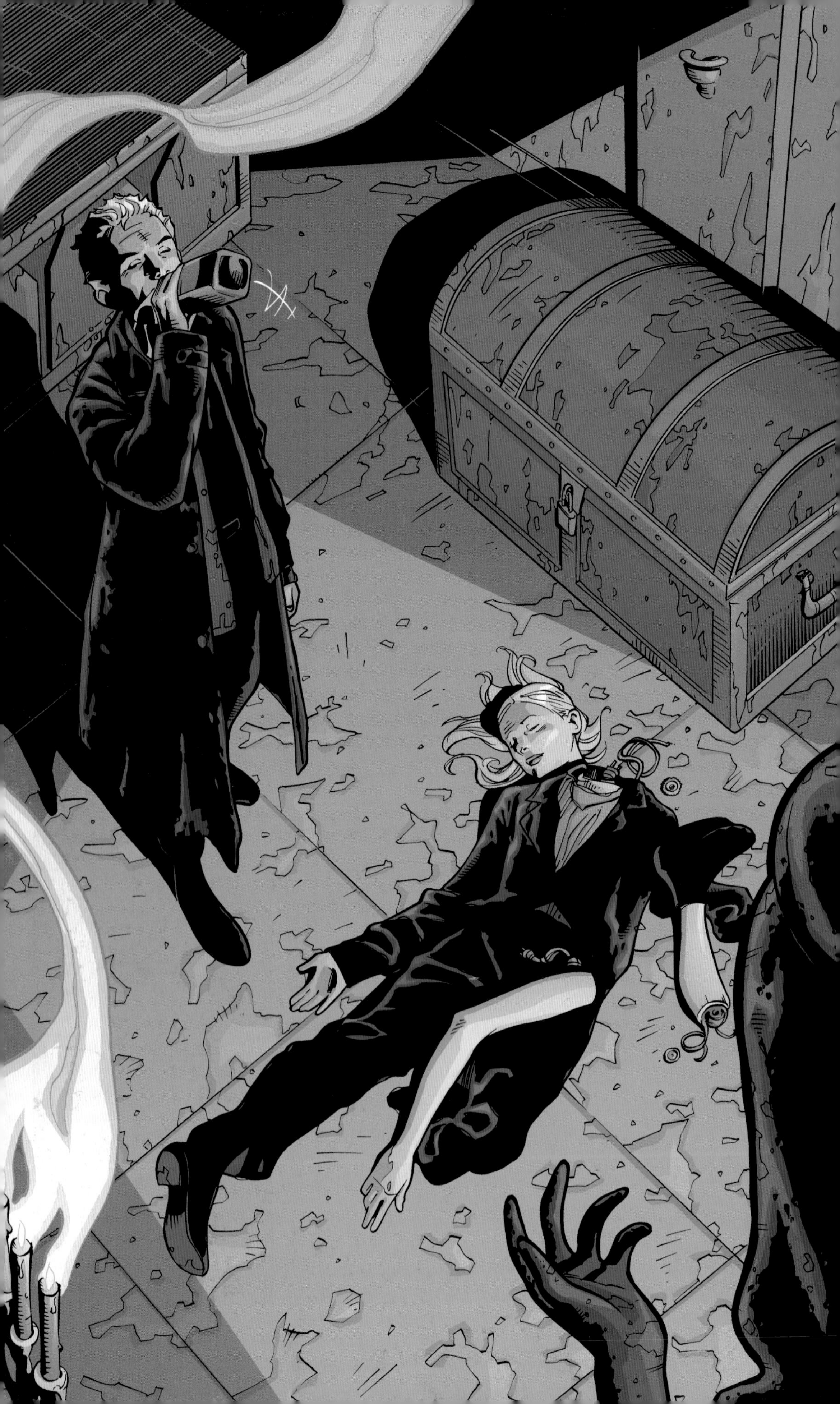

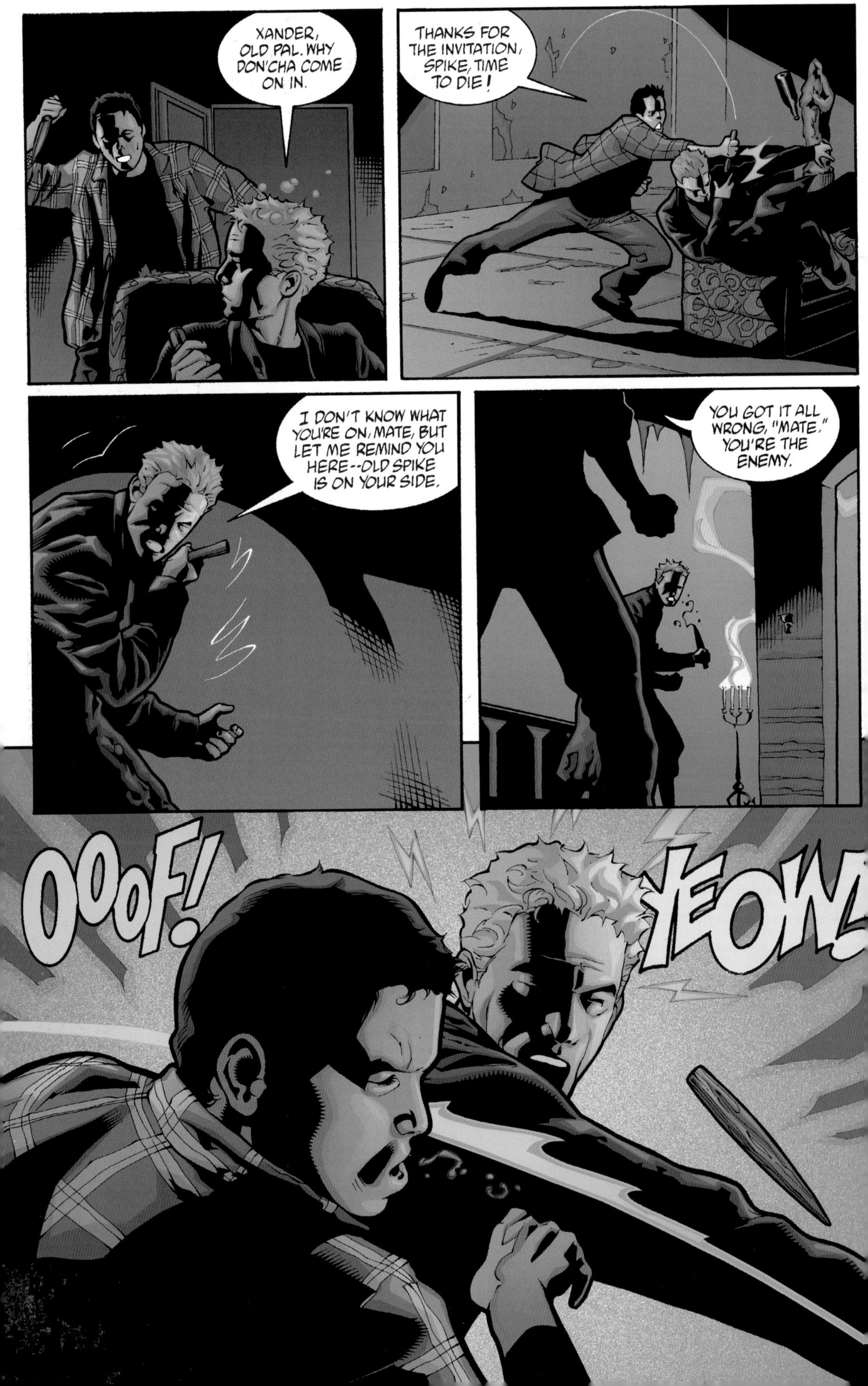
XANDER, OLD PAL. WHY DON'CHA COME ON IN.
THANKS FOR THE INVITATION, SPIKE, TIME TO DIE!
I DON'T KNOW WHAT YOU'RE ON, MATE, BUT LET ME REMIND YOU HERE--OLD SPIKE IS ON YOUR SIDE.
YOU GOT IT ALL WRONG, "MATE." YOU'RE THE ENEMY.
OOOF!
YEOW!

WE HAVE IT AT LAST!

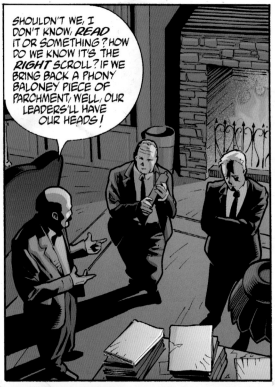

SHOULDN'T WE, I DON'T KNOW, *READ* IT OR SOMETHING? HOW DO WE KNOW IT'S THE *RIGHT* SCROLL? IF WE BRING BACK A PHONY BALONEY PIECE OF PARCHMENT, WELL, OUR LEADERS'LL HAVE OUR HEADS!

AH...HOW *WOULD* WE KNOW IF THIS IS THE RIGHT ONE OR NOT? DO ANY OF US KNOW WHAT IT'S SUPPOSED TO SAY?

BESIDES, WE WERE TOLD *NOT* TO READ IT. THEY MADE THAT PRETTY CLEAR.

GIMME THAT! WHAT KIND OF PANSY DEMONS ARE YOU? JUST BECAUSE SOMEONE TELLS YOU NOT TO...

IT'S BAD, ISN'T IT?

YEP. I'M AFRAID IT IS.

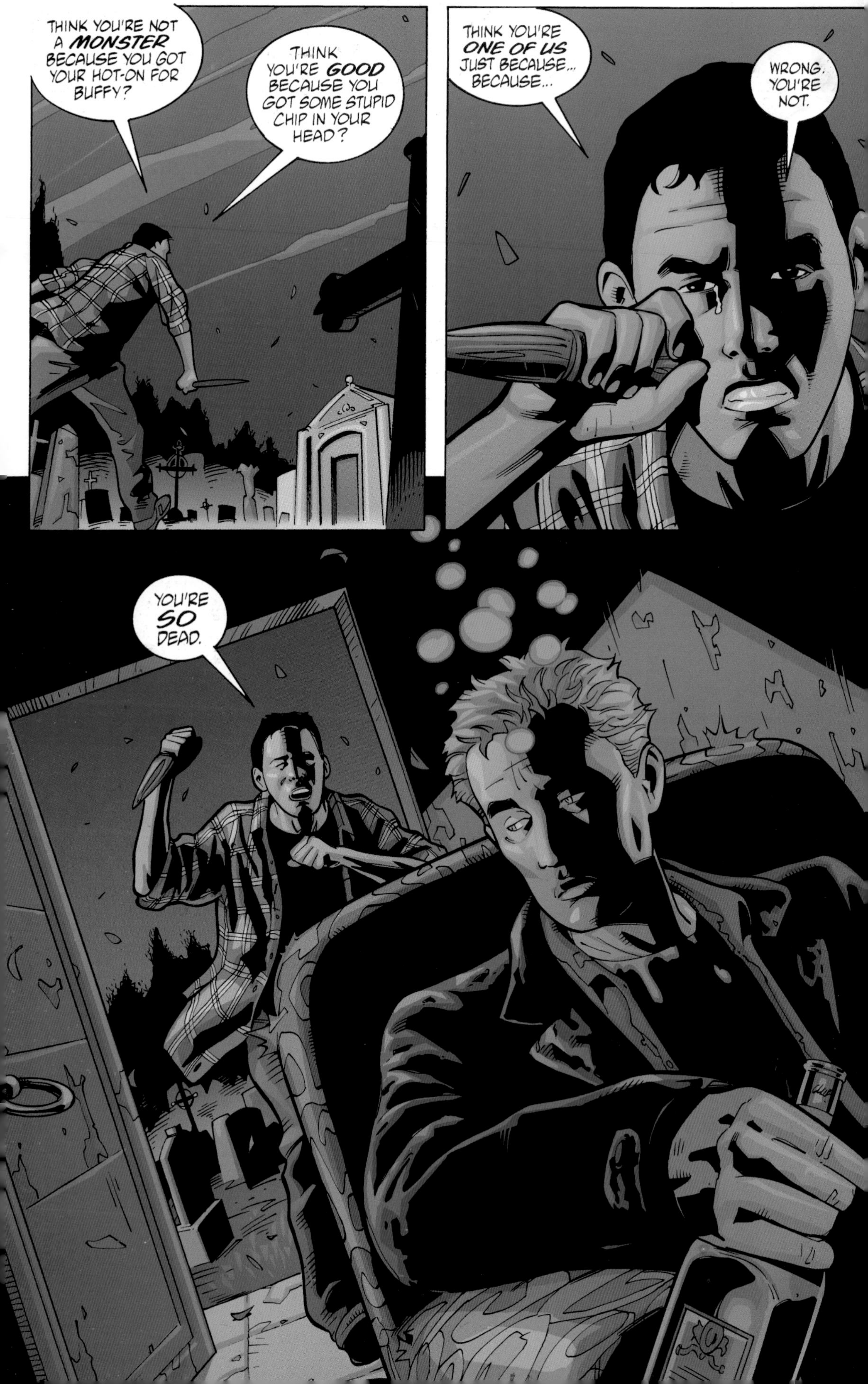
THINK YOU'RE NOT A MONSTER BECAUSE YOU GOT YOUR HOT-ON FOR BUFFY?
THINK YOU'RE GOOD BECAUSE YOU GOT SOME STUPID CHIP IN YOUR HEAD?
THINK YOU'RE ONE OF US JUST BECAUSE... BECAUSE...
WRONG. YOU'RE NOT.
YOU'RE SO DEAD.

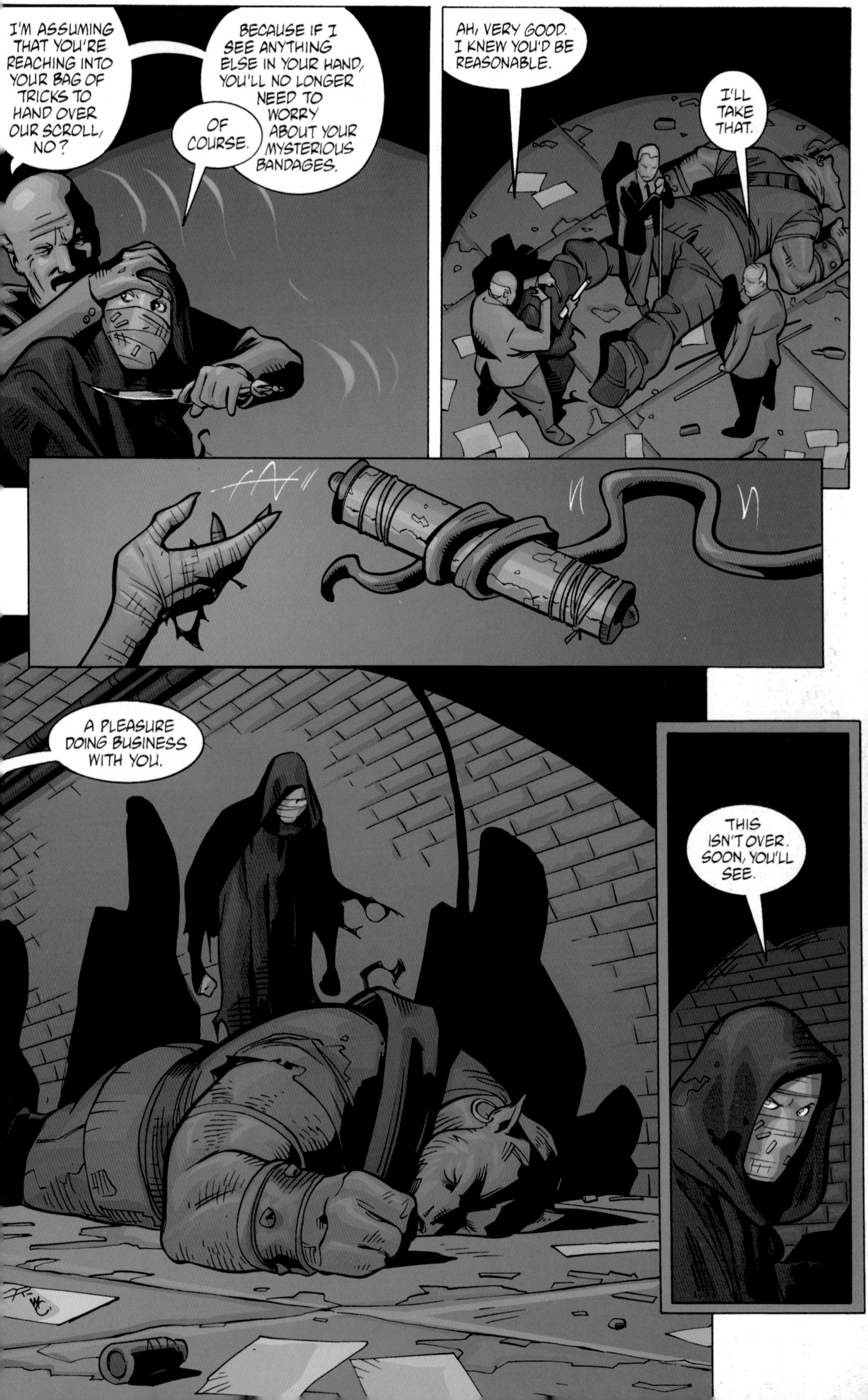

I'M ASSUMING THAT YOU'RE REACHING INTO YOUR BAG OF TRICKS TO HAND OVER OUR SCROLL, NO?
BECAUSE IF I SEE ANYTHING ELSE IN YOUR HAND, YOU'LL NO LONGER NEED TO WORRY ABOUT YOUR MYSTERIOUS BANDAGES.
OF COURSE.
AH, VERY GOOD. I KNEW YOU'D BE REASONABLE.
I'LL TAKE THAT.
A PLEASURE DOING BUSINESS WITH YOU.
THIS ISN'T OVER. SOON, YOU'LL SEE.

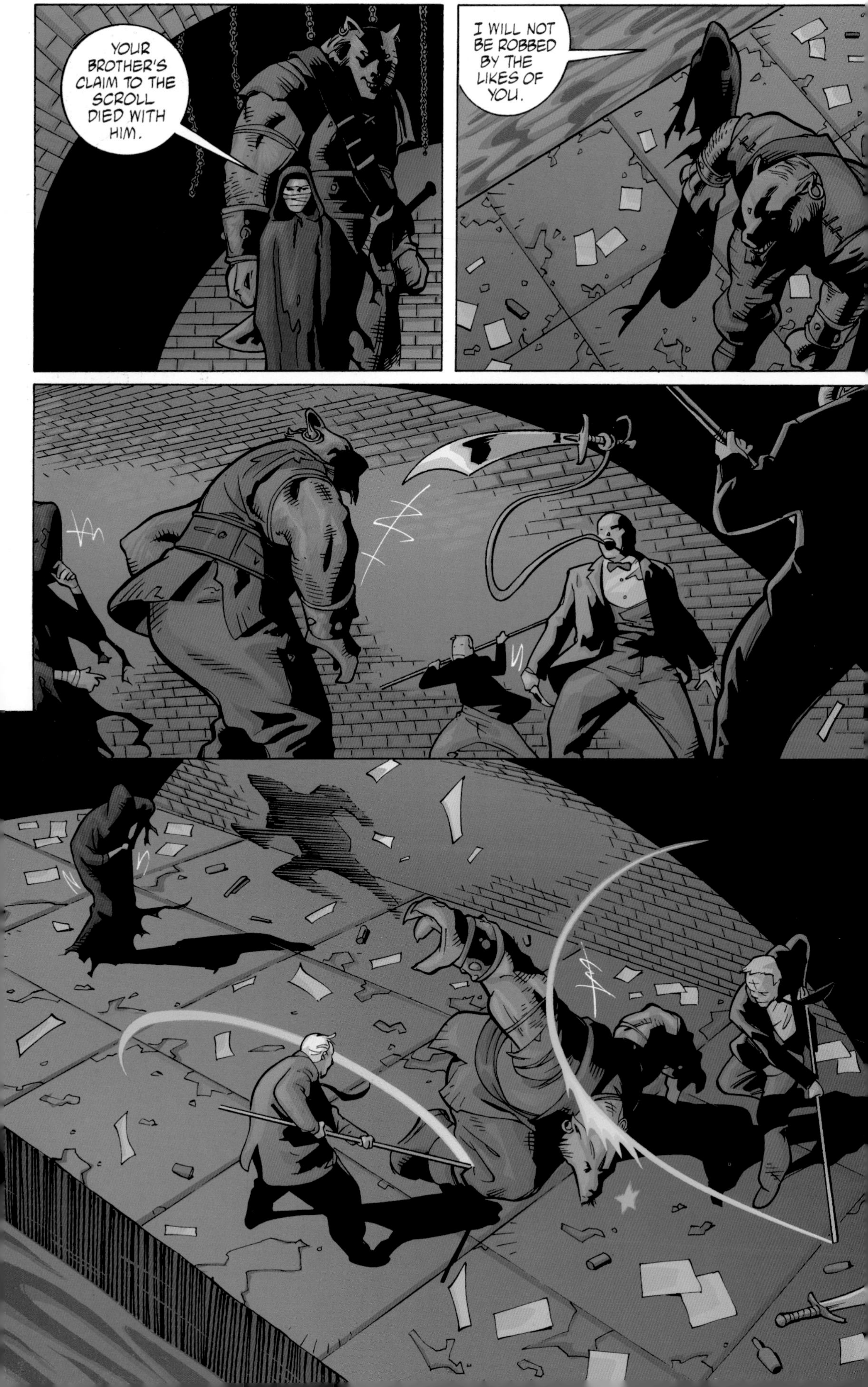
YOUR BROTHER'S CLAIM TO THE SCROLL DIED WITH HIM.
I WILL NOT BE ROBBED BY THE LIKES OF YOU.

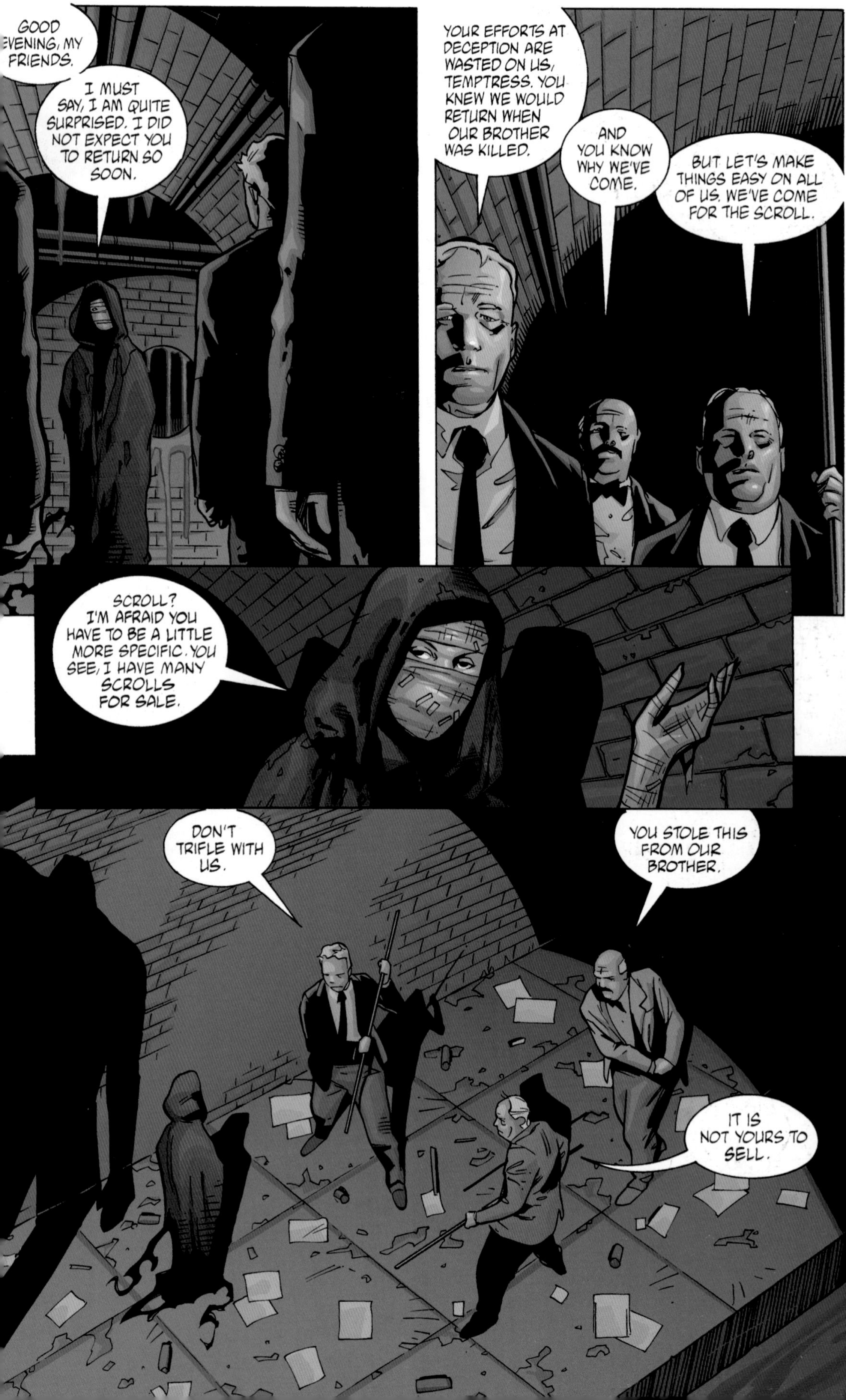
GOOD EVENING, MY FRIENDS.
I MUST SAY, I AM QUITE SURPRISED. I DID NOT EXPECT YOU TO RETURN SO SOON.
YOUR EFFORTS AT DECEPTION ARE WASTED ON US, TEMPTRESS. YOU KNEW WE WOULD RETURN WHEN OUR BROTHER WAS KILLED.
AND YOU KNOW WHY WE'VE COME.
BUT LET'S MAKE THINGS EASY ON ALL OF US. WE'VE COME FOR THE SCROLL.
SCROLL? I'M AFRAID YOU HAVE TO BE A LITTLE MORE SPECIFIC. YOU SEE, I HAVE MANY SCROLLS FOR SALE.
DON'T TRIFLE WITH US.
YOU STOLE THIS FROM OUR BROTHER.
IT IS NOT YOURS TO SELL.

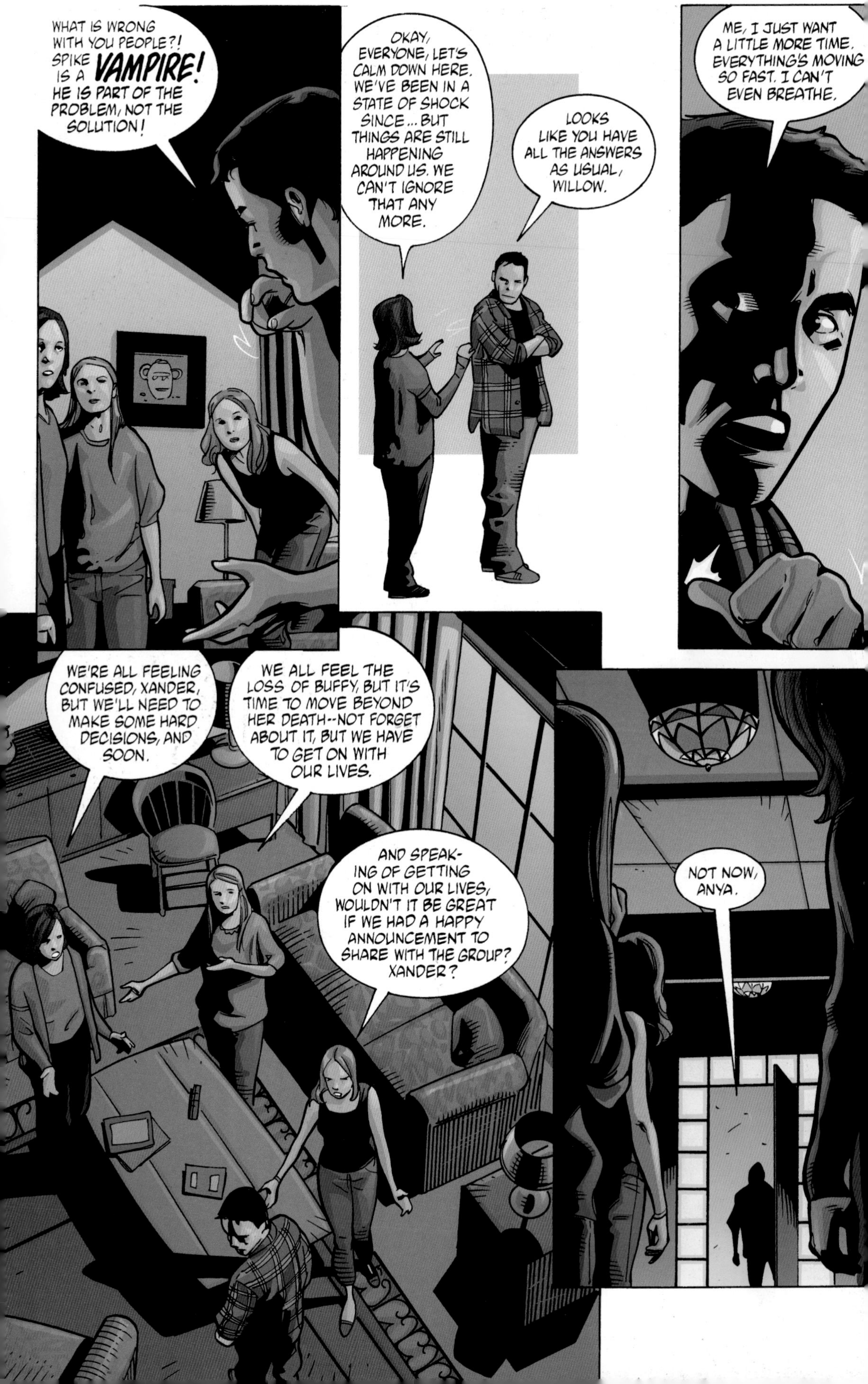
WHAT IS WRONG WITH YOU PEOPLE?! SPIKE IS A VAMPIRE! HE IS PART OF THE PROBLEM, NOT THE SOLUTION!
OKAY, EVERYONE, LET'S CALM DOWN HERE. WE'VE BEEN IN A STATE OF SHOCK SINCE... BUT THINGS ARE STILL HAPPENING AROUND US. WE CAN'T IGNORE THAT ANY MORE.
LOOKS LIKE YOU HAVE ALL THE ANSWERS AS USUAL, WILLOW.
ME, I JUST WANT A LITTLE MORE TIME. EVERYTHING'S MOVING SO FAST. I CAN'T EVEN BREATHE.
WE'RE ALL FEELING CONFUSED, XANDER, BUT WE'LL NEED TO MAKE SOME HARD DECISIONS, AND SOON.
WE ALL FEEL THE LOSS OF BUFFY, BUT IT'S TIME TO MOVE BEYOND HER DEATH--NOT FORGET ABOUT IT, BUT WE HAVE TO GET ON WITH OUR LIVES.
AND SPEAK-ING OF GETTING ON WITH OUR LIVES, WOULDN'T IT BE GREAT IF WE HAD A HAPPY ANNOUNCEMENT TO SHARE WITH THE GROUP? XANDER?
NOT NOW, ANYA.

OKAY, SO GILES MANAGED TO CONVINCE THE PRINCIPAL THAT HE DID NOT NEED TO MEET WITH BUFFY IN PERSON, BUT--

SOMEHOW WE STILL MANAGED TO GET OUR BUTTS KICKED BY A BUNCH OF VAMPIRES WHEN THE VAMPIRE *SLAYER* WAS NOT AROUND TO BACK US UP...

SORRY, I'M STILL ON LAST NIGHT.

IT'S ALL RIGHT, POOKY-BEAR. WE STILL WON. WE ALWAYS WIN.

[CAN] [W]E TALK [AB]OUT [D]AWN [F]OR A [S]ECOND ?

YOU'RE RIGHT. DAWN. AFTER ALL, THE VAMPS ARE GOING TO COME AFTER *ALL* OF US.

WHEN DID YOU BECOME SUCH A FRAIDY CAT? WE'RE ADULTS AND CAN HANDLE OURSELVES AGAINST MONSTERS-- POWERFUL WITCHES, REMEMBER?

I AGREE WITH WILLOW, WE SHOULD BE MORE CONCERNED ABOUT DAWN'S PROBLEM AT SCHOOL.

I CAN'T BELIEVE BUFFY'S ONLY BEEN GONE FOR A COUPLE WEEKS, AND I'M GOING ALL BLUBBER-ING BABY. I GUESS GETTING SLAPPED AROUND BY A VAMP WILL DO THAT TO A GUY.

I...I DON'T KNOW WHAT WE'RE GOING TO DO ABOUT DAWN. WE'LL JUST HAVE TO STRESS TO HER THAT SHE'S GOT. TO KEEP A LOW PROFILE UNTIL....WELL, UNTIL SHE'S IN COLLEGE.

[X]ANDER, [I]T DOESN'T [W]ORK LIKE THAT.

WHAT IF WE GET SPIKE TO HELP US PATROL? THEN WE CAN FOCUS ON MAINTAINING A STABLE HOME ENVIRONMENT--

NO! NO WAY!

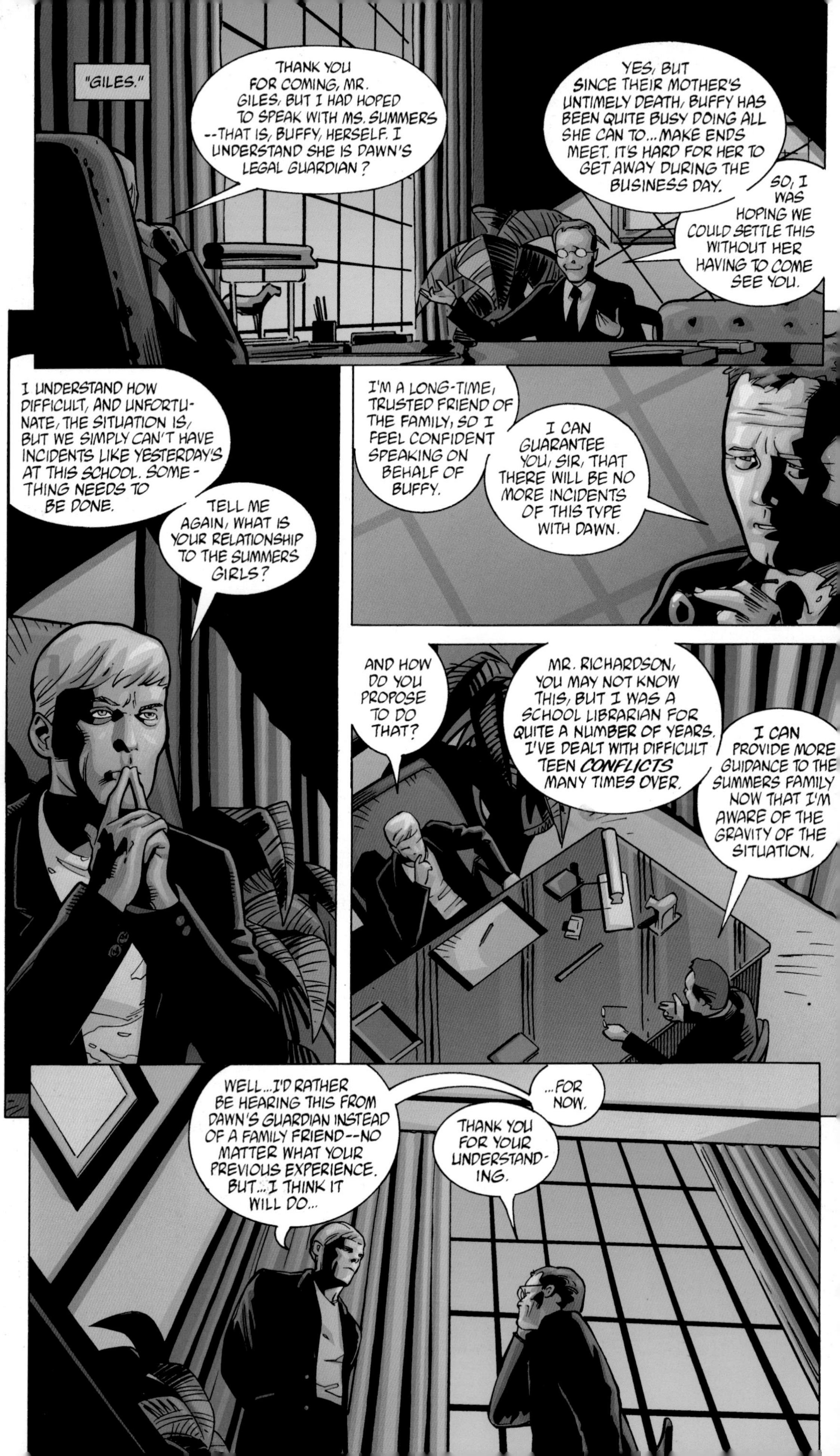
"GILES."
THANK YOU FOR COMING, MR. GILES, BUT I HAD HOPED TO SPEAK WITH MS. SUMMERS --THAT IS, BUFFY, HERSELF. I UNDERSTAND SHE IS DAWN'S LEGAL GUARDIAN?
YES, BUT SINCE THEIR MOTHER'S UNTIMELY DEATH, BUFFY HAS BEEN QUITE BUSY DOING ALL SHE CAN TO...MAKE ENDS MEET. IT'S HARD FOR HER TO GET AWAY DURING THE BUSINESS DAY.
SO, I WAS HOPING WE COULD SETTLE THIS WITHOUT HER HAVING TO COME SEE YOU.
I UNDERSTAND HOW DIFFICULT, AND UNFORTUNATE, THE SITUATION IS, BUT WE SIMPLY CAN'T HAVE INCIDENTS LIKE YESTERDAY'S AT THIS SCHOOL. SOMETHING NEEDS TO BE DONE.
TELL ME AGAIN, WHAT IS YOUR RELATIONSHIP TO THE SUMMERS GIRLS?
I'M A LONG-TIME, TRUSTED FRIEND OF THE FAMILY, SO I FEEL CONFIDENT SPEAKING ON BEHALF OF BUFFY.
I CAN GUARANTEE YOU, SIR, THAT THERE WILL BE NO MORE INCIDENTS OF THIS TYPE WITH DAWN.
AND HOW DO YOU PROPOSE TO DO THAT?
MR. RICHARDSON, YOU MAY NOT KNOW THIS, BUT I WAS A SCHOOL LIBRARIAN FOR QUITE A NUMBER OF YEARS. I'VE DEALT WITH DIFFICULT TEEN CONFLICTS MANY TIMES OVER.
I CAN PROVIDE MORE GUIDANCE TO THE SUMMERS FAMILY NOW THAT I'M AWARE OF THE GRAVITY OF THE SITUATION.
WELL...I'D RATHER BE HEARING THIS FROM DAWN'S GUARDIAN INSTEAD OF A FAMILY FRIEND--NO MATTER WHAT YOUR PREVIOUS EXPERIENCE. BUT...I THINK IT WILL DO...
...FOR NOW.
THANK YOU FOR YOUR UNDERSTANDING.

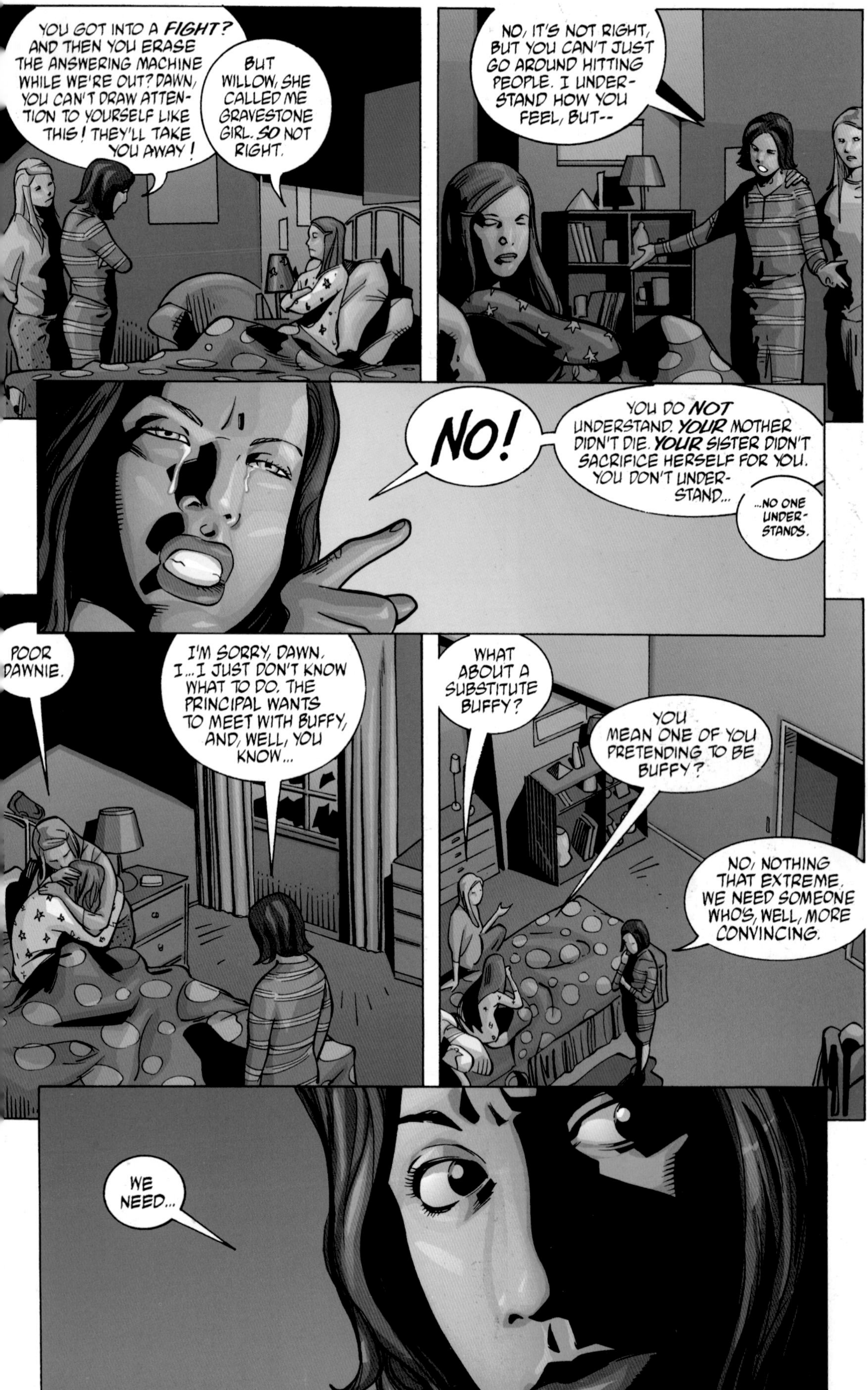
YOU GOT INTO A FIGHT? AND THEN YOU ERASE THE ANSWERING MACHINE WHILE WE'RE OUT? DAWN, YOU CAN'T DRAW ATTENTION TO YOURSELF LIKE THIS! THEY'LL TAKE YOU AWAY!
BUT WILLOW, SHE CALLED ME GRAVESTONE GIRL. SO NOT RIGHT.
NO, IT'S NOT RIGHT, BUT YOU CAN'T JUST GO AROUND HITTING PEOPLE. I UNDERSTAND HOW YOU FEEL, BUT--
NO!
YOU DO NOT UNDERSTAND. YOUR MOTHER DIDN'T DIE. YOUR SISTER DIDN'T SACRIFICE HERSELF FOR YOU. YOU DON'T UNDERSTAND...
...NO ONE UNDERSTANDS.
POOR DAWNIE.
I'M SORRY, DAWN. I... I JUST DON'T KNOW WHAT TO DO. THE PRINCIPAL WANTS TO MEET WITH BUFFY, AND, WELL, YOU KNOW...
WHAT ABOUT A SUBSTITUTE BUFFY?
YOU MEAN ONE OF YOU PRETENDING TO BE BUFFY?
NO, NOTHING THAT EXTREME. WE NEED SOMEONE WHO'S, WELL, MORE CONVINCING.
WE NEED...

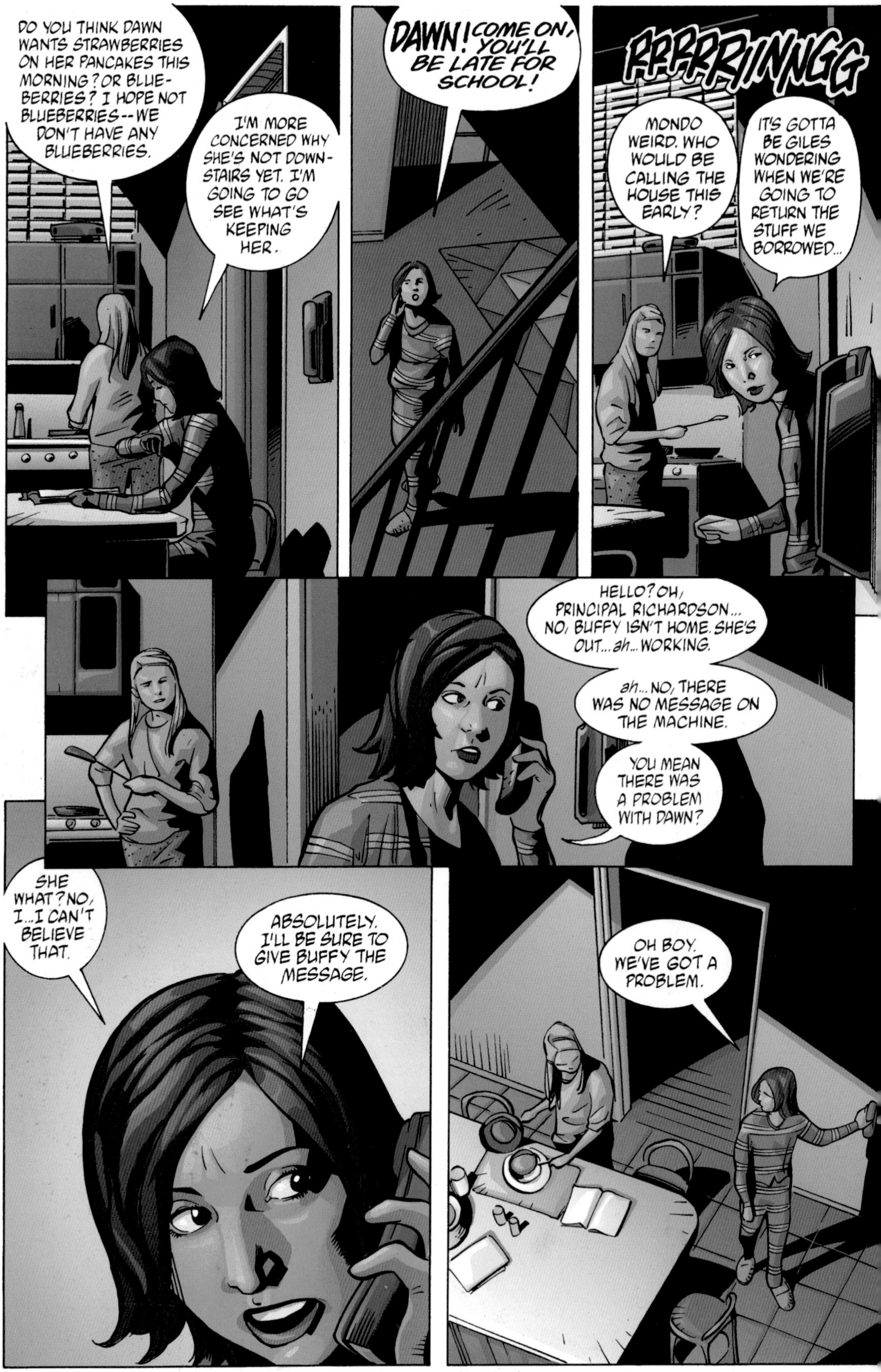
DO YOU THINK DAWN WANTS STRAWBERRIES ON HER PANCAKES THIS MORNING? OR BLUE-BERRIES? I HOPE NOT BLUEBERRIES--WE DON'T HAVE ANY BLUEBERRIES.
I'M MORE CONCERNED WHY SHE'S NOT DOWN-STAIRS YET. I'M GOING TO GO SEE WHAT'S KEEPING HER.
DAWN! COME ON, YOU'LL BE LATE FOR SCHOOL!
RRRRRIINNGG
MONDO WEIRD. WHO WOULD BE CALLING THE HOUSE THIS EARLY?
IT'S GOTTA BE GILES WONDERING WHEN WE'RE GOING TO RETURN THE STUFF WE BORROWED...
HELLO? OH, PRINCIPAL RICHARDSON... NO, BUFFY ISN'T HOME. SHE'S OUT... ah... WORKING.
ah... NO, THERE WAS NO MESSAGE ON THE MACHINE.
YOU MEAN THERE WAS A PROBLEM WITH DAWN?
SHE WHAT? NO, I... I CAN'T BELIEVE THAT.
ABSOLUTELY. I'LL BE SURE TO GIVE BUFFY THE MESSAGE.
OH BOY. WE'VE GOT A PROBLEM.

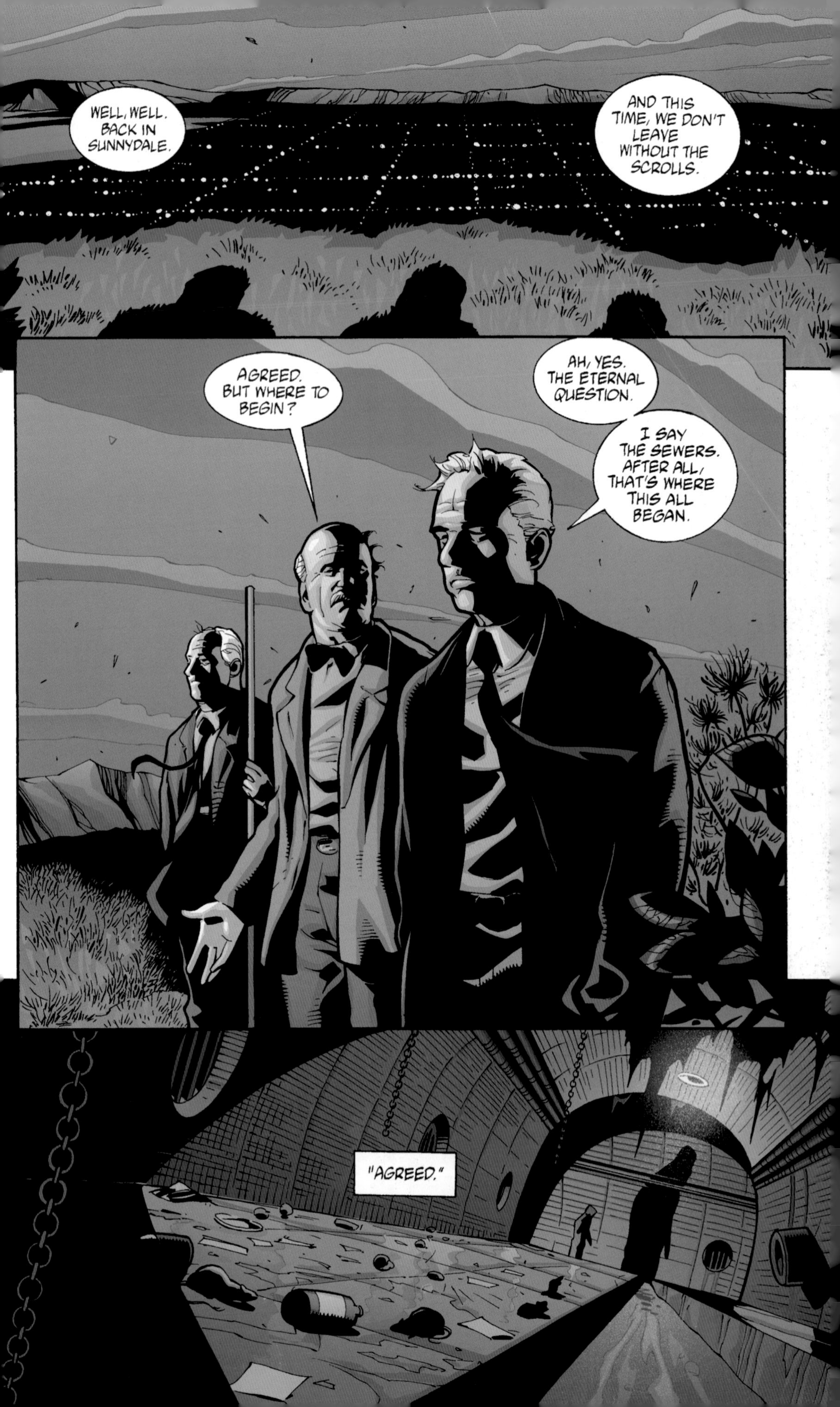
WELL, WELL. BACK IN SUNNYDALE.
AND THIS TIME, WE DON'T LEAVE WITHOUT THE SCROLLS.
AGREED. BUT WHERE TO BEGIN?
AH, YES. THE ETERNAL QUESTION.
I SAY THE SEWERS. AFTER ALL, THAT'S WHERE THIS ALL BEGAN.
"AGREED."

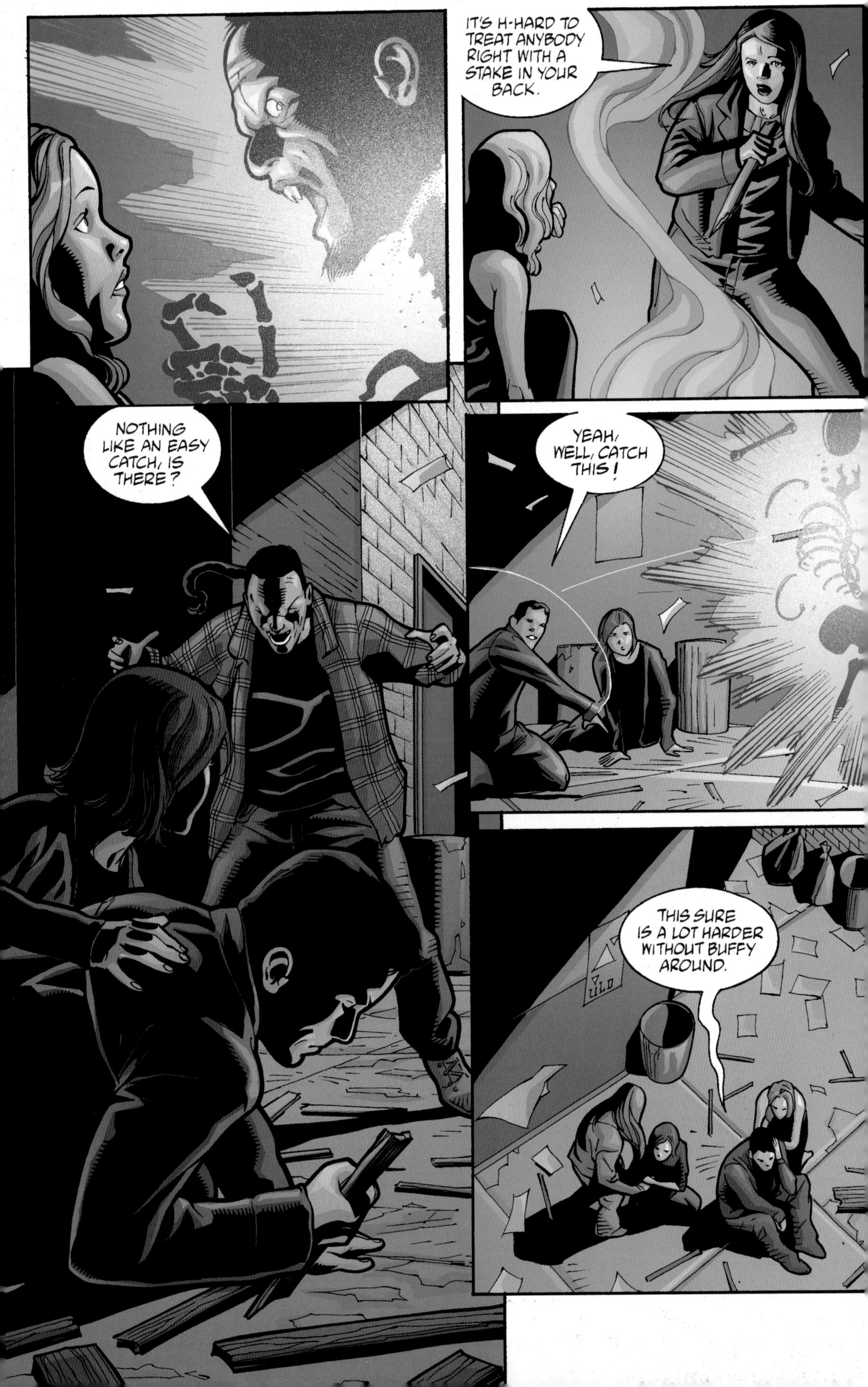
IT'S H-HARD TO TREAT ANYBODY RIGHT WITH A STAKE IN YOUR BACK.
NOTHING LIKE AN EASY CATCH, IS THERE?
YEAH, WELL, CATCH THIS!
THIS SURE IS A LOT HARDER WITHOUT BUFFY AROUND.

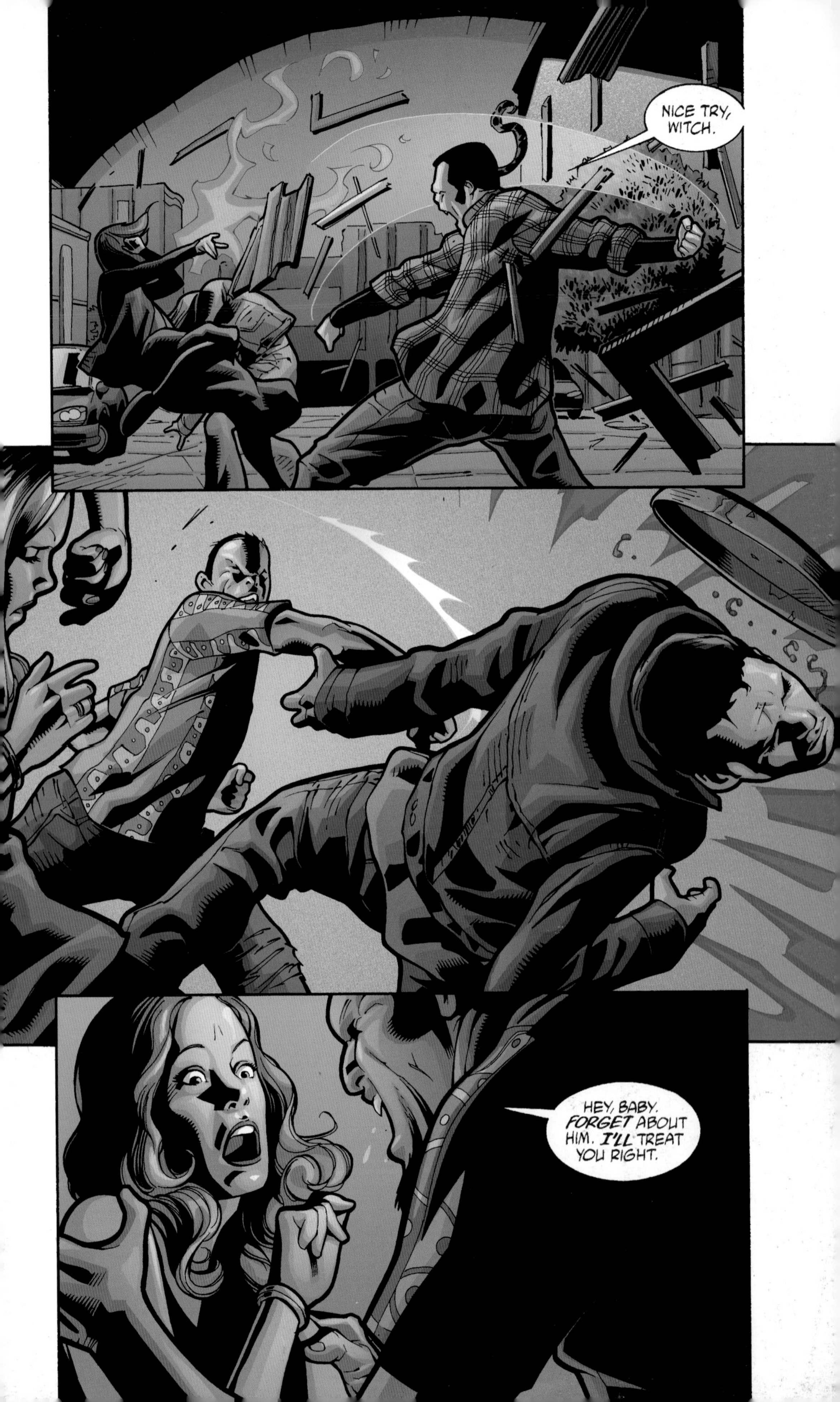

NICE TRY, WITCH.
HEY, BABY. FORGET ABOUT HIM. I'LL TREAT YOU RIGHT.

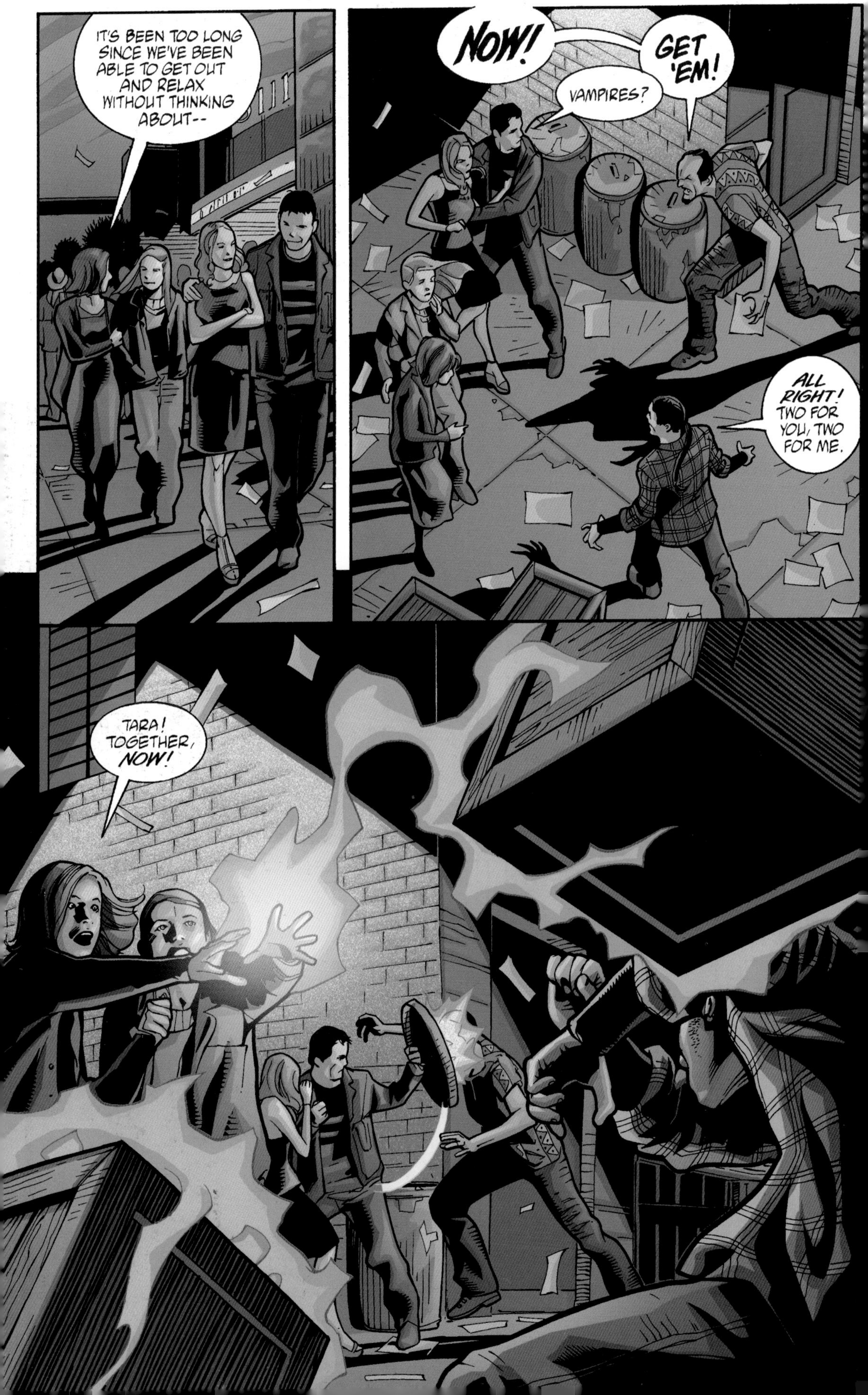
IT'S BEEN TOO LONG SINCE WE'VE BEEN ABLE TO GET OUT AND RELAX WITHOUT THINKING ABOUT--
NOW!
GET 'EM!
VAMPIRES?
ALL RIGHT! TWO FOR YOU, TWO FOR ME.
TARA! TOGETHER, NOW!

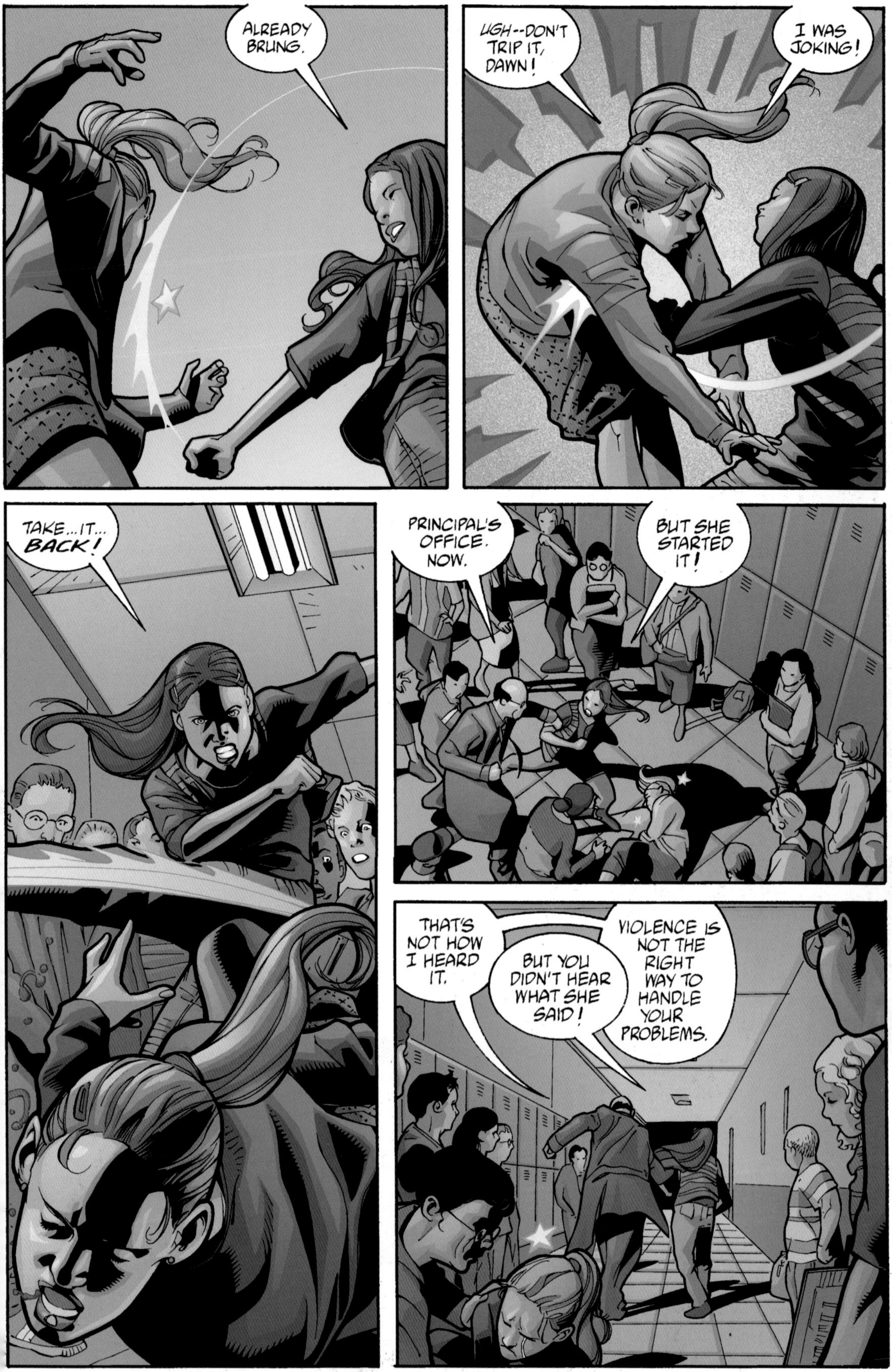
ALREADY BRUNG.
UGH--DON'T TRIP IT, DAWN!
I WAS JOKING!
TAKE... IT... BACK!
PRINCIPAL'S OFFICE. NOW.
BUT SHE STARTED IT!
THAT'S NOT HOW I HEARD IT.
BUT YOU DIDN'T HEAR WHAT SHE SAID!
VIOLENCE IS NOT THE RIGHT WAY TO HANDLE YOUR PROBLEMS.

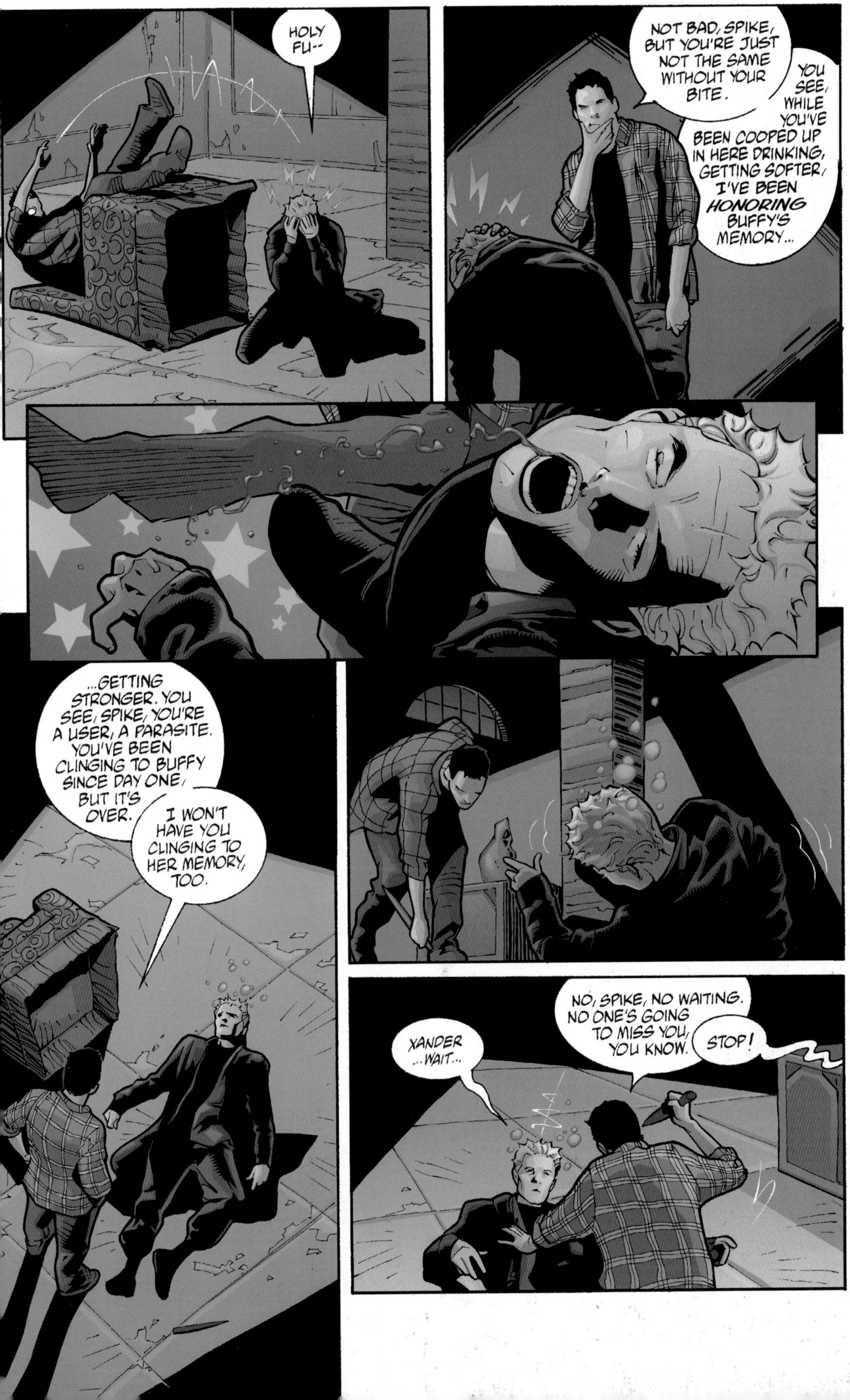
HOLY FU--
NOT BAD, SPIKE, BUT YOU'RE JUST NOT THE SAME WITHOUT YOUR BITE.
YOU SEE, WHILE YOU'VE BEEN COOPED UP IN HERE DRINKING, GETTING SOFTER, I'VE BEEN *HONORING* BUFFY'S MEMORY...
...GETTING STRONGER. YOU SEE, SPIKE, YOU'RE A USER, A PARASITE. YOU'VE BEEN CLINGING TO BUFFY SINCE DAY ONE, BUT IT'S OVER.
I WON'T HAVE YOU CLINGING TO HER MEMORY, TOO.
XANDER ...WAIT...
NO, SPIKE, NO WAITING. NO ONE'S GOING TO MISS YOU, YOU KNOW.
STOP!

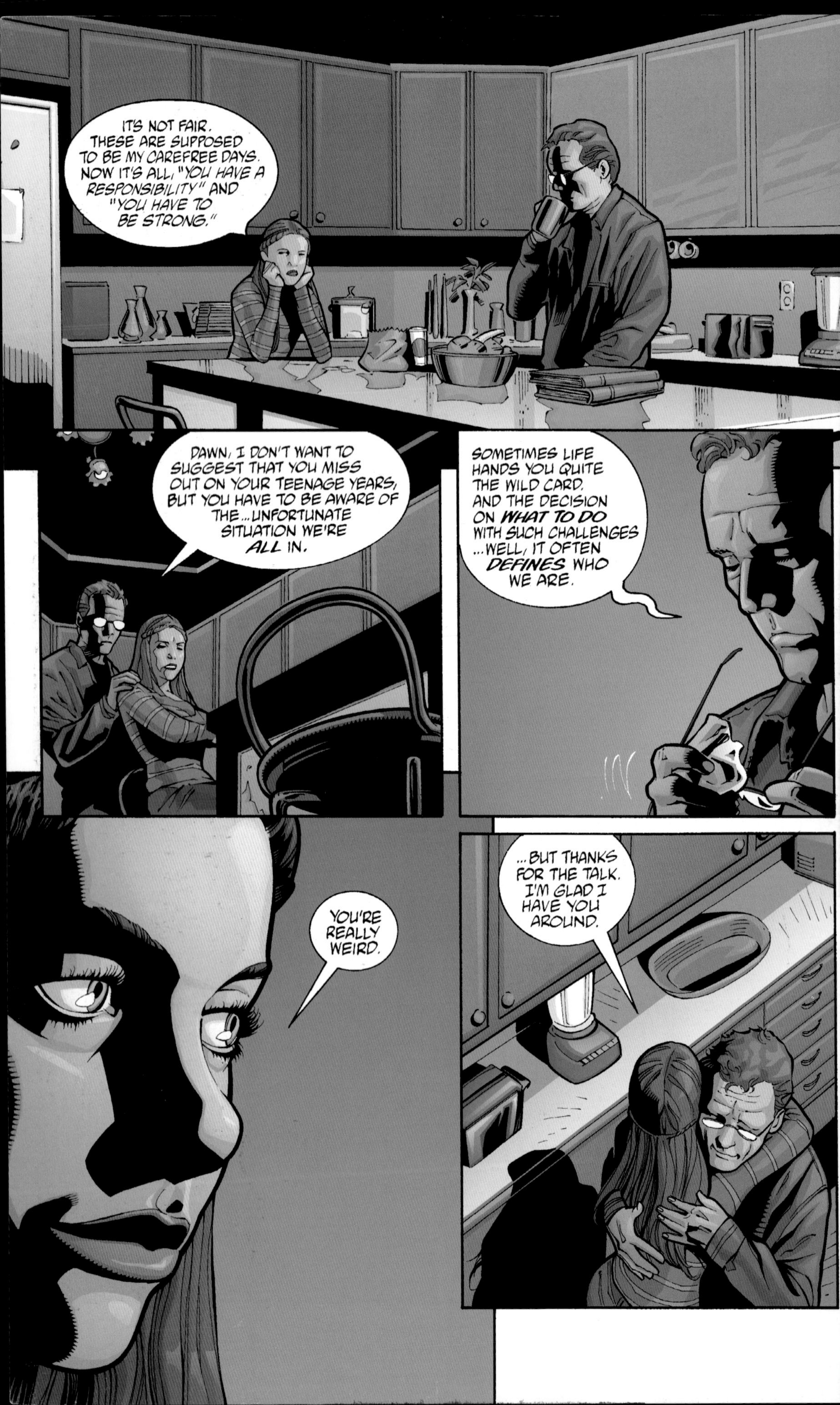
IT'S NOT FAIR. THESE ARE SUPPOSED TO BE MY CAREFREE DAYS. NOW IT'S ALL, "YOU HAVE A RESPONSIBILITY" AND "YOU HAVE TO BE STRONG."
DAWN, I DON'T WANT TO SUGGEST THAT YOU MISS OUT ON YOUR TEENAGE YEARS, BUT YOU HAVE TO BE AWARE OF THE...UNFORTUNATE SITUATION WE'RE ALL IN.
SOMETIMES LIFE HANDS YOU QUITE THE WILD CARD. AND THE DECISION ON WHAT TO DO WITH SUCH CHALLENGES ...WELL, IT OFTEN DEFINES WHO WE ARE.
YOU'RE REALLY WEIRD.
...BUT THANKS FOR THE TALK. I'M GLAD I HAVE YOU AROUND.

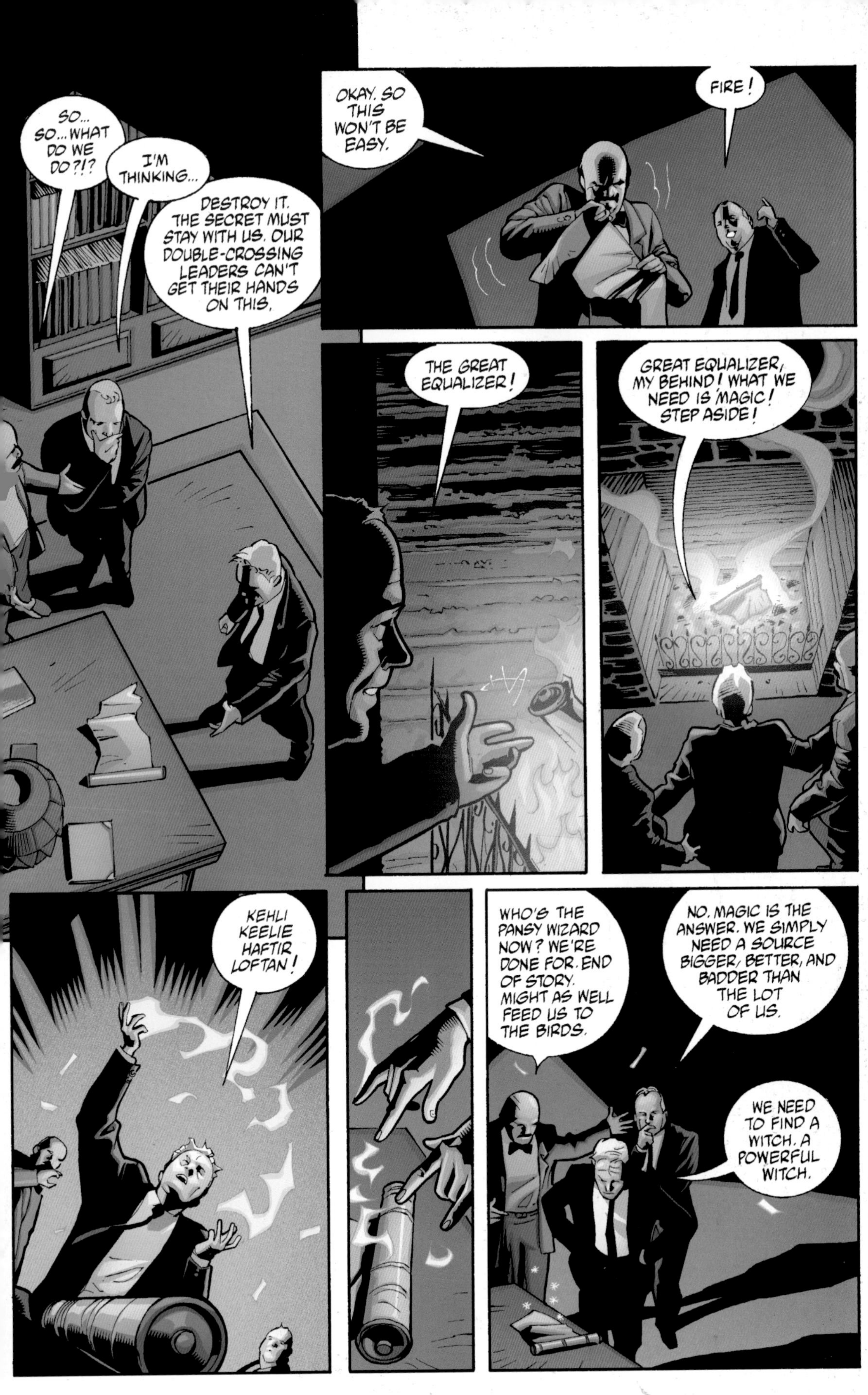
SO... SO...WHAT DO WE DO?!?
I'M THINKING...
DESTROY IT. THE SECRET MUST STAY WITH US. OUR DOUBLE-CROSSING LEADERS CAN'T GET THEIR HANDS ON THIS.
OKAY. SO THIS WON'T BE EASY.
FIRE!
THE GREAT EQUALIZER!
GREAT EQUALIZER, MY BEHIND! WHAT WE NEED IS MAGIC! STEP ASIDE!
KEHLI KEELIE HAFTIR LOFTAN!
WHO'S THE PANSY WIZARD NOW? WE'RE DONE FOR. END OF STORY. MIGHT AS WELL FEED US TO THE BIRDS.
NO. MAGIC IS THE ANSWER. WE SIMPLY NEED A SOURCE BIGGER, BETTER, AND BADDER THAN THE LOT OF US.
WE NEED TO FIND A WITCH. A POWERFUL WITCH.

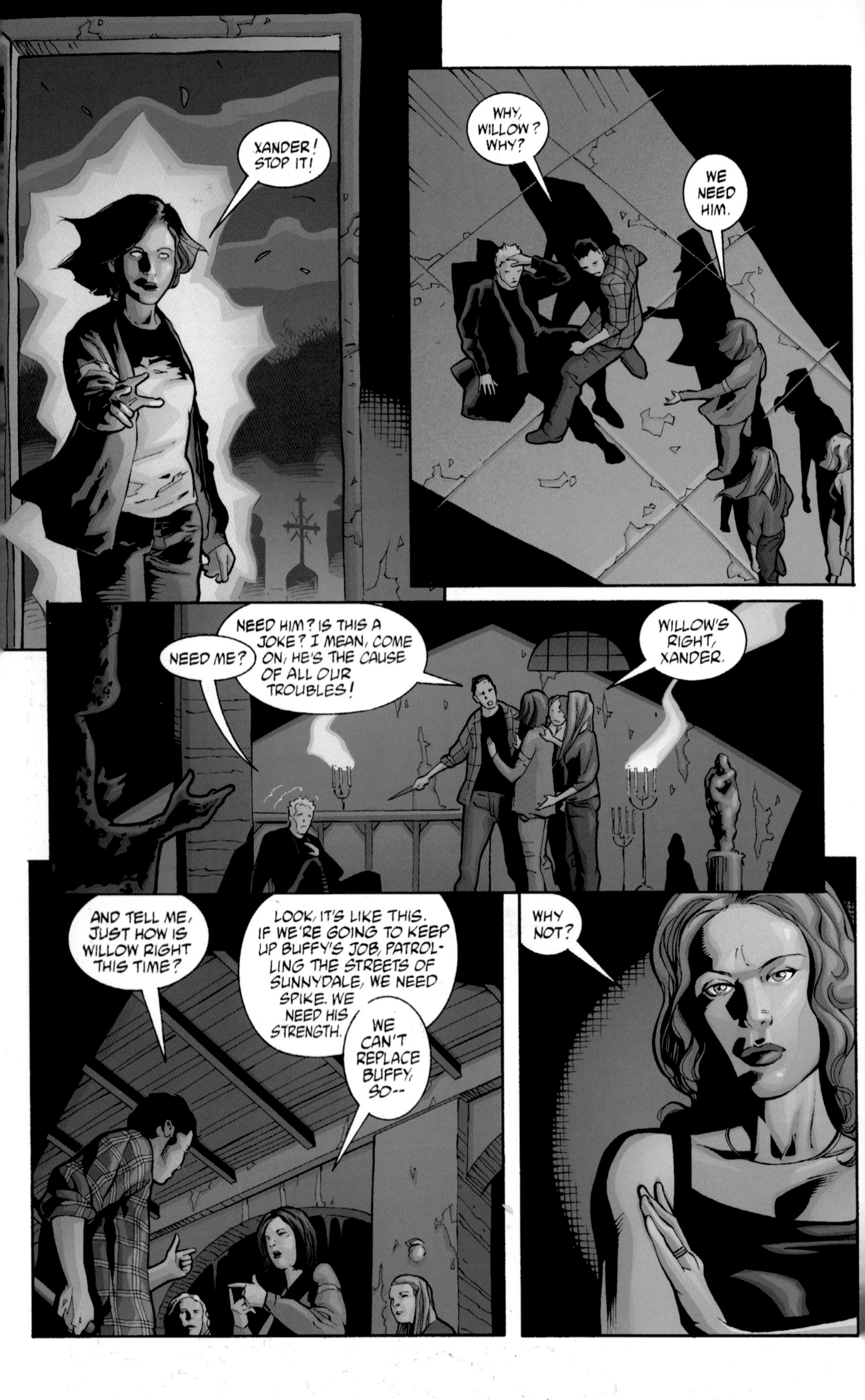
XANDER! STOP IT!
WHY, WILLOW? WHY?
WE NEED HIM.
NEED ME?
NEED HIM? IS THIS A JOKE? I MEAN, COME ON, HE'S THE CAUSE OF ALL OUR TROUBLES!
WILLOW'S RIGHT, XANDER.
AND TELL ME, JUST HOW IS WILLOW RIGHT THIS TIME?
LOOK, IT'S LIKE THIS. IF WE'RE GOING TO KEEP UP BUFFY'S JOB, PATROL-LING THE STREETS OF SUNNYDALE, WE NEED SPIKE. WE NEED HIS STRENGTH.
WE CAN'T REPLACE BUFFY, SO--
WHY NOT?

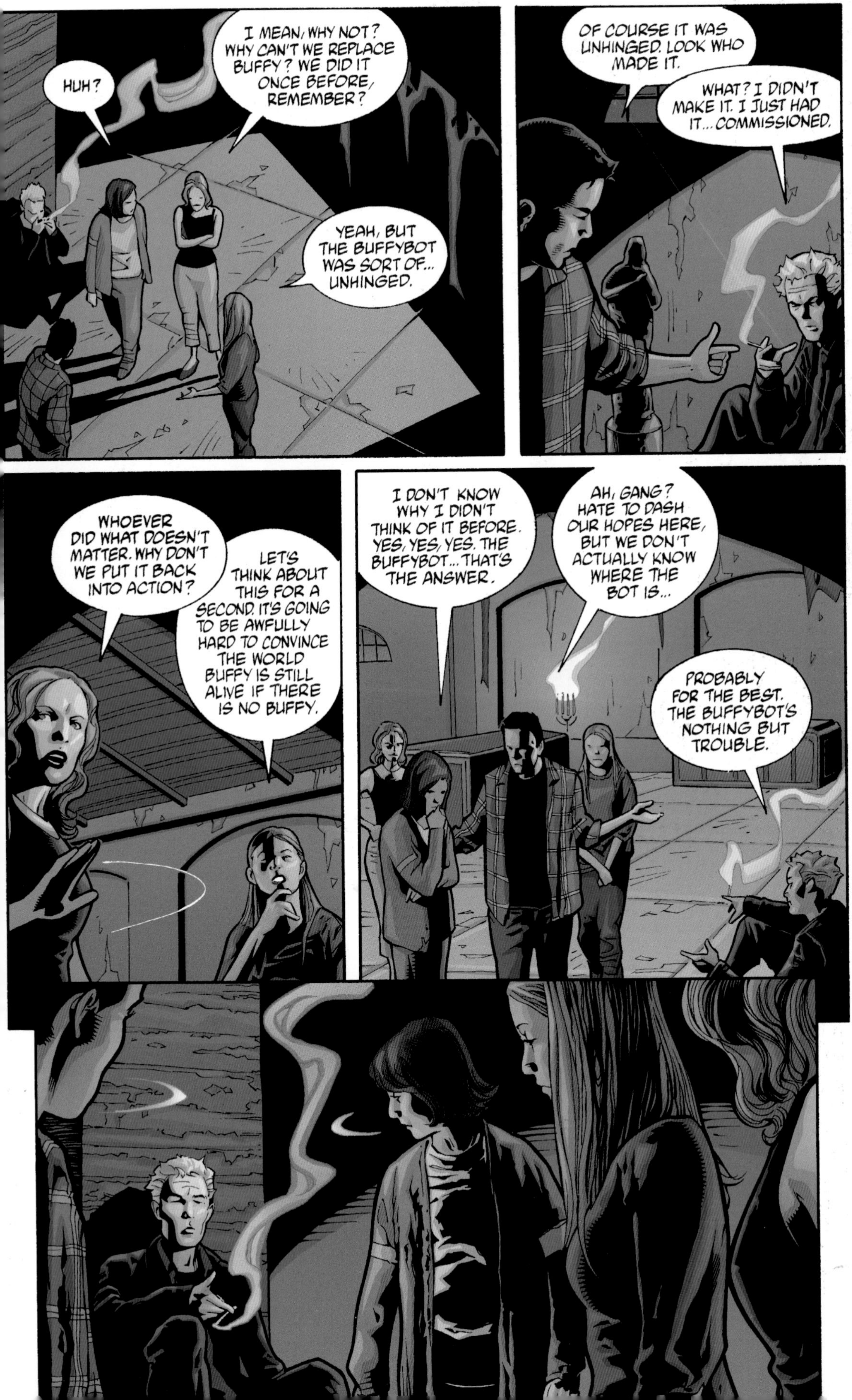
HUH?
I MEAN, WHY NOT? WHY CAN'T WE REPLACE BUFFY? WE DID IT ONCE BEFORE, REMEMBER?
YEAH, BUT THE BUFFYBOT WAS SORT OF... UNHINGED.
OF COURSE IT WAS UNHINGED. LOOK WHO MADE IT.
WHAT? I DIDN'T MAKE IT. I JUST HAD IT... COMMISSIONED.
WHOEVER DID WHAT DOESN'T MATTER. WHY DON'T WE PUT IT BACK INTO ACTION?
LET'S THINK ABOUT THIS FOR A SECOND. IT'S GOING TO BE AWFULLY HARD TO CONVINCE THE WORLD BUFFY IS STILL ALIVE IF THERE IS NO BUFFY.
I DON'T KNOW WHY I DIDN'T THINK OF IT BEFORE. YES, YES, YES. THE BUFFYBOT... THAT'S THE ANSWER.
AH, GANG? HATE TO DASH OUR HOPES HERE, BUT WE DON'T ACTUALLY KNOW WHERE THE BOT IS...
PROBABLY FOR THE BEST. THE BUFFYBOT'S NOTHING BUT TROUBLE.

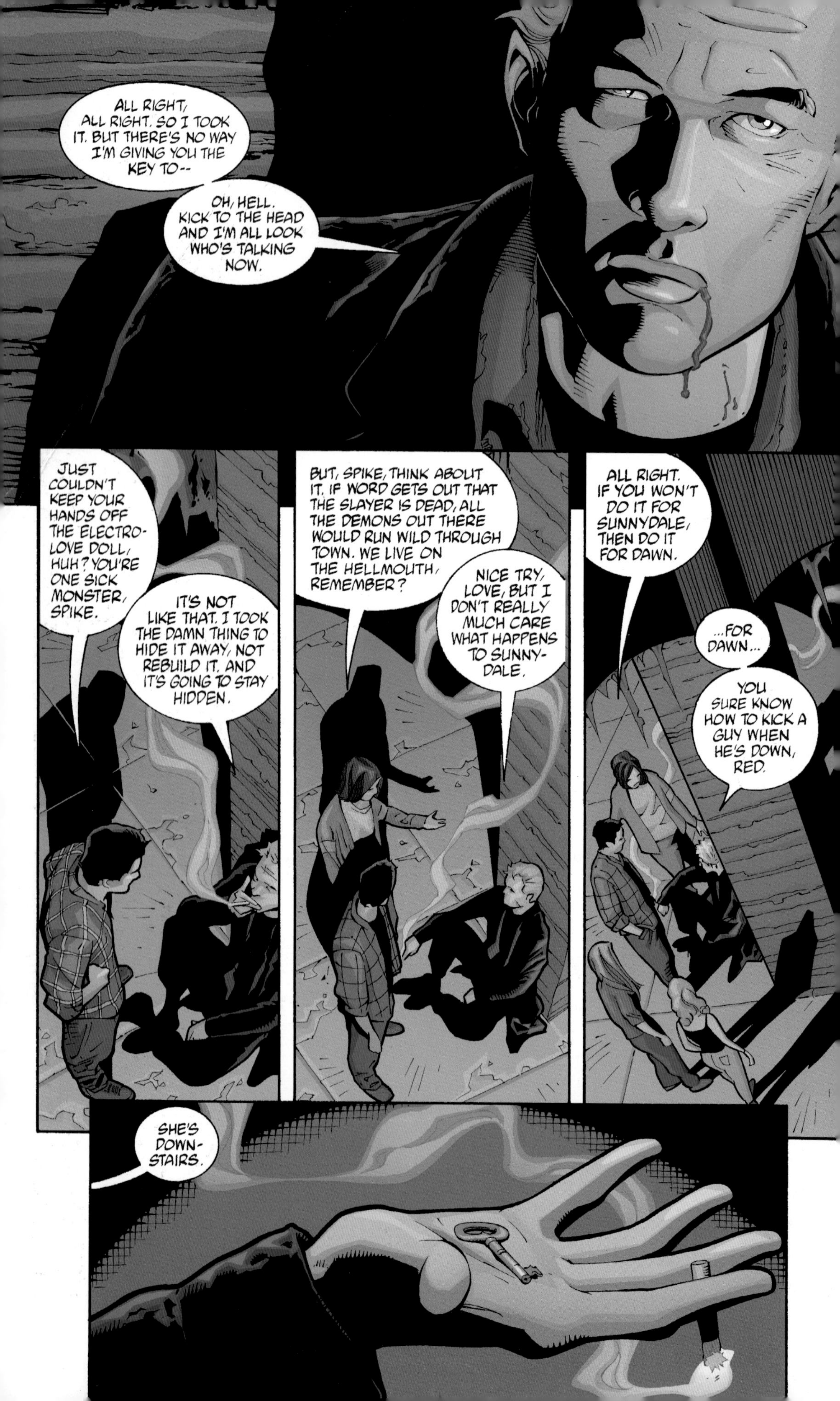
ALL RIGHT, ALL RIGHT. SO I TOOK IT. BUT THERE'S NO WAY I'M GIVING YOU THE KEY TO--
OH, HELL. KICK TO THE HEAD AND I'M ALL LOOK WHO'S TALKING NOW.
JUST COULDN'T KEEP YOUR HANDS OFF THE ELECTRO-LOVE DOLL, HUH? YOU'RE ONE SICK MONSTER, SPIKE.
IT'S NOT LIKE THAT. I TOOK THE DAMN THING TO HIDE IT AWAY, NOT REBUILD IT. AND IT'S GOING TO STAY HIDDEN.
BUT, SPIKE, THINK ABOUT IT. IF WORD GETS OUT THAT THE SLAYER IS DEAD, ALL THE DEMONS OUT THERE WOULD RUN WILD THROUGH TOWN. WE LIVE ON THE HELLMOUTH, REMEMBER?
NICE TRY, LOVE, BUT I DON'T REALLY MUCH CARE WHAT HAPPENS TO SUNNY-DALE.
ALL RIGHT. IF YOU WON'T DO IT FOR SUNNYDALE, THEN DO IT FOR DAWN.
...FOR DAWN...
YOU SURE KNOW HOW TO KICK A GUY WHEN HE'S DOWN, RED.
SHE'S DOWN-STAIRS.

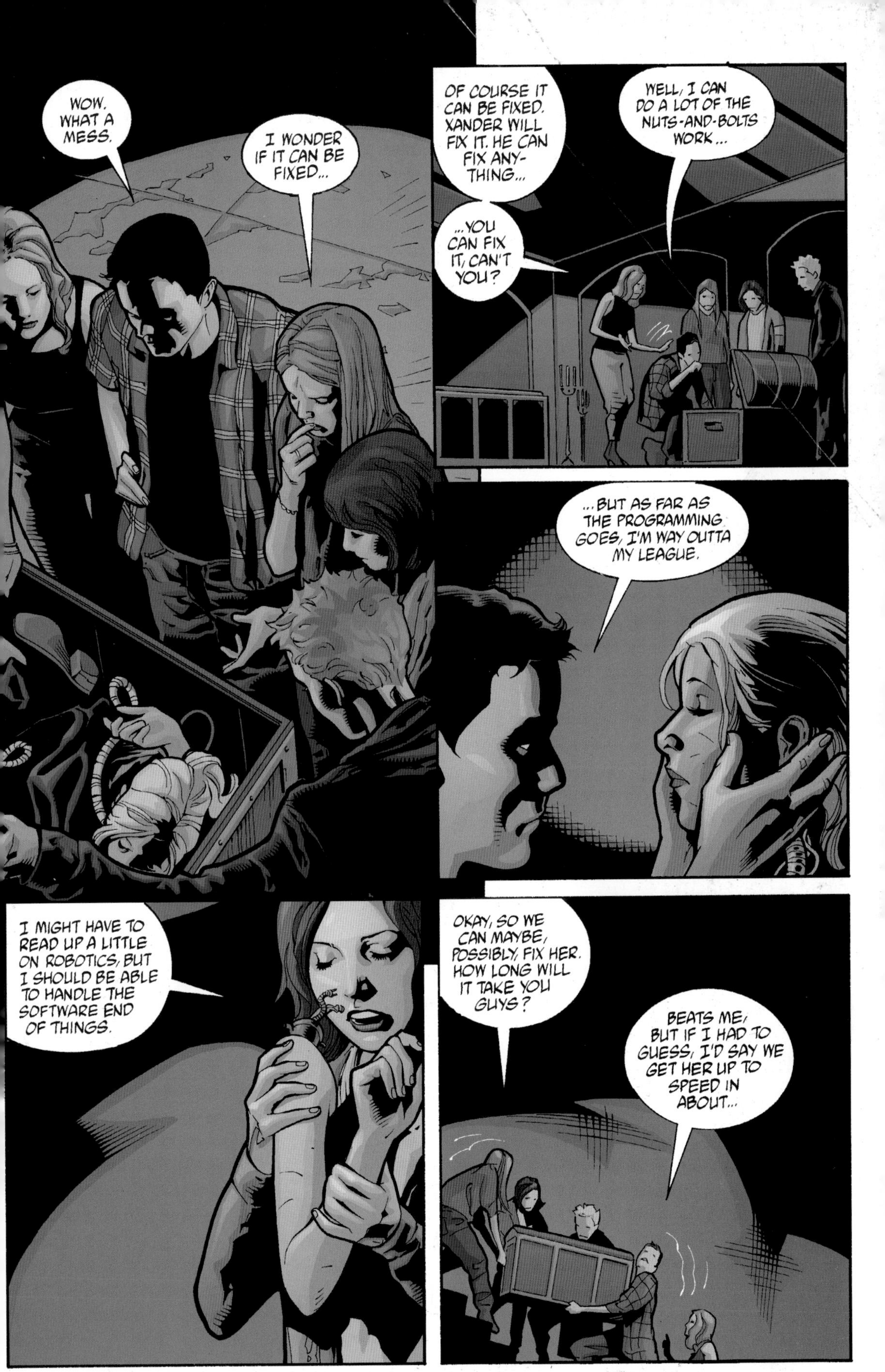
WOW. WHAT A MESS.
I WONDER IF IT CAN BE FIXED...
OF COURSE IT CAN BE FIXED. XANDER WILL FIX IT. HE CAN FIX ANY-THING...
...YOU CAN FIX IT, CAN'T YOU?
WELL, I CAN DO A LOT OF THE NUTS-AND-BOLTS WORK...
...BUT AS FAR AS THE PROGRAMMING GOES, I'M WAY OUTTA MY LEAGUE.
I MIGHT HAVE TO READ UP A LITTLE ON ROBOTICS, BUT I SHOULD BE ABLE TO HANDLE THE SOFTWARE END OF THINGS.
OKAY, SO WE CAN MAYBE, POSSIBLY, FIX HER. HOW LONG WILL IT TAKE YOU GUYS?
BEATS ME, BUT IF I HAD TO GUESS, I'D SAY WE GET HER UP TO SPEED IN ABOUT...

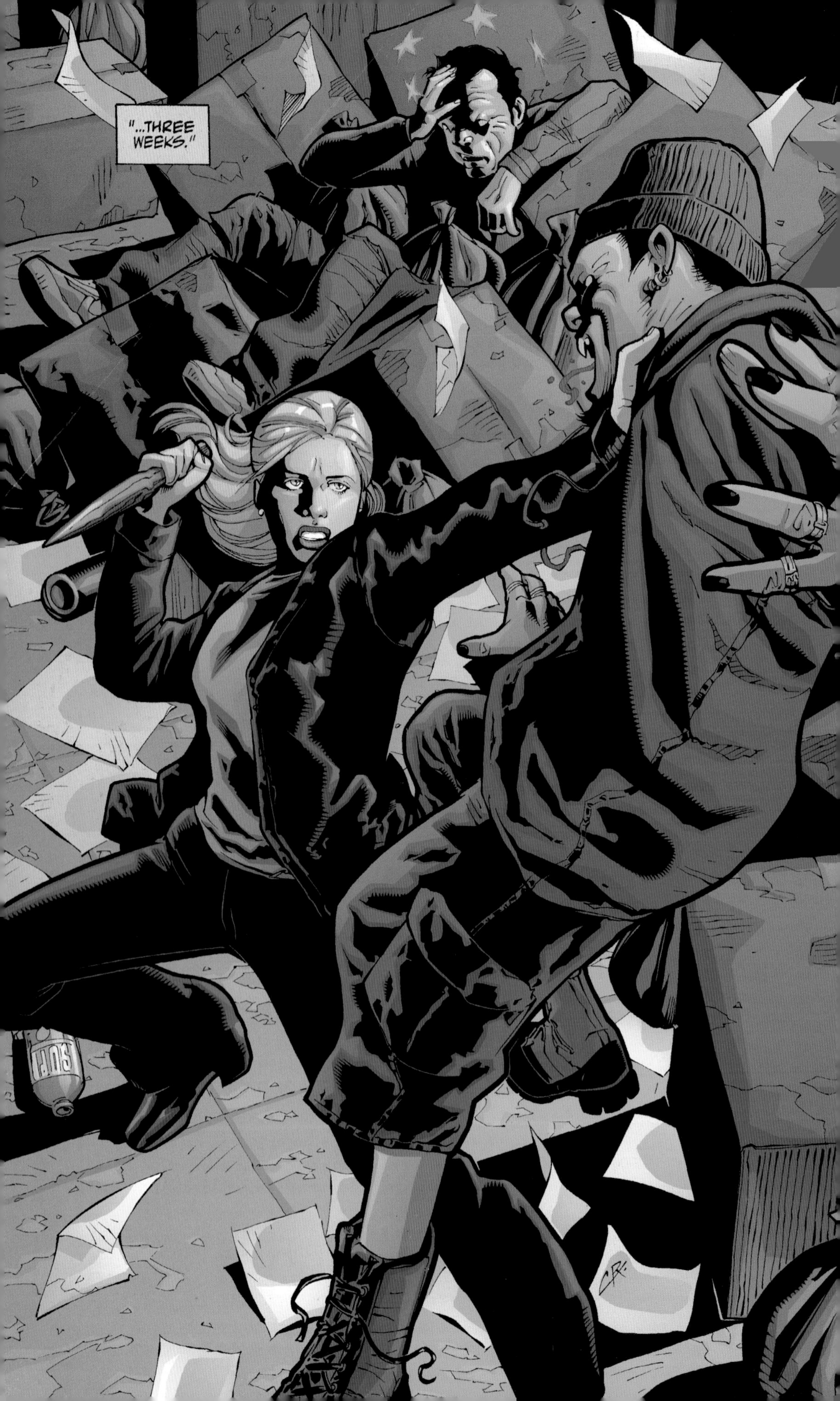
"...THREE WEEKS."

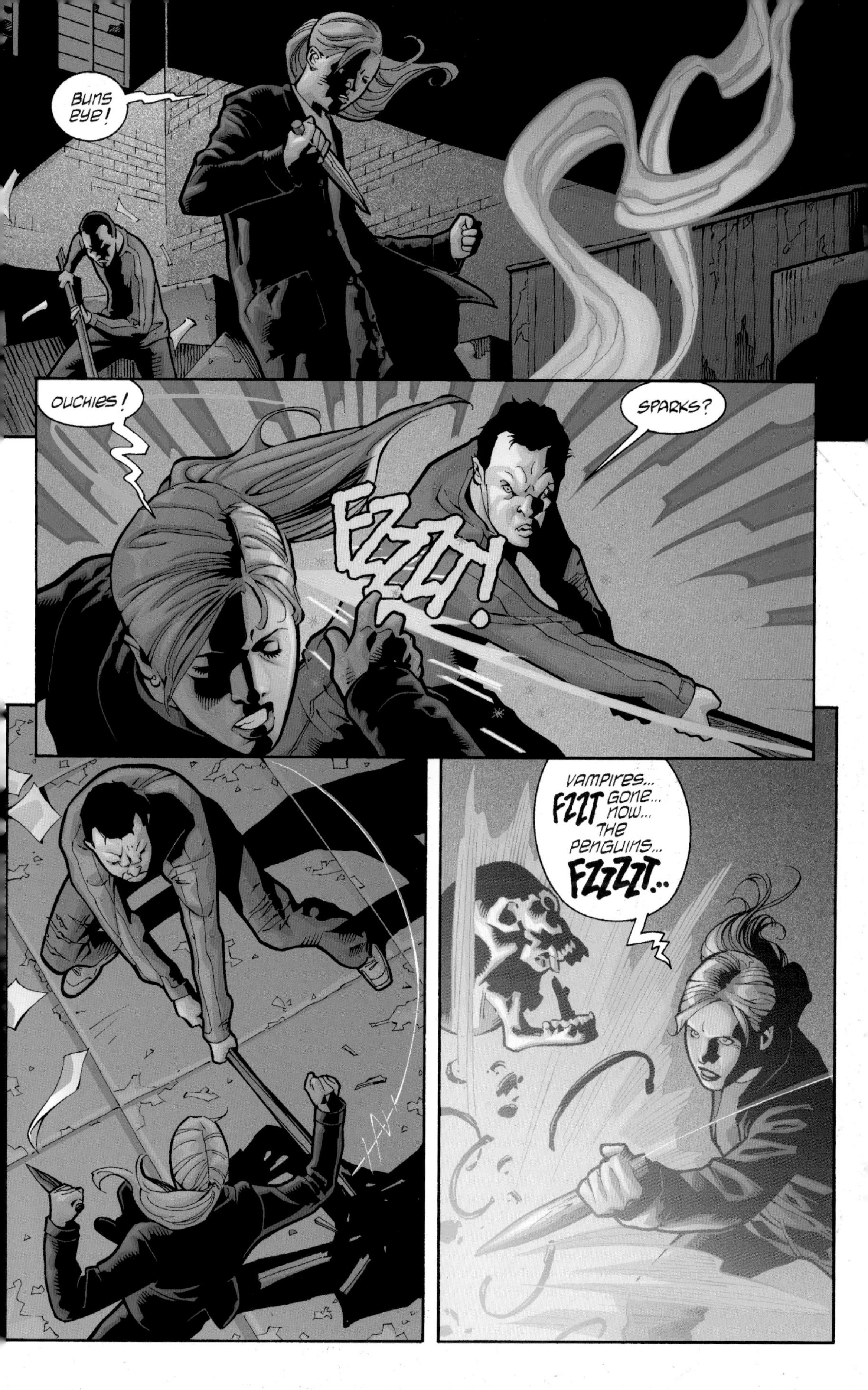
BUNS EYE!
OUCHIES!
SPARKS?
FZZZT!
VAMPIRES... FZZT GONE... NOW... THE PENGUINS... FZZZZT...

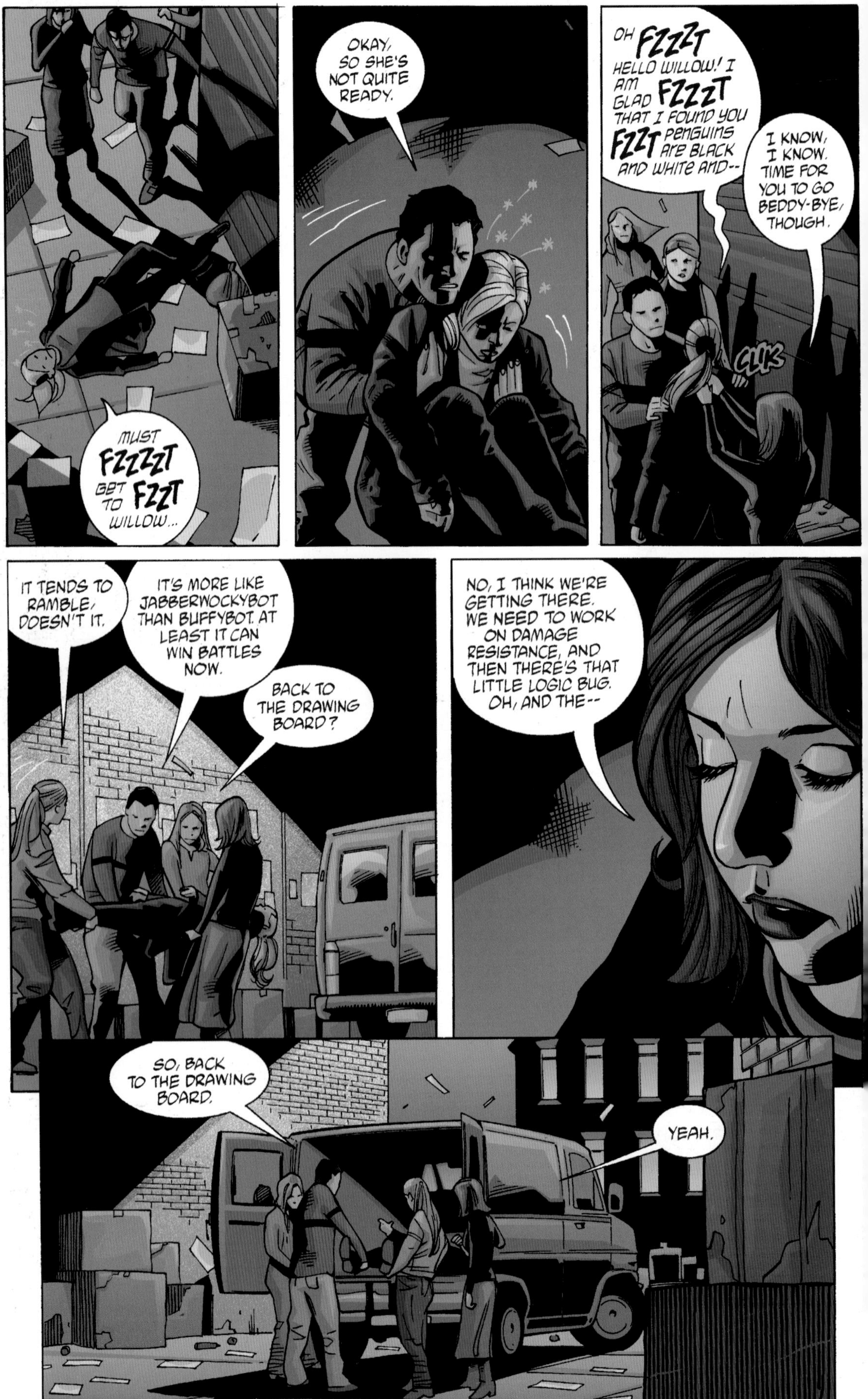

MUST FZZZZT GET TO FZZT WILLOW...
OKAY, SO SHE'S NOT QUITE READY.
OH FZZZT HELLO WILLOW! I AM GLAD FZZZT THAT I FOUND YOU FZZT PENGUINS ARE BLACK AND WHITE AND--
I KNOW, I KNOW. TIME FOR YOU TO GO BEDDY-BYE, THOUGH.
CLIK
IT TENDS TO RAMBLE, DOESN'T IT.
IT'S MORE LIKE JABBERWOCKYBOT THAN BUFFYBOT. AT LEAST IT CAN WIN BATTLES NOW.
BACK TO THE DRAWING BOARD?
NO, I THINK WE'RE GETTING THERE. WE NEED TO WORK ON DAMAGE RESISTANCE, AND THEN THERE'S THAT LITTLE LOGIC BUG. OH, AND THE--
SO, BACK TO THE DRAWING BOARD.
YEAH.

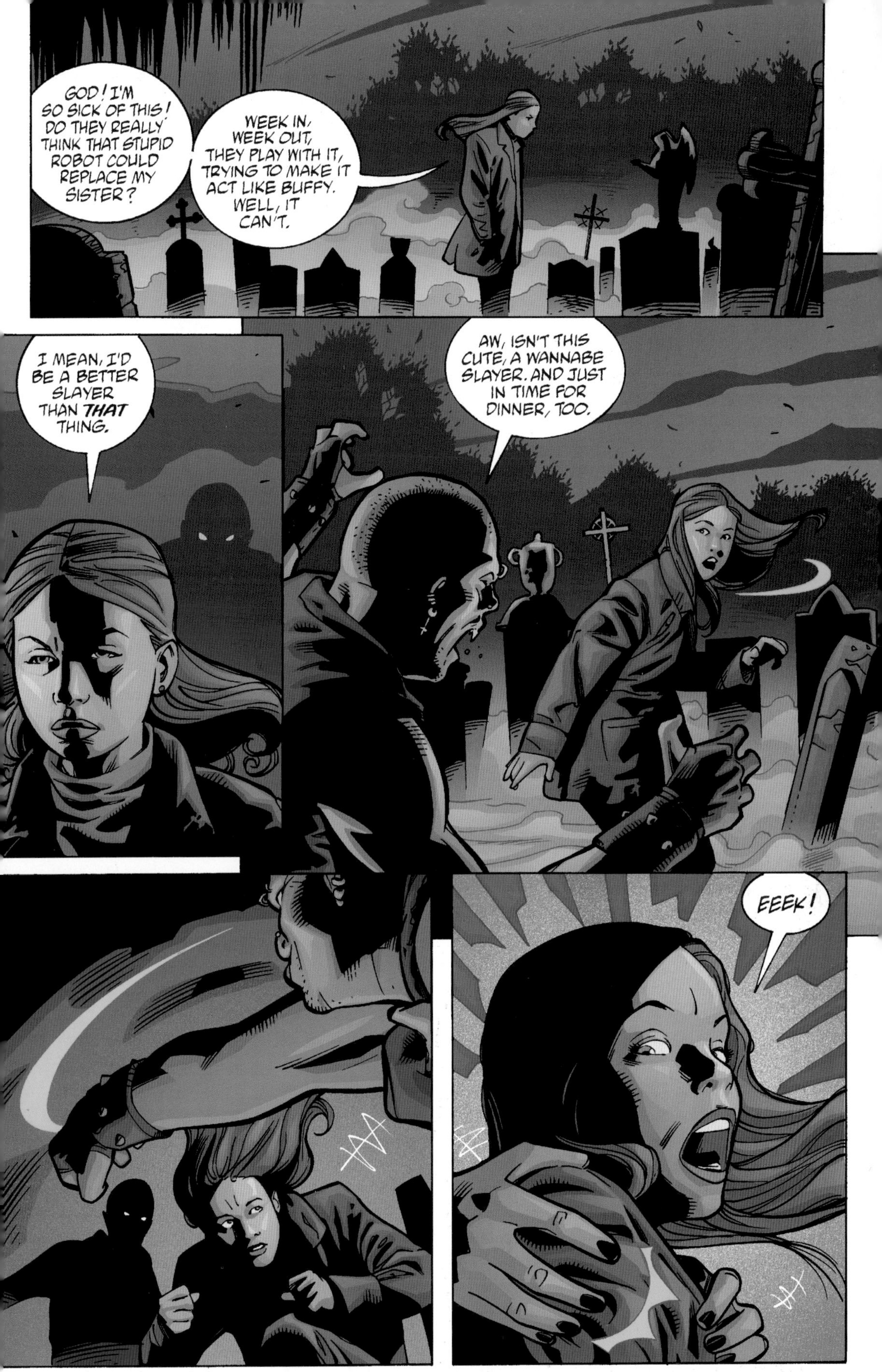
GOD! I'M SO SICK OF THIS! DO THEY REALLY THINK THAT STUPID ROBOT COULD REPLACE MY SISTER?
WEEK IN, WEEK OUT, THEY PLAY WITH IT, TRYING TO MAKE IT ACT LIKE BUFFY. WELL, IT CAN'T.
I MEAN, I'D BE A BETTER SLAYER THAN THAT THING.
AW, ISN'T THIS CUTE, A WANNABE SLAYER. AND JUST IN TIME FOR DINNER, TOO.
EEEK!

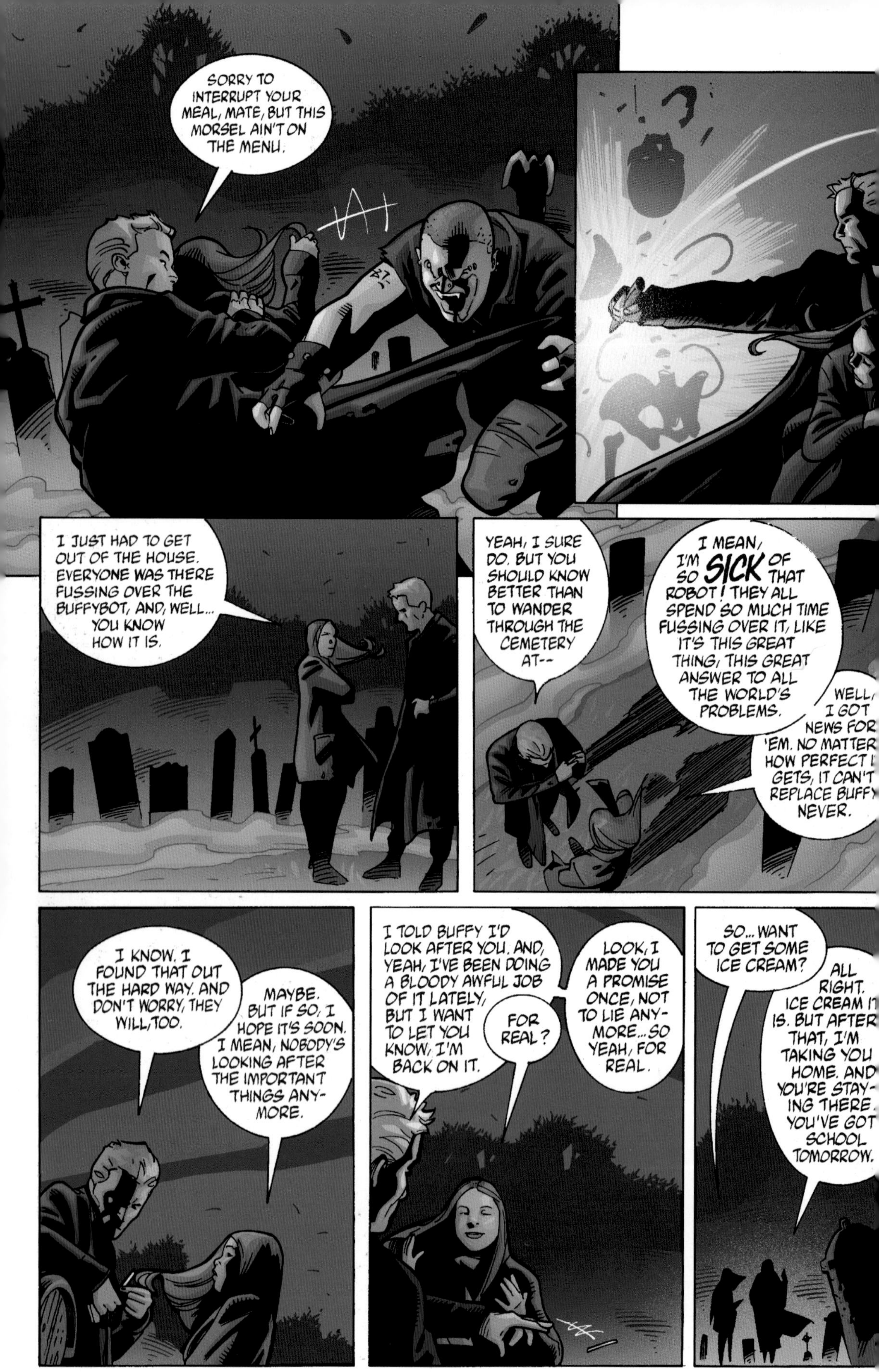

SORRY TO INTERRUPT YOUR MEAL, MATE, BUT THIS MORSEL AIN'T ON THE MENU.
I JUST HAD TO GET OUT OF THE HOUSE. EVERYONE WAS THERE FUSSING OVER THE BUFFYBOT, AND, WELL... YOU KNOW HOW IT IS.
YEAH, I SURE DO. BUT YOU SHOULD KNOW BETTER THAN TO WANDER THROUGH THE CEMETERY AT--
I MEAN, I'M SO SICK OF THAT ROBOT! THEY ALL SPEND SO MUCH TIME FUSSING OVER IT, LIKE IT'S THIS GREAT THING, THIS GREAT ANSWER TO ALL THE WORLD'S PROBLEMS.
WELL, I GOT NEWS FOR 'EM. NO MATTER HOW PERFECT I GETS, IT CAN'T REPLACE BUFFY NEVER.
I KNOW. I FOUND THAT OUT THE HARD WAY. AND DON'T WORRY, THEY WILL, TOO.
MAYBE. BUT IF SO, I HOPE IT'S SOON. I MEAN, NOBODY'S LOOKING AFTER THE IMPORTANT THINGS ANY-MORE.
I TOLD BUFFY I'D LOOK AFTER YOU. AND, YEAH, I'VE BEEN DOING A BLOODY AWFUL JOB OF IT LATELY, BUT I WANT TO LET YOU KNOW, I'M BACK ON IT.
FOR REAL?
LOOK, I MADE YOU A PROMISE ONCE, NOT TO LIE ANY-MORE... SO YEAH, FOR REAL.
SO... WANT TO GET SOME ICE CREAM?
ALL RIGHT. ICE CREAM I IS. BUT AFTER THAT, I'M TAKING YOU HOME. AND YOU'RE STAY-ING THERE. YOU'VE GOT SCHOOL TOMORROW.

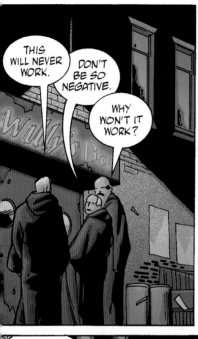

THIS WILL NEVER WORK.

DON'T BE SO NEGATIVE.

WHY WON'T IT WORK?

IT'S A DUMB PLAN. I FEEL LIKE AN IDIOT IN THESE ROBES.

WE'VE BEEN PLAYING THIS YOUR WAY, LOOKING FOR A WITCH FOR WEEKS. WELL, LET ME TELL YOU, ONE ISN'T GOING TO COME TO US. WE HAVE TO GET OUT IN PUBLIC AND FIND ONE.

I THINK IT'S A GOOD PLAN, COMING HERE TO WILLY'S, BUT TELL ME AGAIN WHY WE HAVE TO WEAR THESE ROBES...

HAVE YOU BEEN PAYING ATTENTION? WE WERE HIRED TO DO A JOB, AND WE BOTCHED IT--

HE'S THE ONE WHO BOTCHED IT.

DID NOT!

CAN IT! IT DOESN'T MATTER WHO BOTCHED IT, THE FACT IS NOW OUR LEADERS WANT TO KILL US, SO WE NEED A DISGUISE.

HENCE THE ROBES, YOU NIMWIT.

IT SEEMS LIKE A DESPERATE PLAN.

IT IS.

FINE! IF IT'S SUCH A BAD PLAN, I'D LIKE TO HEAR SOME OTHER IDEAS.

ALL RIGHT THEN. HOODS UP, LET'S GO.

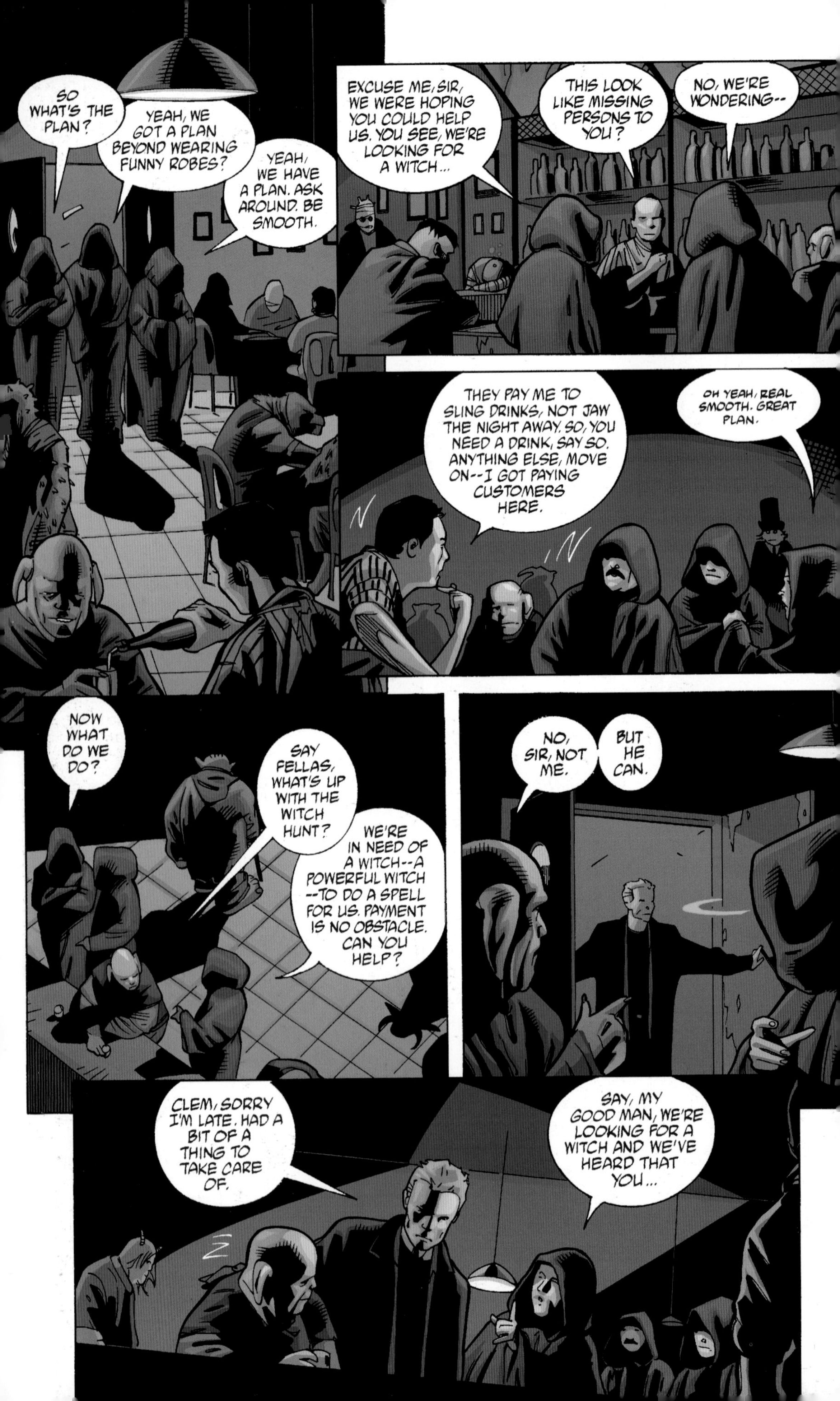
SO WHAT'S THE PLAN?
YEAH, WE GOT A PLAN BEYOND WEARING FUNNY ROBES?
YEAH, WE HAVE A PLAN. ASK AROUND. BE SMOOTH.
EXCUSE ME, SIR, WE WERE HOPING YOU COULD HELP US. YOU SEE, WE'RE LOOKING FOR A WITCH...
THIS LOOK LIKE MISSING PERSONS TO YOU?
NO, WE'RE WONDERING--
THEY PAY ME TO SLING DRINKS, NOT JAW THE NIGHT AWAY. SO, YOU NEED A DRINK, SAY SO. ANYTHING ELSE, MOVE ON--I GOT PAYING CUSTOMERS HERE.
OH YEAH, REAL SMOOTH. GREAT PLAN.
NOW WHAT DO WE DO?
SAY FELLAS, WHAT'S UP WITH THE WITCH HUNT?
WE'RE IN NEED OF A WITCH--A POWERFUL WITCH --TO DO A SPELL FOR US. PAYMENT IS NO OBSTACLE. CAN YOU HELP?
NO, SIR, NOT ME.
BUT HE CAN.
CLEM, SORRY I'M LATE. HAD A BIT OF A THING TO TAKE CARE OF.
SAY, MY GOOD MAN, WE'RE LOOKING FOR A WITCH AND WE'VE HEARD THAT YOU...

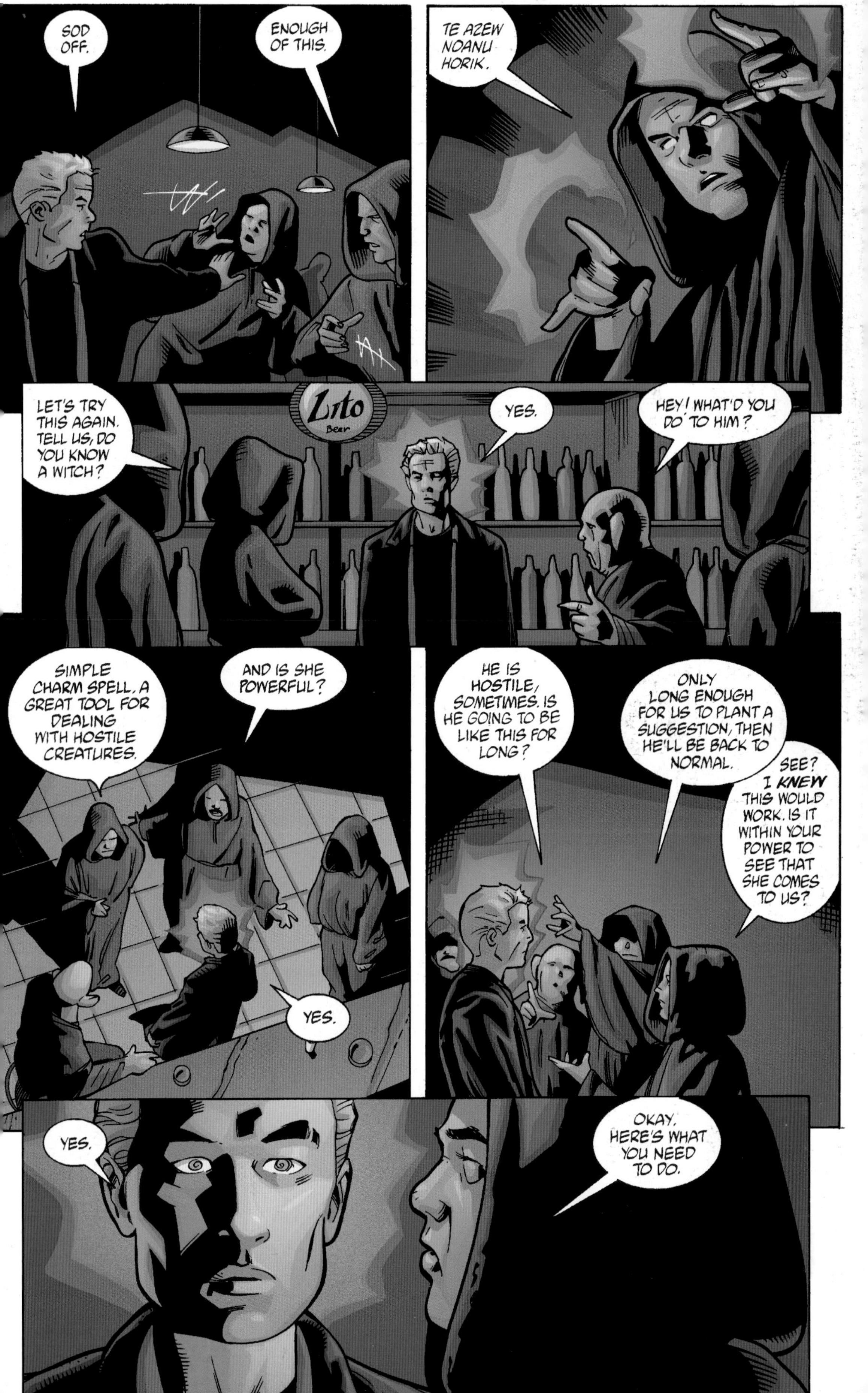
SOD OFF.
ENOUGH OF THIS.
TE AZEW NOANU HORIK.
LET'S TRY THIS AGAIN. TELL US, DO YOU KNOW A WITCH?
Lito Beer
YES.
HEY! WHAT'D YOU DO TO HIM?
SIMPLE CHARM SPELL, A GREAT TOOL FOR DEALING WITH HOSTILE CREATURES.
AND IS SHE POWERFUL?
YES.
HE IS HOSTILE, SOMETIMES. IS HE GOING TO BE LIKE THIS FOR LONG?
ONLY LONG ENOUGH FOR US TO PLANT A SUGGESTION, THEN HE'LL BE BACK TO NORMAL.
SEE? I KNEW THIS WOULD WORK. IS IT WITHIN YOUR POWER TO SEE THAT SHE COMES TO US?
YES.
OKAY, HERE'S WHAT YOU NEED TO DO.

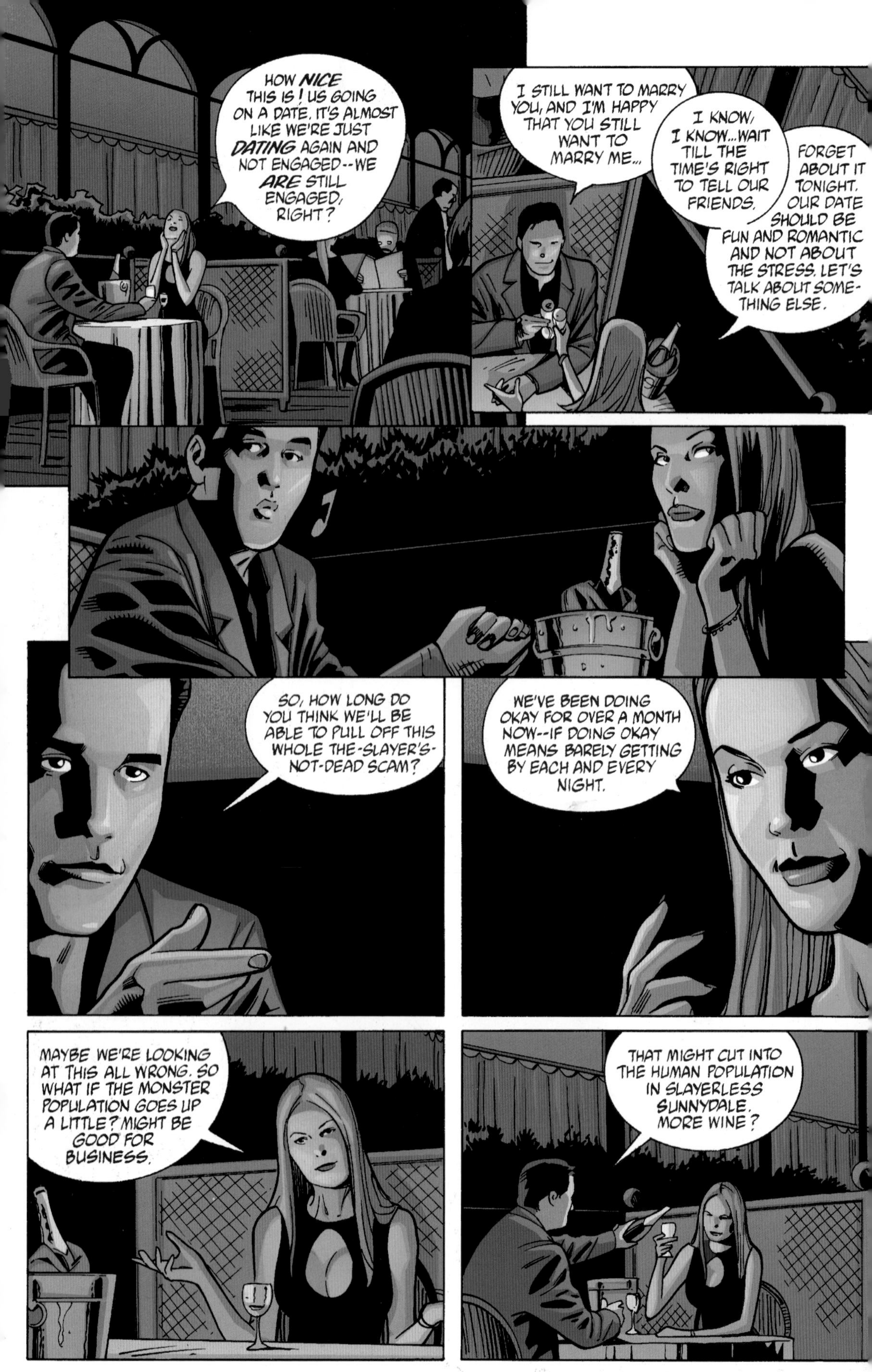

HOW NICE THIS IS! US GOING ON A DATE. IT'S ALMOST LIKE WE'RE JUST DATING AGAIN AND NOT ENGAGED--WE ARE STILL ENGAGED, RIGHT?
I STILL WANT TO MARRY YOU, AND I'M HAPPY THAT YOU STILL WANT TO MARRY ME...
I KNOW, I KNOW...WAIT TILL THE TIME'S RIGHT TO TELL OUR FRIENDS.
FORGET ABOUT IT TONIGHT. OUR DATE SHOULD BE FUN AND ROMANTIC AND NOT ABOUT THE STRESS. LET'S TALK ABOUT SOMETHING ELSE.
SO, HOW LONG DO YOU THINK WE'LL BE ABLE TO PULL OFF THIS WHOLE THE-SLAYER'S-NOT-DEAD SCAM?
WE'VE BEEN DOING OKAY FOR OVER A MONTH NOW--IF DOING OKAY MEANS BARELY GETTING BY EACH AND EVERY NIGHT.
MAYBE WE'RE LOOKING AT THIS ALL WRONG. SO WHAT IF THE MONSTER POPULATION GOES UP A LITTLE? MIGHT BE GOOD FOR BUSINESS.
THAT MIGHT CUT INTO THE HUMAN POPULATION IN SLAYERLESS SUNNYDALE. MORE WINE?

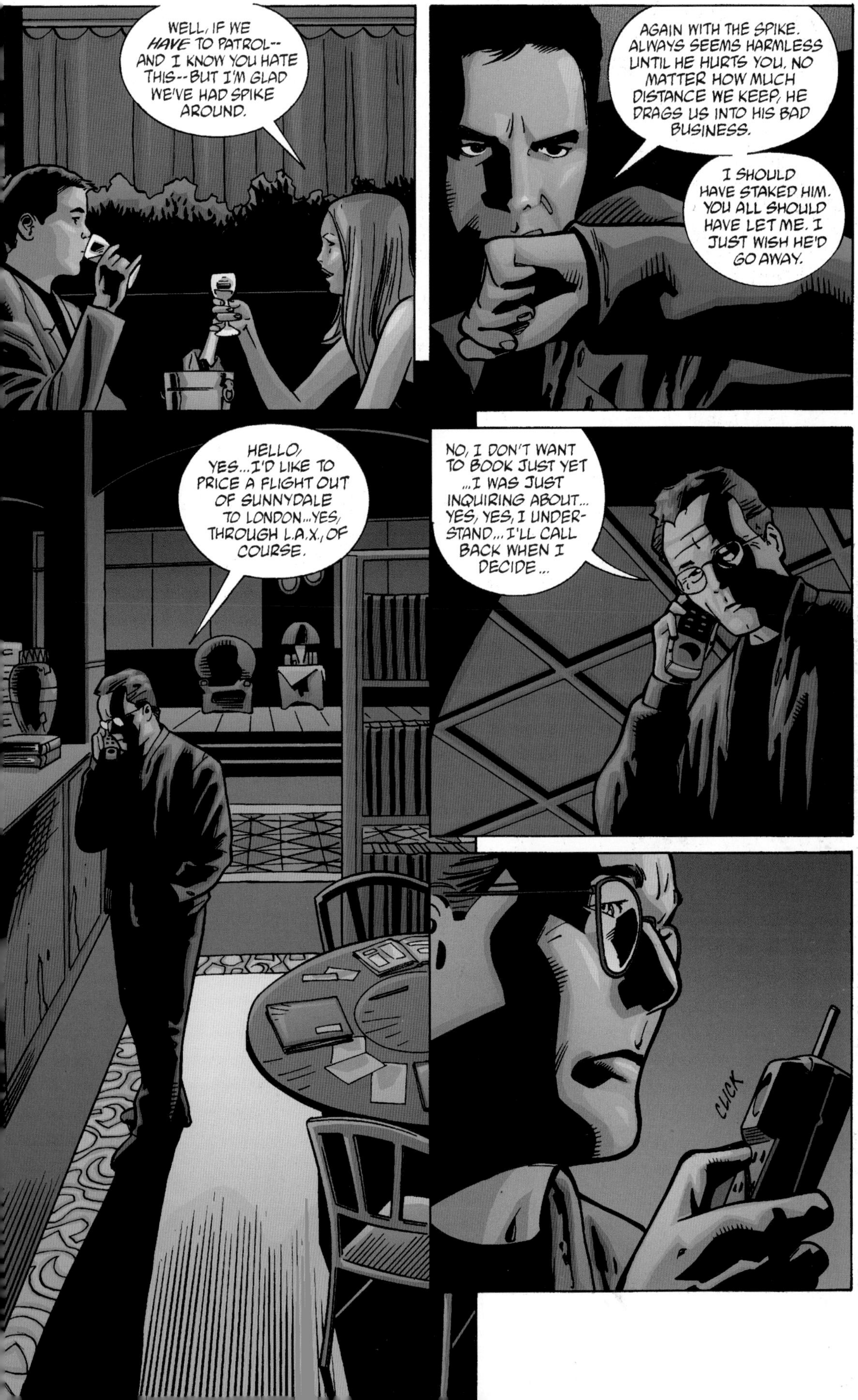
WELL, IF WE *HAVE* TO PATROL-- AND I KNOW YOU HATE THIS--BUT I'M GLAD WE'VE HAD SPIKE AROUND.
AGAIN WITH THE SPIKE. ALWAYS SEEMS HARMLESS UNTIL HE HURTS YOU. NO MATTER HOW MUCH DISTANCE WE KEEP, HE DRAGS US INTO HIS BAD BUSINESS.
I SHOULD HAVE STAKED HIM. YOU ALL SHOULD HAVE LET ME. I JUST WISH HE'D GO AWAY.
HELLO, YES...I'D LIKE TO PRICE A FLIGHT OUT OF SUNNYDALE TO LONDON...YES, THROUGH L.A.X., OF COURSE.
NO, I DON'T WANT TO BOOK JUST YET ...I WAS JUST INQUIRING ABOUT... YES, YES, I UNDER-STAND... I'LL CALL BACK WHEN I DECIDE...
CLICK

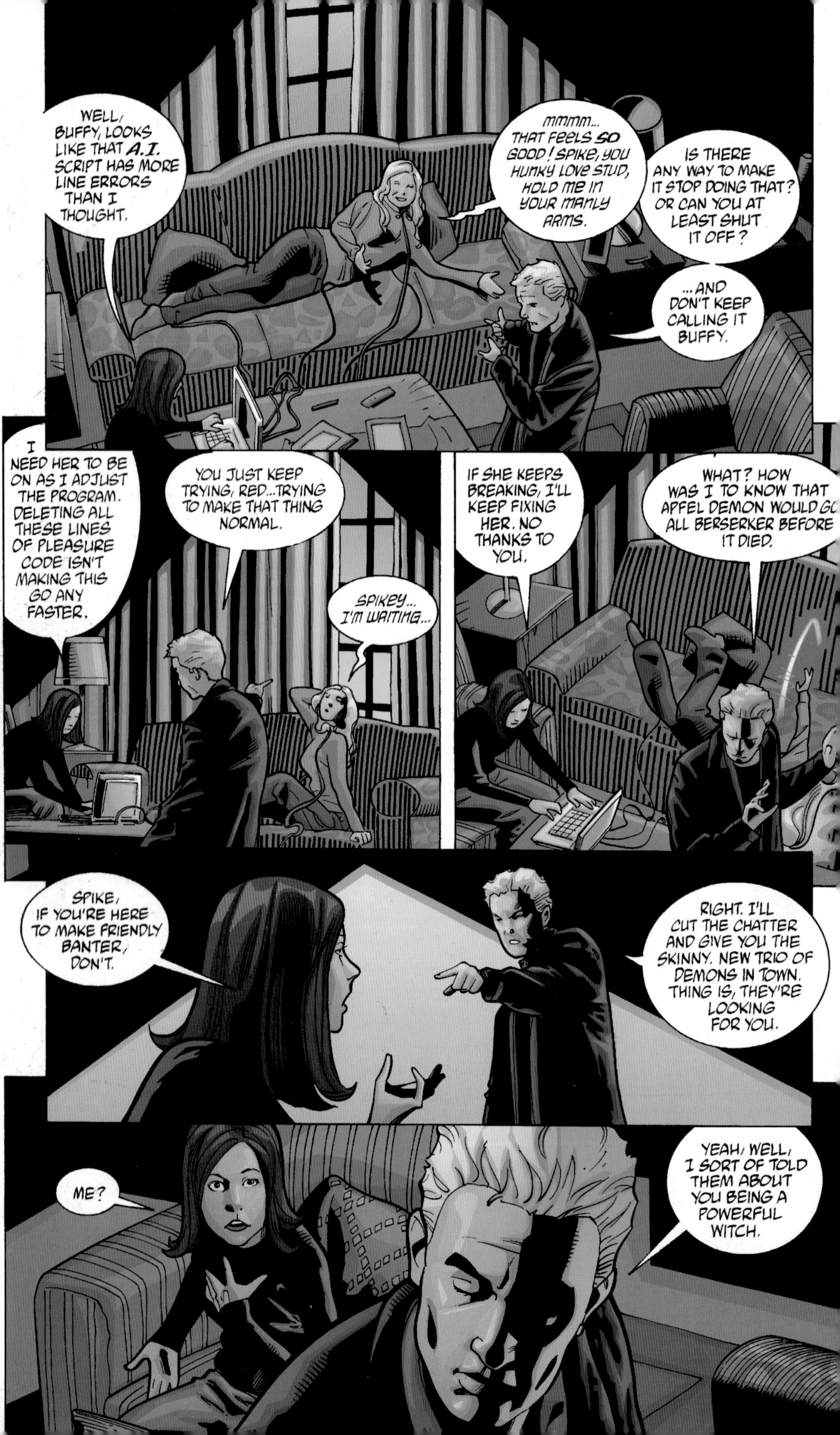
WELL, BUFFY, LOOKS LIKE THAT A.I. SCRIPT HAS MORE LINE ERRORS THAN I THOUGHT.
MMMM... THAT FEELS SO GOOD! SPIKE, YOU HUNKY LOVE STUD, HOLD ME IN YOUR MANLY ARMS.
IS THERE ANY WAY TO MAKE IT STOP DOING THAT? OR CAN YOU AT LEAST SHUT IT OFF?
...AND DON'T KEEP CALLING IT BUFFY.
I NEED HER TO BE ON AS I ADJUST THE PROGRAM. DELETING ALL THESE LINES OF PLEASURE CODE ISN'T MAKING THIS GO ANY FASTER.
YOU JUST KEEP TRYING, RED...TRYING TO MAKE THAT THING NORMAL.
SPIKEY... I'M WAITING...
IF SHE KEEPS BREAKING, I'LL KEEP FIXING HER. NO THANKS TO YOU.
WHAT? HOW WAS I TO KNOW THAT APFEL DEMON WOULD GO ALL BERSERKER BEFORE IT DIED.
SPIKE, IF YOU'RE HERE TO MAKE FRIENDLY BANTER, DON'T.
RIGHT. I'LL CUT THE CHATTER AND GIVE YOU THE SKINNY. NEW TRIO OF DEMONS IN TOWN. THING IS, THEY'RE LOOKING FOR YOU.
ME?
YEAH, WELL, I SORT OF TOLD THEM ABOUT YOU BEING A POWERFUL WITCH.

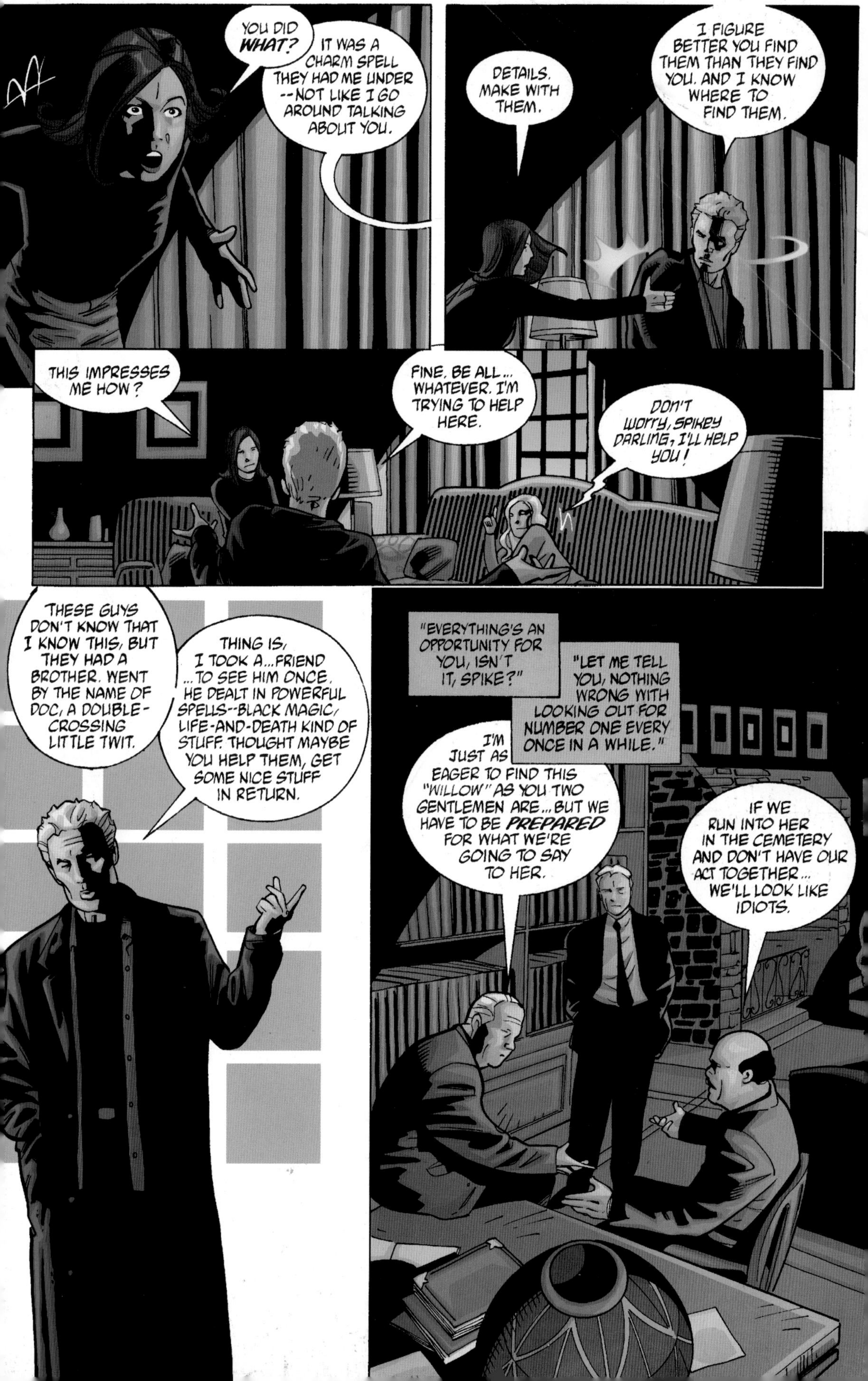
YOU DID **WHAT?**
IT WAS A CHARM SPELL THEY HAD ME UNDER --NOT LIKE I GO AROUND TALKING ABOUT YOU.
DETAILS. MAKE WITH THEM.
I FIGURE BETTER YOU FIND THEM THAN THEY FIND YOU. AND I KNOW WHERE TO FIND THEM.
THIS IMPRESSES ME HOW?
FINE. BE ALL... WHATEVER. I'M TRYING TO HELP HERE.
DON'T WORRY, SPIKEY DARLING, I'LL HELP YOU!
THESE GUYS DON'T KNOW THAT I KNOW THIS, BUT THEY HAD A BROTHER. WENT BY THE NAME OF DOC, A DOUBLE-CROSSING LITTLE TWIT.
THING IS, I TOOK A...FRIEND ...TO SEE HIM ONCE. HE DEALT IN POWERFUL SPELLS--BLACK MAGIC, LIFE-AND-DEATH KIND OF STUFF. THOUGHT MAYBE YOU HELP THEM, GET SOME NICE STUFF IN RETURN.
"EVERYTHING'S AN OPPORTUNITY FOR YOU, ISN'T IT, SPIKE?"
"LET ME TELL YOU, NOTHING WRONG WITH LOOKING OUT FOR NUMBER ONE EVERY ONCE IN A WHILE."
I'M JUST AS EAGER TO FIND THIS "WILLOW" AS YOU TWO GENTLEMEN ARE... BUT WE HAVE TO BE ***PREPARED*** FOR WHAT WE'RE GOING TO SAY TO HER.
IF WE RUN INTO HER IN THE CEMETERY AND DON'T HAVE OUR ACT TOGETHER... WE'LL LOOK LIKE IDIOTS.

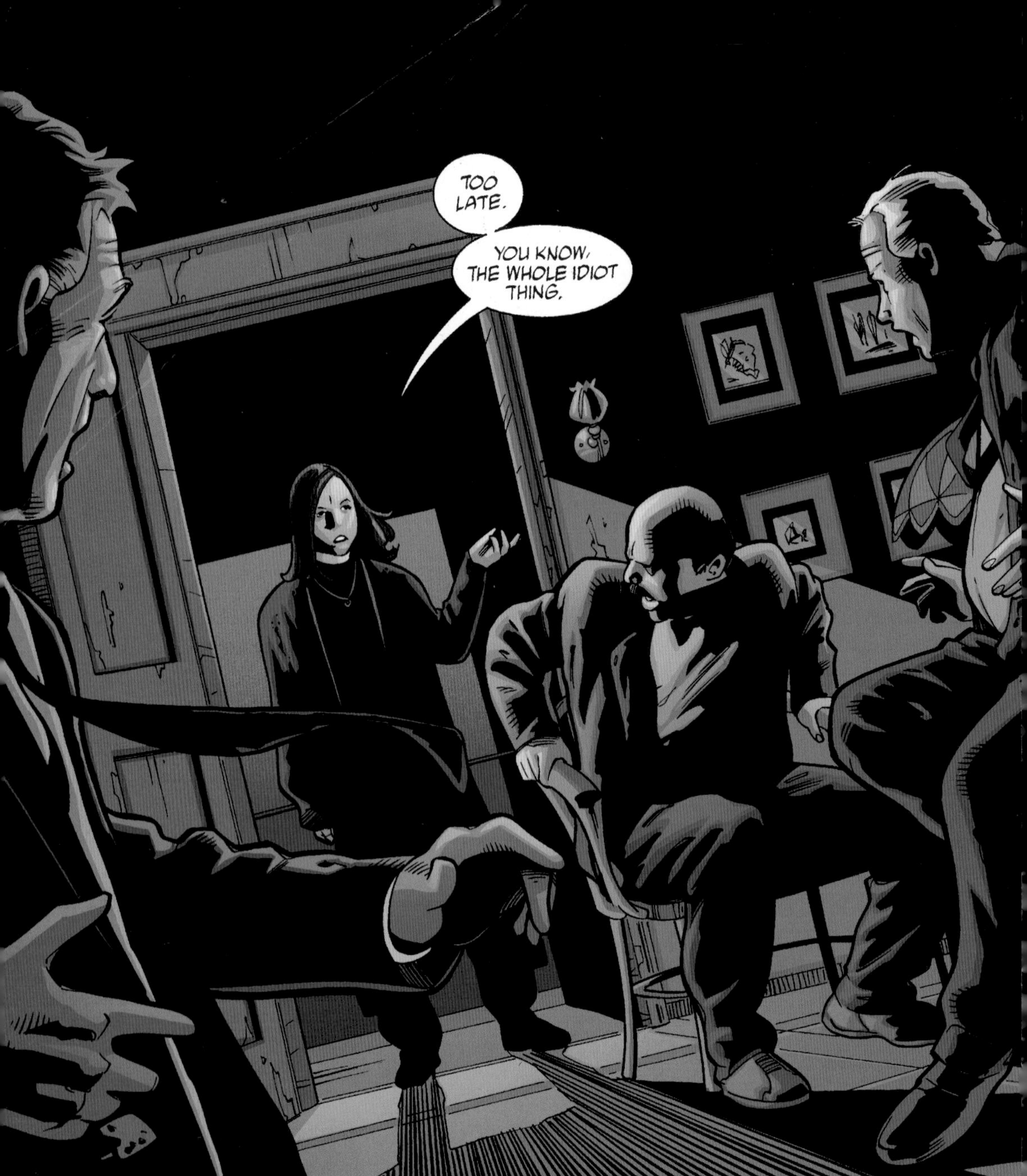
TOO LATE.
YOU KNOW, THE WHOLE IDIOT THING.

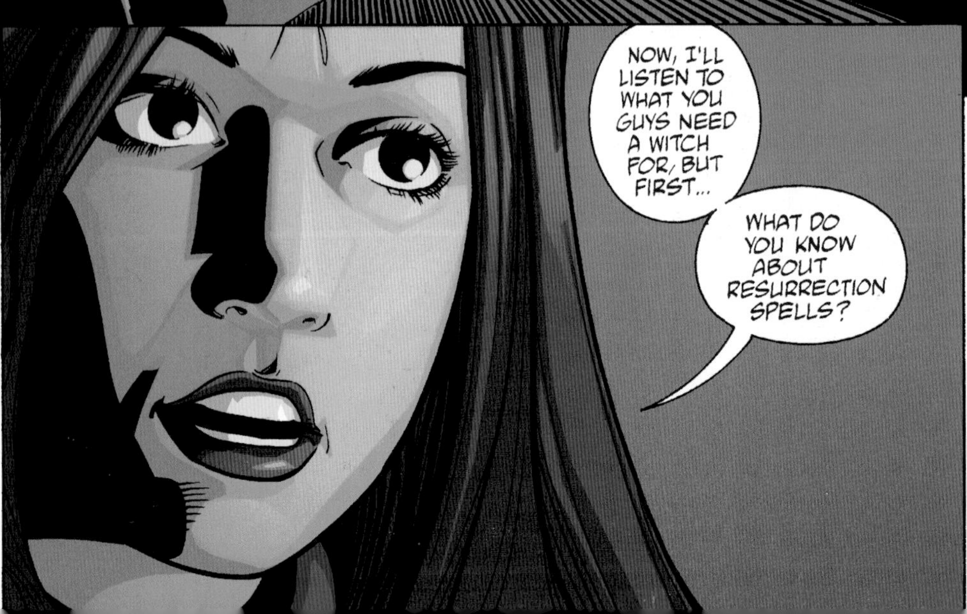
NOW, I'LL LISTEN TO WHAT YOU GUYS NEED A WITCH FOR, BUT FIRST...
WHAT DO YOU KNOW ABOUT RESURRECTION SPELLS?

ABOUT TIME YOU SHOWED.

HEY, MAN, IT WASN'T EASY SLIPPING AWAY FROM--

SAVE THE EXCUSES, MATE. I'VE HEARD 'EM ALL, MOST OF 'EM MORE THAN ONCE.

SO, uh, DID YOU GET IT, OR WHAT?

OF COURSE I GOT IT. BUT THE REAL QUESTION IS, DO YOU HAVE THE MALIAN TWIGS?

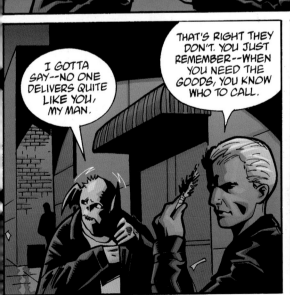

I GOTTA SAY--NO ONE DELIVERS QUITE LIKE YOU, MY MAN.

THAT'S RIGHT THEY DON'T. YOU JUST REMEMBER--WHEN YOU NEED THE GOODS, YOU KNOW WHO TO CALL.

WELL, WELL. NOT A BAD NIGHT'S WORK.

GOTCHA.

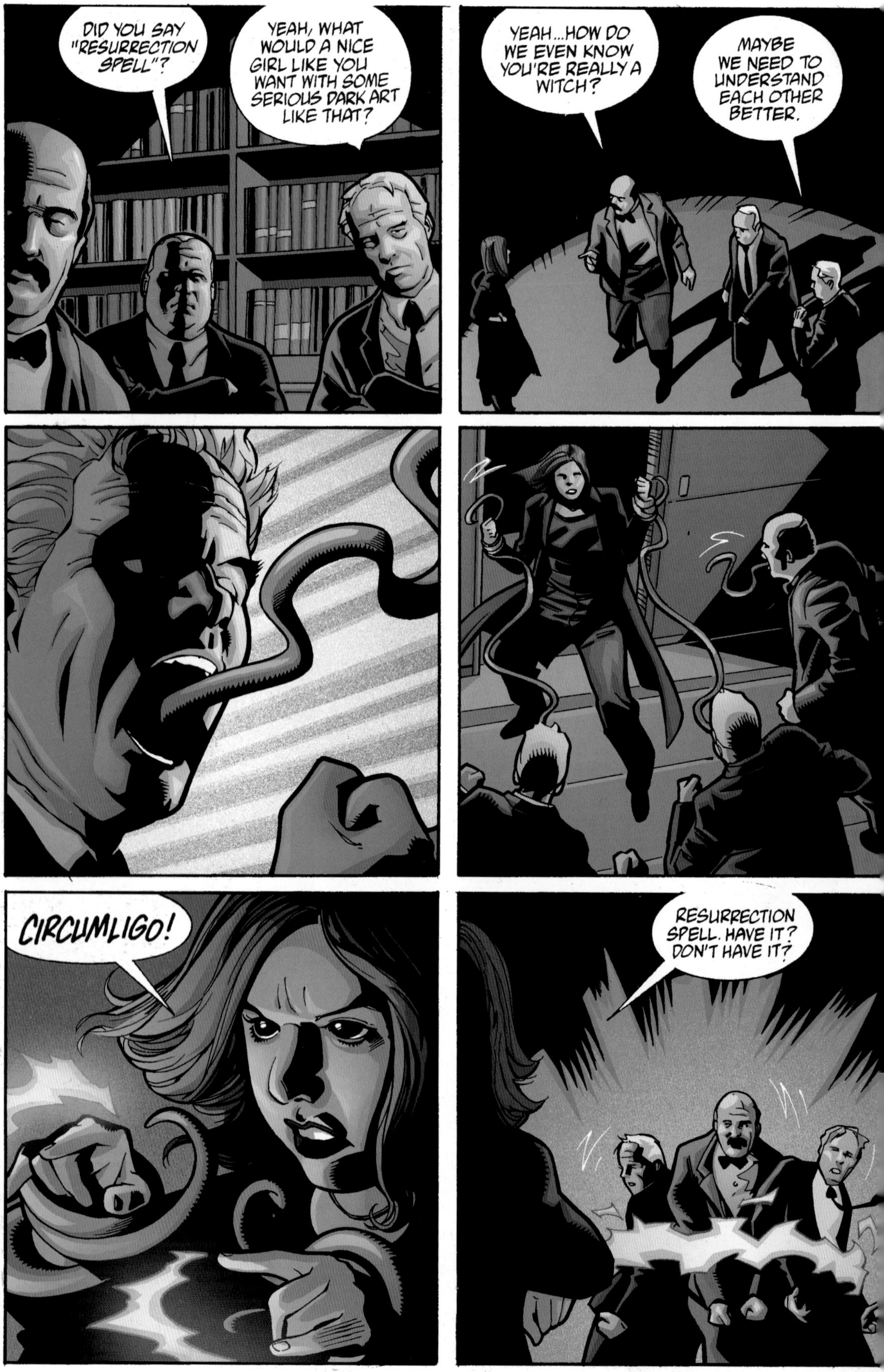
DID YOU SAY "RESURRECTION SPELL"?
YEAH, WHAT WOULD A NICE GIRL LIKE YOU WANT WITH SOME SERIOUS DARK ART LIKE THAT?
YEAH...HOW DO WE EVEN KNOW YOU'RE REALLY A WITCH?
MAYBE WE NEED TO UNDERSTAND EACH OTHER BETTER.
CIRCUMLIGO!
RESURRECTION SPELL. HAVE IT? DON'T HAVE IT?

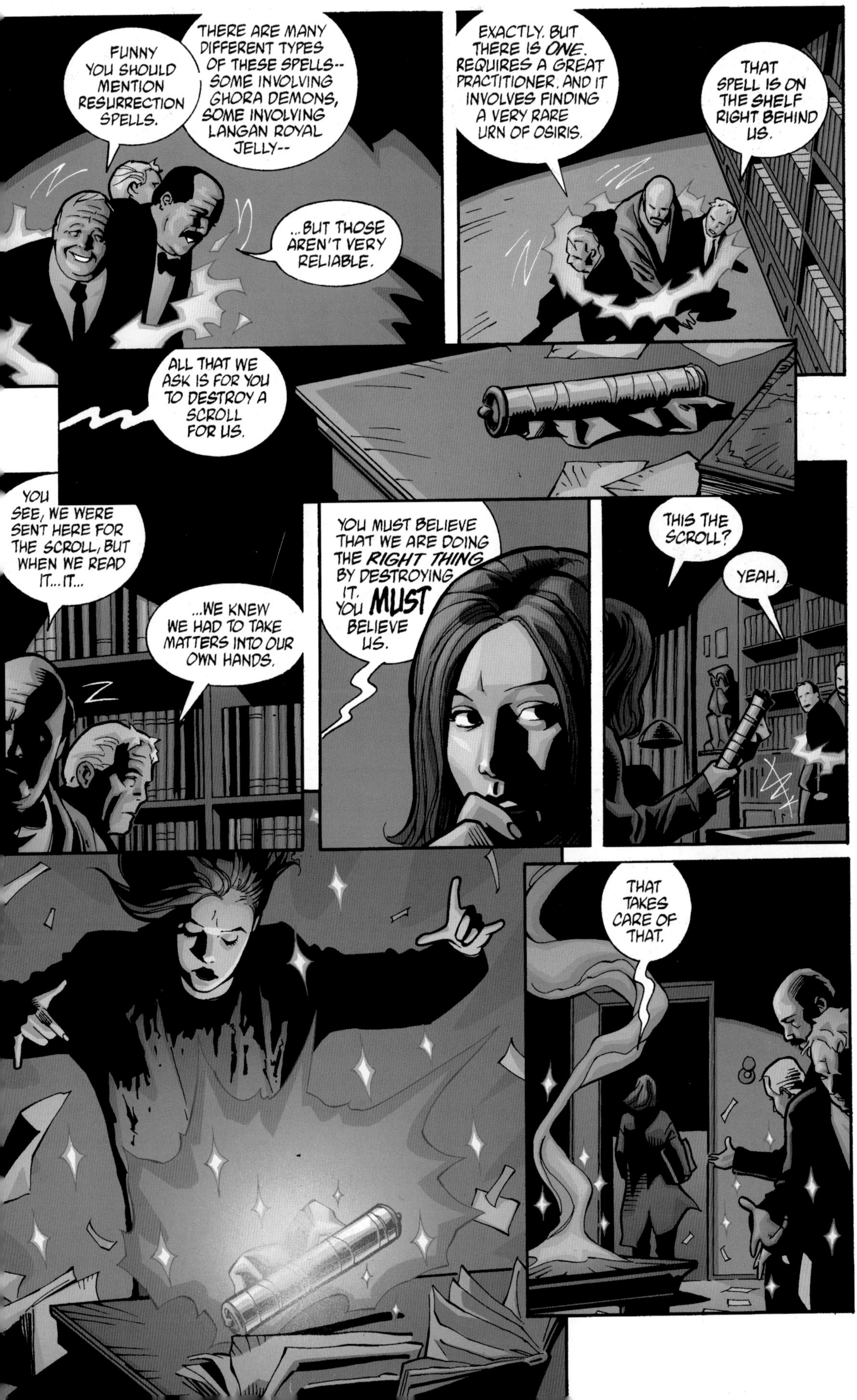
FUNNY YOU SHOULD MENTION RESURRECTION SPELLS.
THERE ARE MANY DIFFERENT TYPES OF THESE SPELLS-- SOME INVOLVING GHORA DEMONS, SOME INVOLVING LANGAN ROYAL JELLY--
...BUT THOSE AREN'T VERY RELIABLE.
EXACTLY. BUT THERE IS ONE. REQUIRES A GREAT PRACTITIONER, AND IT INVOLVES FINDING A VERY RARE URN OF OSIRIS.
THAT SPELL IS ON THE SHELF RIGHT BEHIND US.
ALL THAT WE ASK IS FOR YOU TO DESTROY A SCROLL FOR US.
YOU SEE, WE WERE SENT HERE FOR THE SCROLL, BUT WHEN WE READ IT... IT...
...WE KNEW WE HAD TO TAKE MATTERS INTO OUR OWN HANDS.
YOU MUST BELIEVE THAT WE ARE DOING THE RIGHT THING BY DESTROYING IT. YOU MUST BELIEVE US.
THIS THE SCROLL?
YEAH.
THAT TAKES CARE OF THAT.

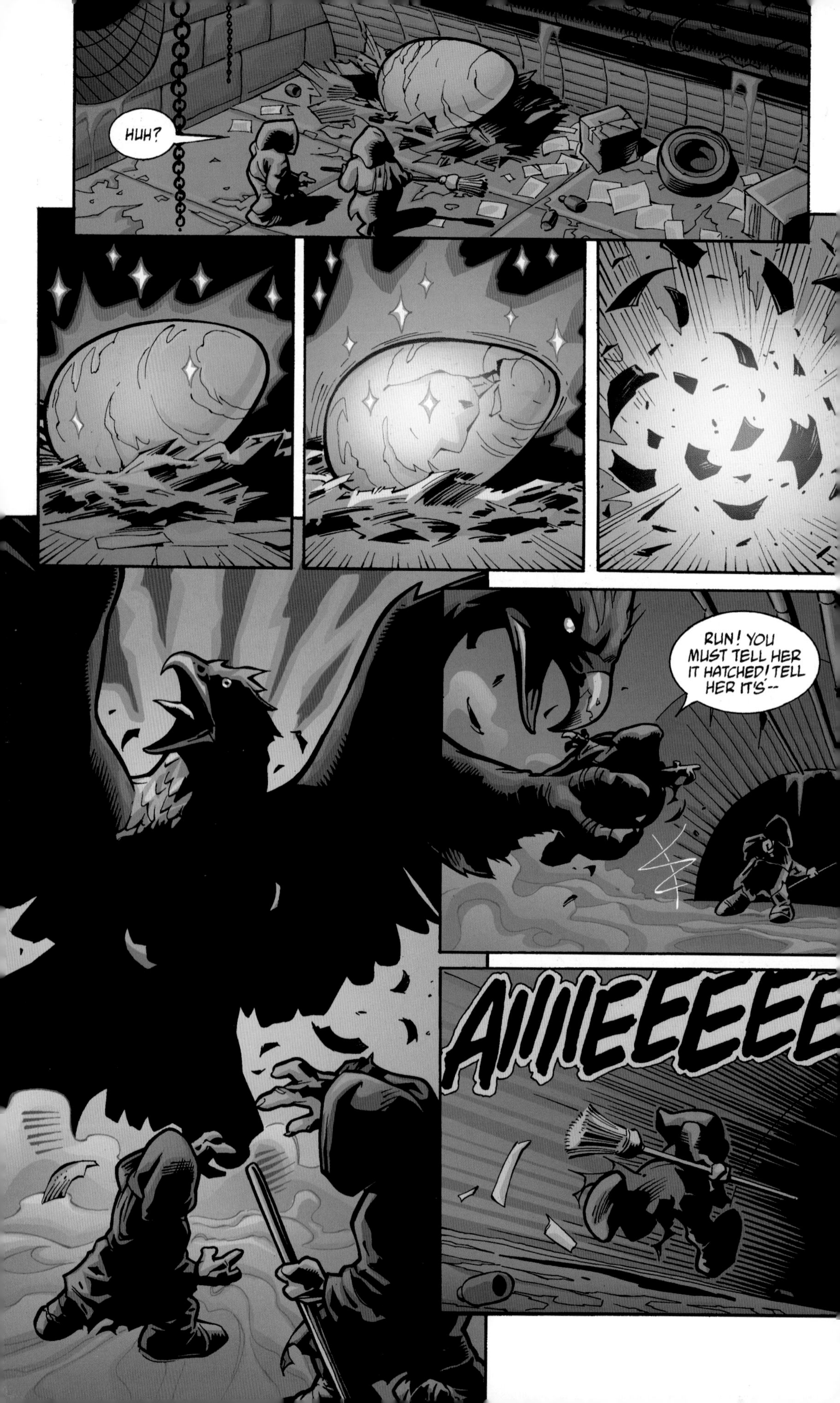

HUH?
RUN! YOU MUST TELL HER IT HATCHED! TELL HER IT'S--
AIIIEEEEEE

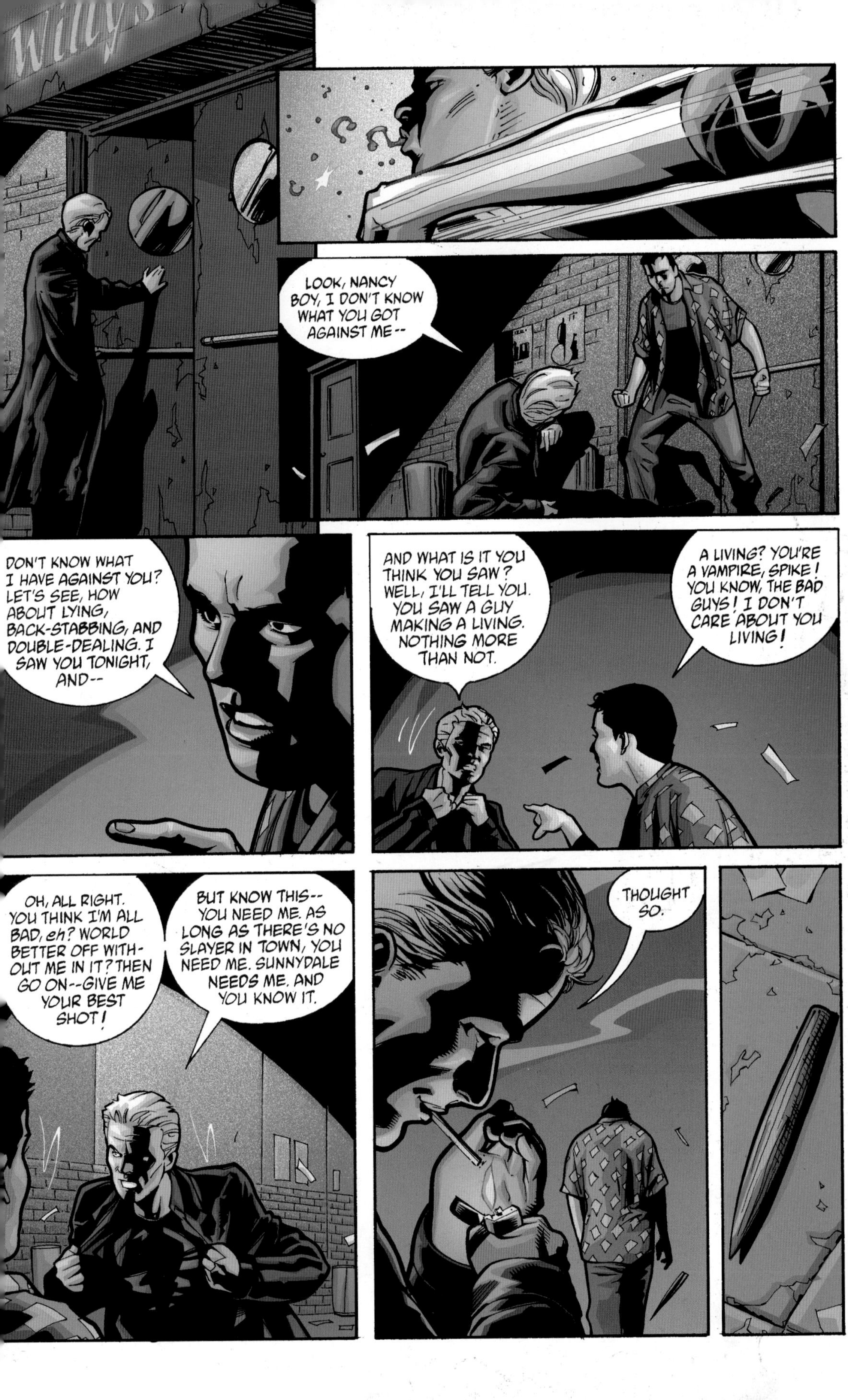
Willy's
LOOK, NANCY BOY, I DON'T KNOW WHAT YOU GOT AGAINST ME--
DON'T KNOW WHAT I HAVE AGAINST YOU? LET'S SEE, HOW ABOUT LYING, BACK-STABBING, AND DOUBLE-DEALING. I SAW YOU TONIGHT, AND--
AND WHAT IS IT YOU THINK YOU SAW? WELL, I'LL TELL YOU. YOU SAW A GUY MAKING A LIVING. NOTHING MORE THAN NOT.
A LIVING? YOU'RE A VAMPIRE, SPIKE! YOU KNOW, THE BAD GUYS! I DON'T CARE ABOUT YOU LIVING!
OH, ALL RIGHT. YOU THINK I'M ALL BAD, eh? WORLD BETTER OFF WITH-OUT ME IN IT? THEN GO ON--GIVE ME YOUR BEST SHOT!
BUT KNOW THIS-- YOU NEED ME. AS LONG AS THERE'S NO SLAYER IN TOWN, YOU NEED ME. SUNNYDALE NEEDS ME. AND YOU KNOW IT.
THOUGHT SO.

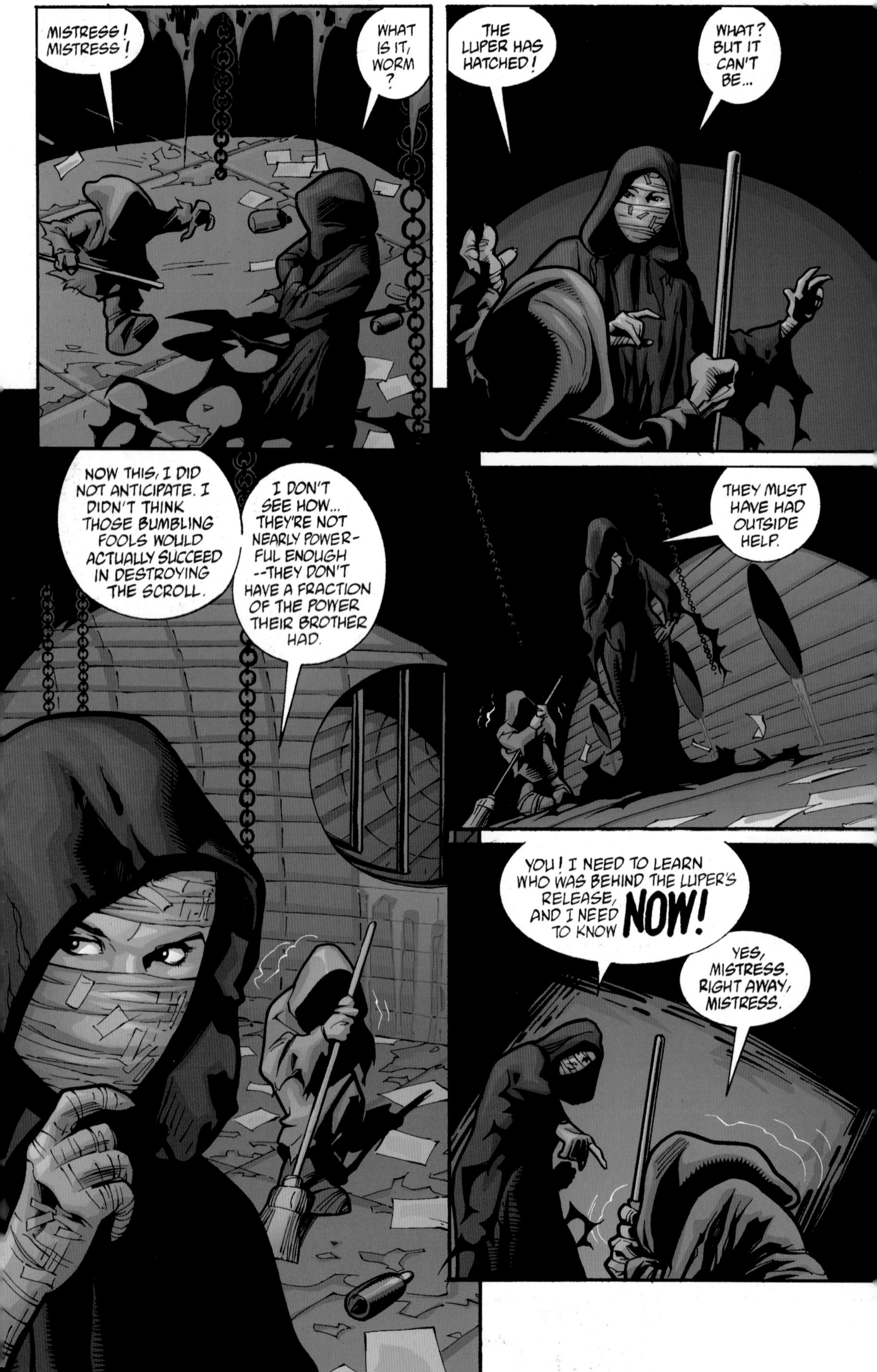
MISTRESS! MISTRESS!
WHAT IS IT, WORM?
THE LUPER HAS HATCHED!
WHAT? BUT IT CAN'T BE...
NOW THIS, I DID NOT ANTICIPATE. I DIDN'T THINK THOSE BUMBLING FOOLS WOULD ACTUALLY SUCCEED IN DESTROYING THE SCROLL.
I DON'T SEE HOW... THEY'RE NOT NEARLY POWER-FUL ENOUGH --THEY DON'T HAVE A FRACTION OF THE POWER THEIR BROTHER HAD.
THEY MUST HAVE HAD OUTSIDE HELP.
YOU! I NEED TO LEARN WHO WAS BEHIND THE LUPER'S RELEASE, AND I NEED TO KNOW NOW!
YES, MISTRESS. RIGHT AWAY, MISTRESS.

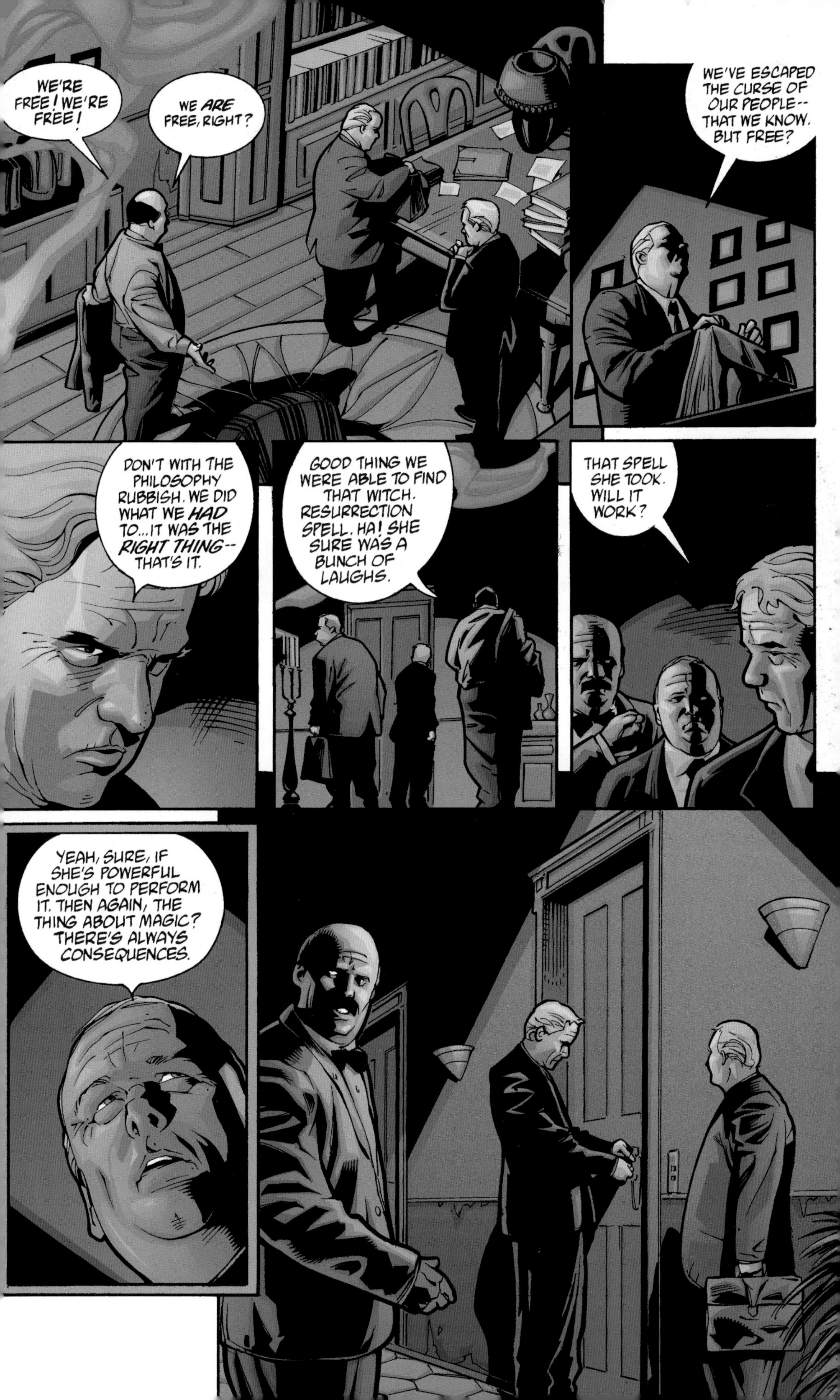

WE'RE FREE! WE'RE FREE!
WE ARE FREE, RIGHT?
WE'VE ESCAPED THE CURSE OF OUR PEOPLE-- THAT WE KNOW. BUT FREE?
DON'T WITH THE PHILOSOPHY RUBBISH. WE DID WHAT WE HAD TO...IT WAS THE RIGHT THING-- THAT'S IT.
GOOD THING WE WERE ABLE TO FIND THAT WITCH. RESURRECTION SPELL. HA! SHE SURE WAS A BUNCH OF LAUGHS.
THAT SPELL SHE TOOK. WILL IT WORK?
YEAH, SURE, IF SHE'S POWERFUL ENOUGH TO PERFORM IT. THEN AGAIN, THE THING ABOUT MAGIC? THERE'S ALWAYS CONSEQUENCES.

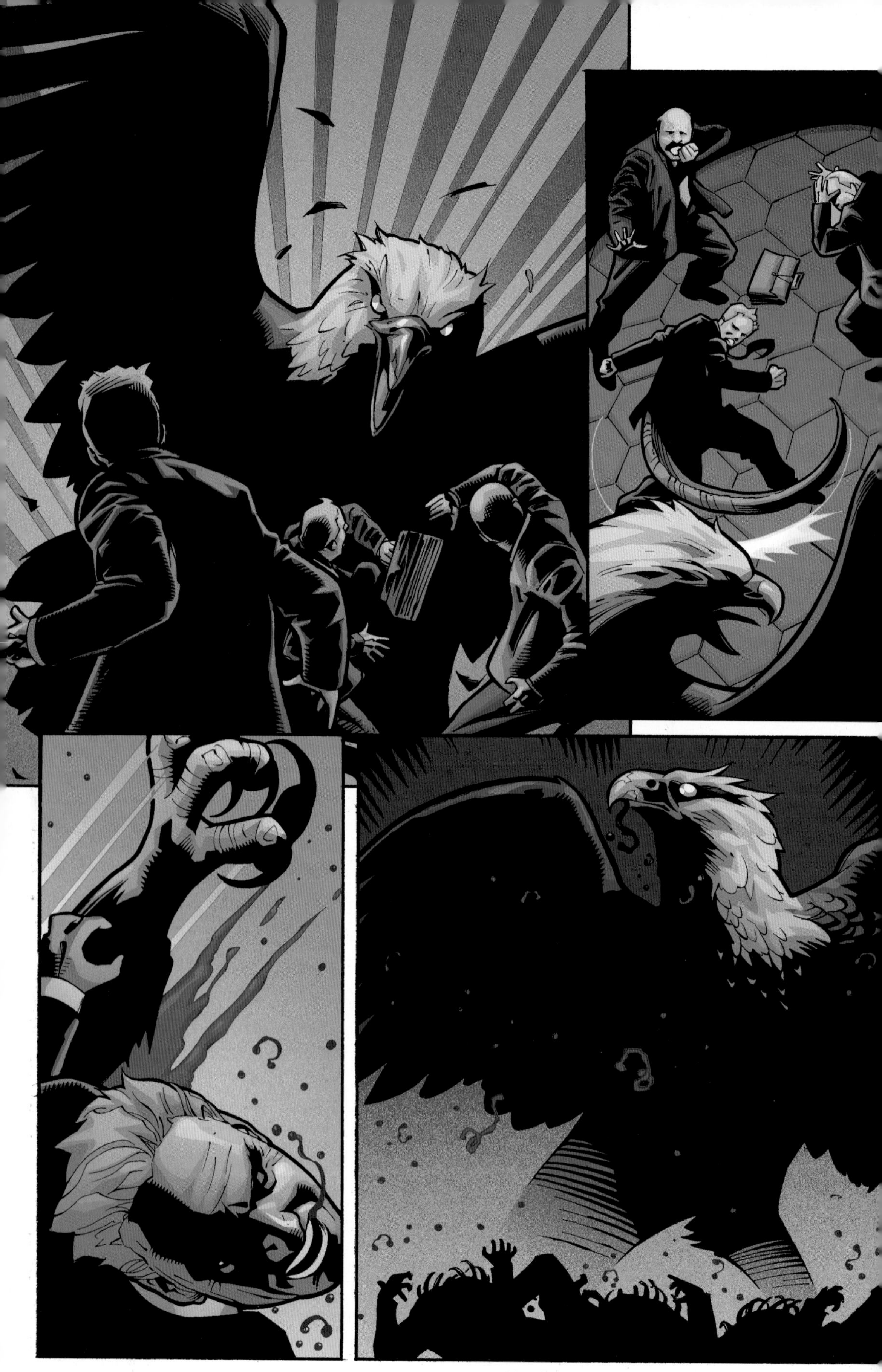

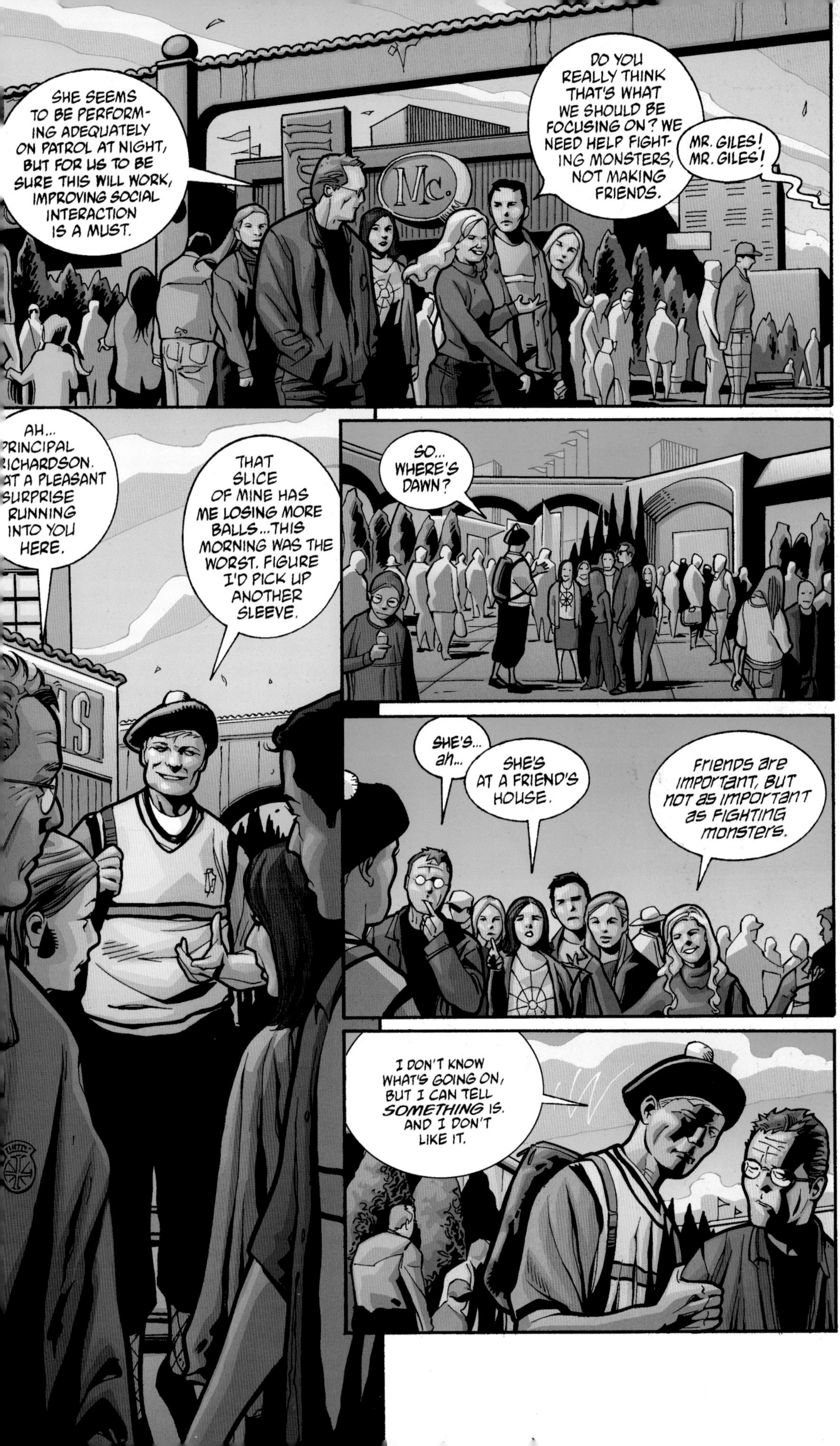
SHE SEEMS TO BE PERFORMING ADEQUATELY ON PATROL AT NIGHT, BUT FOR US TO BE SURE THIS WILL WORK, IMPROVING SOCIAL INTERACTION IS A MUST.
DO YOU REALLY THINK THAT'S WHAT WE SHOULD BE FOCUSING ON? WE NEED HELP FIGHTING MONSTERS, NOT MAKING FRIENDS.
MR. GILES! MR. GILES!
Mc.
AH... PRINCIPAL RICHARDSON. AT A PLEASANT SURPRISE RUNNING INTO YOU HERE.
THAT SLICE OF MINE HAS ME LOSING MORE BALLS...THIS MORNING WAS THE WORST. FIGURE I'D PICK UP ANOTHER SLEEVE.
SO... WHERE'S DAWN?
SHE'S... ah...
SHE'S AT A FRIEND'S HOUSE.
Friends are important, but not as important as fighting monsters.
I DON'T KNOW WHAT'S GOING ON, BUT I CAN TELL SOMETHING IS. AND I DON'T LIKE IT.

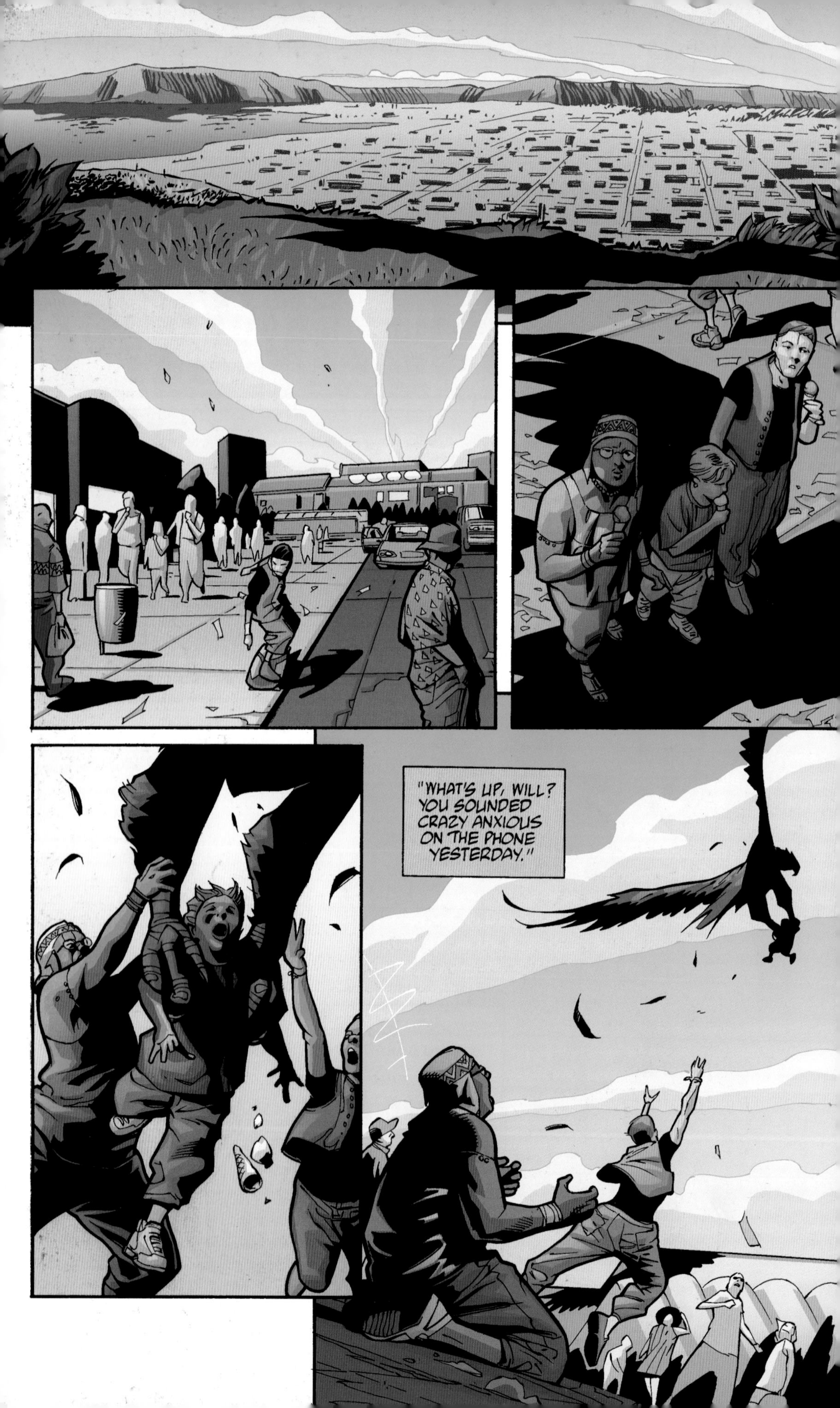
"WHAT'S UP, WILL? YOU SOUNDED CRAZY ANXIOUS ON THE PHONE YESTERDAY."

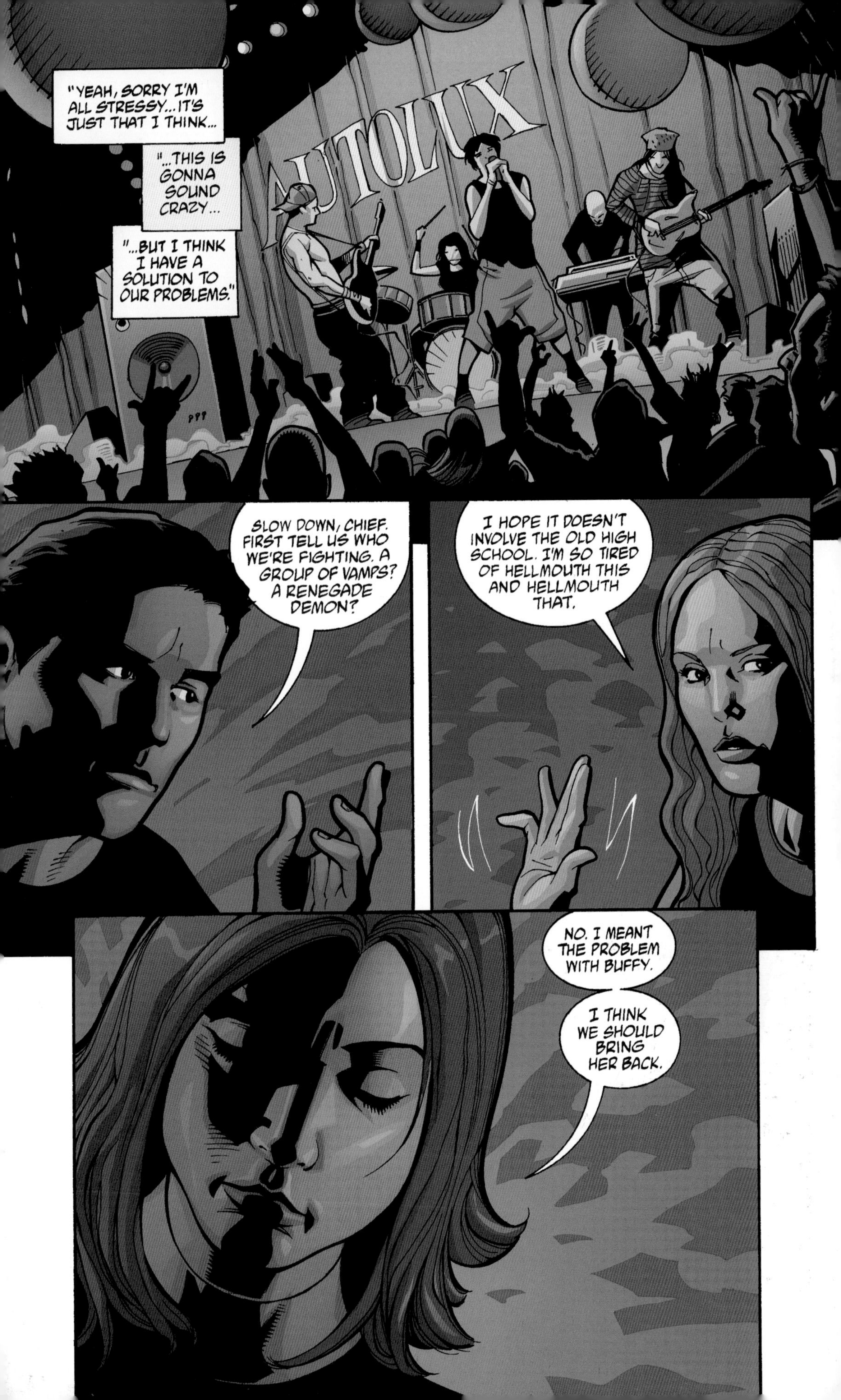
"YEAH, SORRY I'M ALL STRESSY... IT'S JUST THAT I THINK...
"...THIS IS GONNA SOUND CRAZY...
"...BUT I THINK I HAVE A SOLUTION TO OUR PROBLEMS."
AUTOLUX
SLOW DOWN, CHIEF. FIRST TELL US WHO WE'RE FIGHTING. A GROUP OF VAMPS? A RENEGADE DEMON?
I HOPE IT DOESN'T INVOLVE THE OLD HIGH SCHOOL. I'M SO TIRED OF HELLMOUTH THIS AND HELLMOUTH THAT.
NO. I MEANT THE PROBLEM WITH BUFFY.
I THINK WE SHOULD BRING HER BACK.

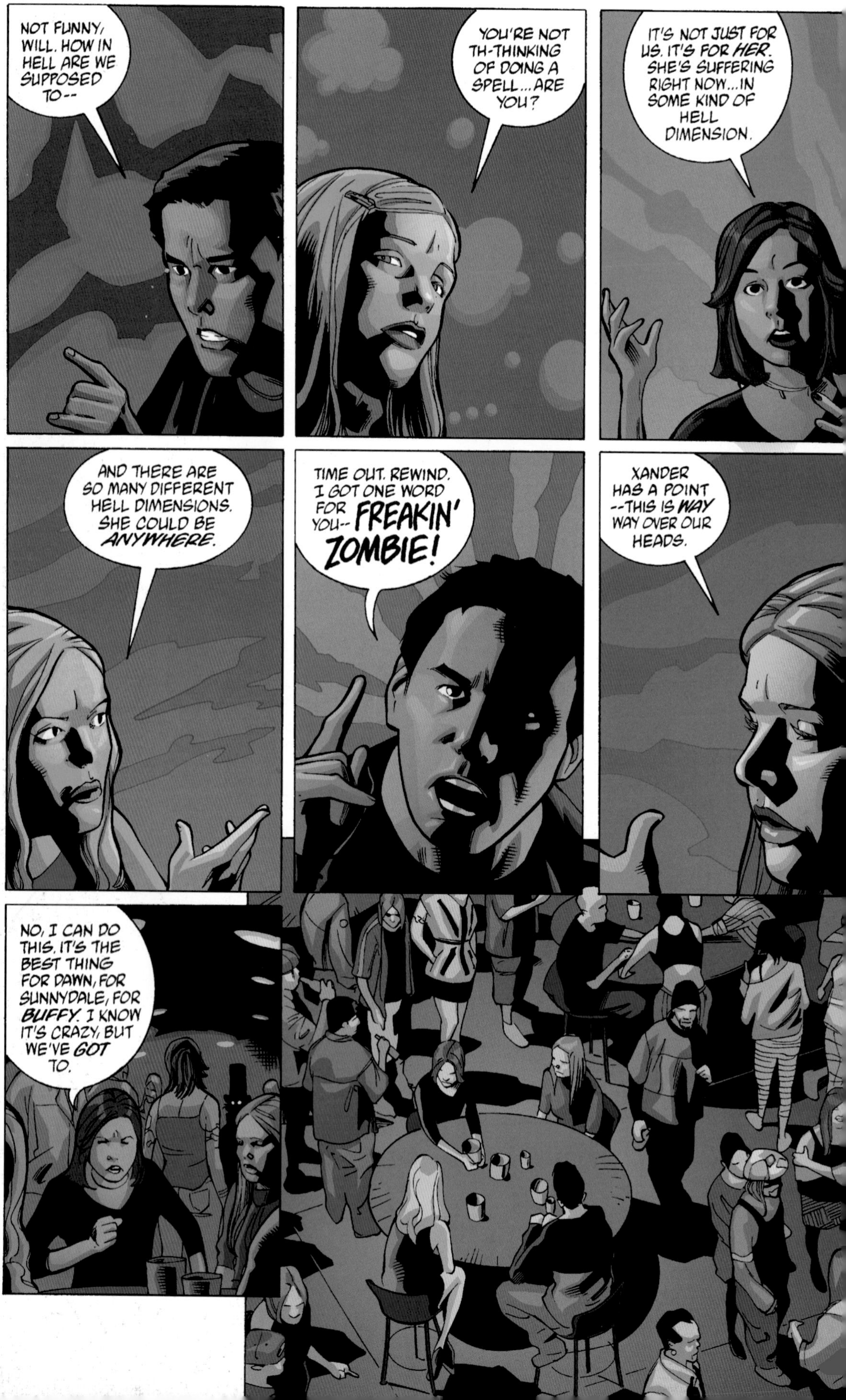
NOT FUNNY, WILL. HOW IN HELL ARE WE SUPPOSED TO--
YOU'RE NOT TH-THINKING OF DOING A SPELL... ARE YOU?
IT'S NOT JUST FOR US. IT'S FOR HER. SHE'S SUFFERING RIGHT NOW... IN SOME KIND OF HELL DIMENSION.
AND THERE ARE SO MANY DIFFERENT HELL DIMENSIONS. SHE COULD BE ANYWHERE.
TIME OUT. REWIND. I GOT ONE WORD FOR YOU-- FREAKIN' ZOMBIE!
XANDER HAS A POINT --THIS IS WAY WAY OVER OUR HEADS.
NO, I CAN DO THIS. IT'S THE BEST THING FOR DAWN, FOR SUNNYDALE, FOR BUFFY. I KNOW IT'S CRAZY, BUT WE'VE GOT TO.

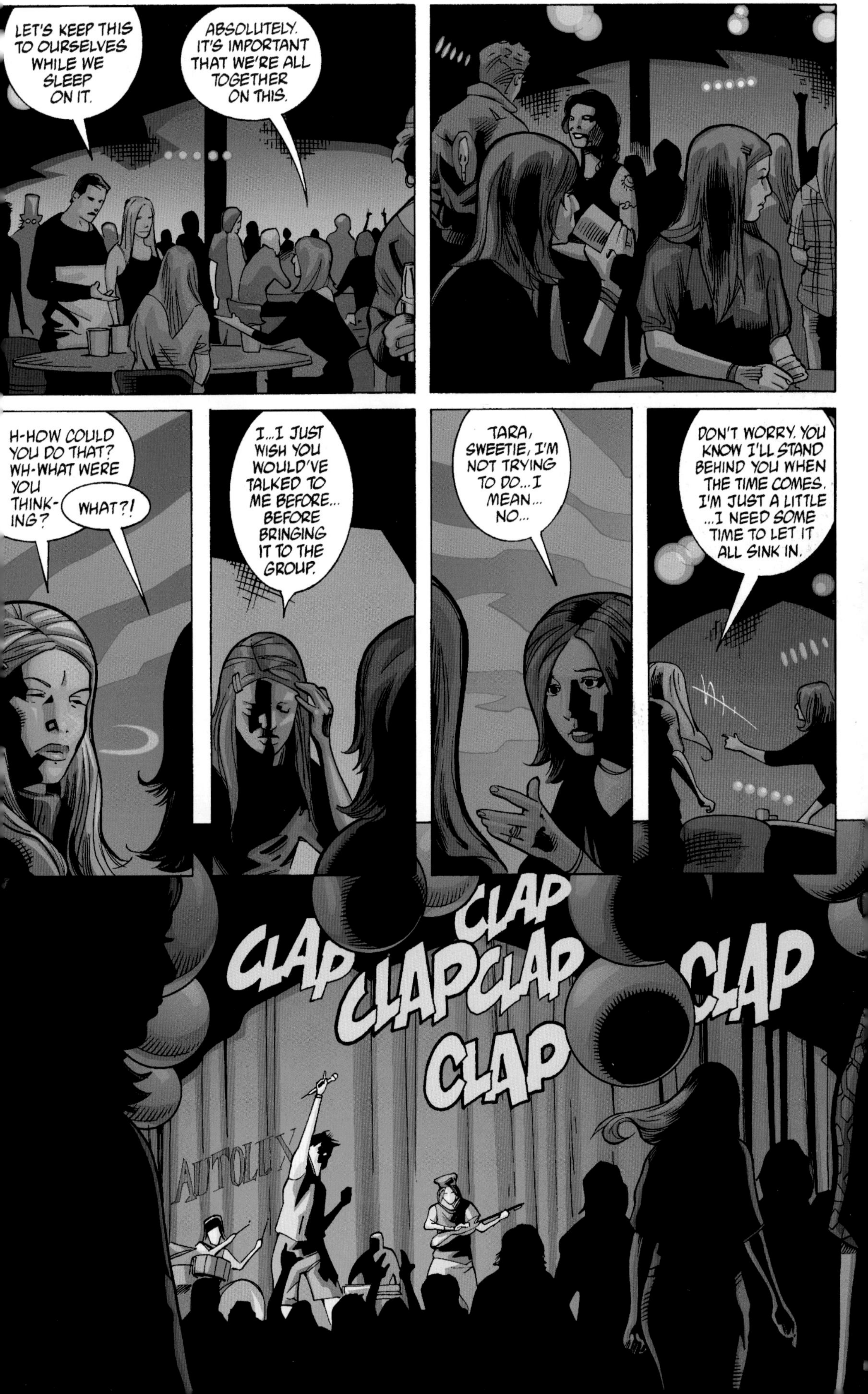
LET'S KEEP THIS TO OURSELVES WHILE WE SLEEP ON IT.
ABSOLUTELY. IT'S IMPORTANT THAT WE'RE ALL TOGETHER ON THIS.
H-HOW COULD YOU DO THAT? WH-WHAT WERE YOU THINKING?
WHAT?!
I...I JUST WISH YOU WOULD'VE TALKED TO ME BEFORE... BEFORE BRINGING IT TO THE GROUP.
TARA, SWEETIE, I'M NOT TRYING TO DO...I MEAN... NO...
DON'T WORRY. YOU KNOW I'LL STAND BEHIND YOU WHEN THE TIME COMES. I'M JUST A LITTLE ...I NEED SOME TIME TO LET IT ALL SINK IN.
CLAP
CLAP
CLAP CLAP
CLAP
CLAP
AUTOLUX

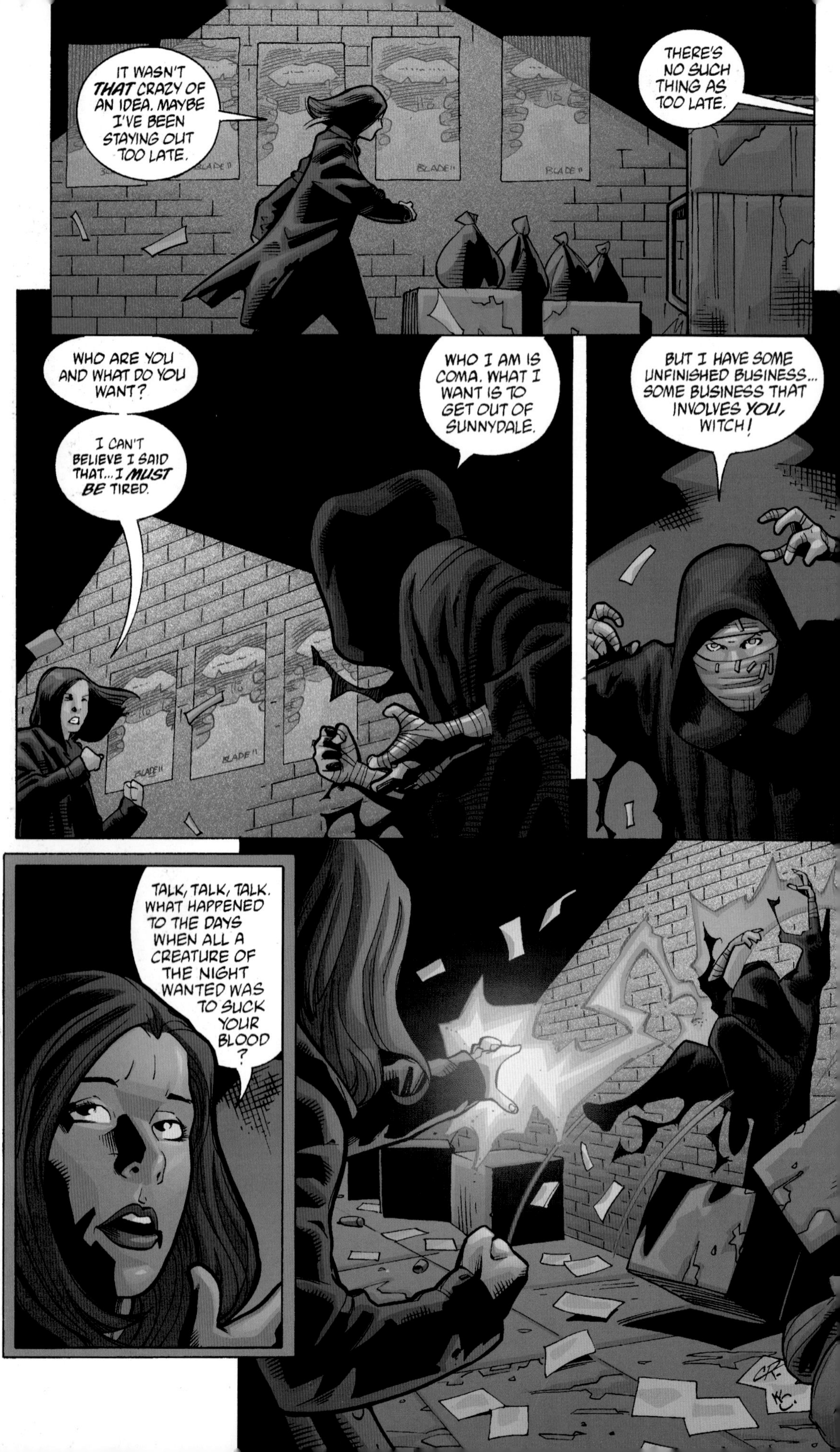
IT WASN'T THAT CRAZY OF AN IDEA. MAYBE I'VE BEEN STAYING OUT TOO LATE.
THERE'S NO SUCH THING AS TOO LATE.
WHO ARE YOU AND WHAT DO YOU WANT?
I CAN'T BELIEVE I SAID THAT... I MUST BE TIRED.
WHO I AM IS COMA. WHAT I WANT IS TO GET OUT OF SUNNYDALE.
BUT I HAVE SOME UNFINISHED BUSINESS... SOME BUSINESS THAT INVOLVES YOU, WITCH!
TALK, TALK, TALK. WHAT HAPPENED TO THE DAYS WHEN ALL A CREATURE OF THE NIGHT WANTED WAS TO SUCK YOUR BLOOD?

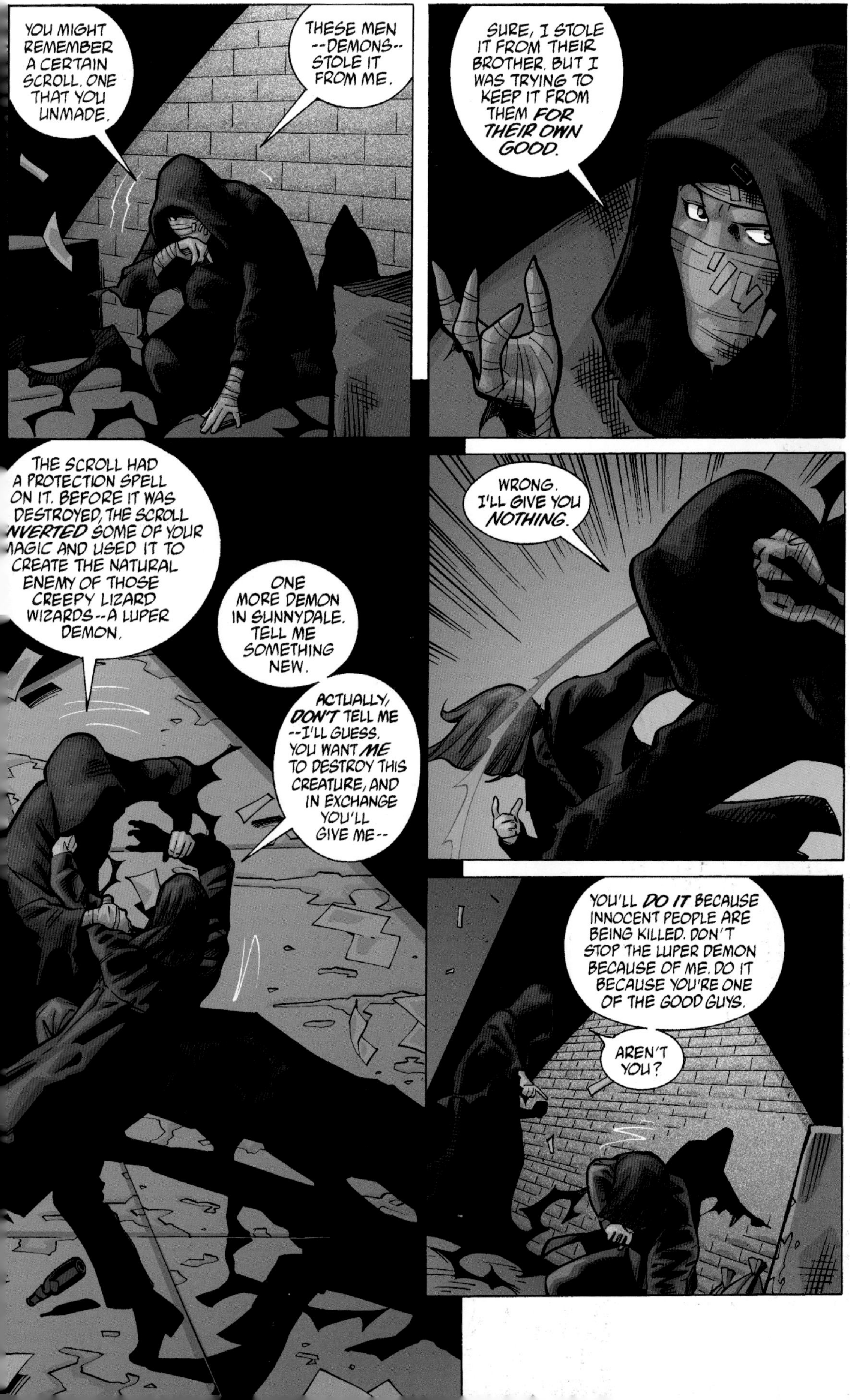
YOU MIGHT REMEMBER A CERTAIN SCROLL. ONE THAT YOU UNMADE.
THESE MEN --DEMONS-- STOLE IT FROM ME.
SURE, I STOLE IT FROM THEIR BROTHER. BUT I WAS TRYING TO KEEP IT FROM THEM FOR THEIR OWN GOOD.
THE SCROLL HAD A PROTECTION SPELL ON IT. BEFORE IT WAS DESTROYED, THE SCROLL NVERTED SOME OF YOUR MAGIC AND USED IT TO CREATE THE NATURAL ENEMY OF THOSE CREEPY LIZARD WIZARDS--A LUPER DEMON.
ONE MORE DEMON IN SUNNYDALE. TELL ME SOMETHING NEW.
ACTUALLY, DON'T TELL ME --I'LL GUESS. YOU WANT ME TO DESTROY THIS CREATURE, AND IN EXCHANGE YOU'LL GIVE ME--
WRONG. I'LL GIVE YOU NOTHING.
YOU'LL DO IT BECAUSE INNOCENT PEOPLE ARE BEING KILLED. DON'T STOP THE LUPER DEMON BECAUSE OF ME. DO IT BECAUSE YOU'RE ONE OF THE GOOD GUYS.
AREN'T YOU?

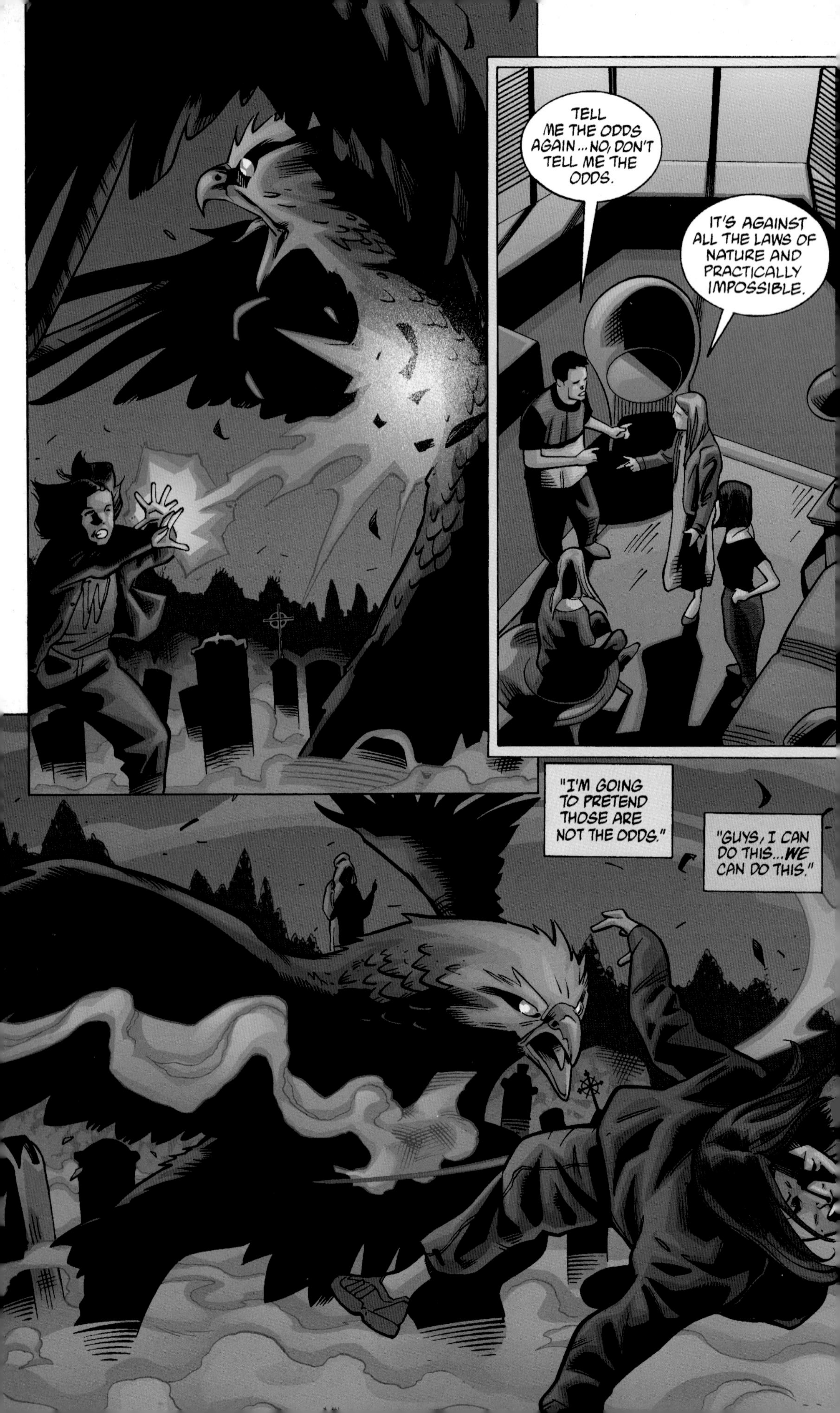
TELL ME THE ODDS AGAIN... NO, DON'T TELL ME THE ODDS.
IT'S AGAINST ALL THE LAWS OF NATURE AND PRACTICALLY IMPOSSIBLE.
"I'M GOING TO PRETEND THOSE ARE NOT THE ODDS."
"GUYS, I CAN DO THIS... WE CAN DO THIS."

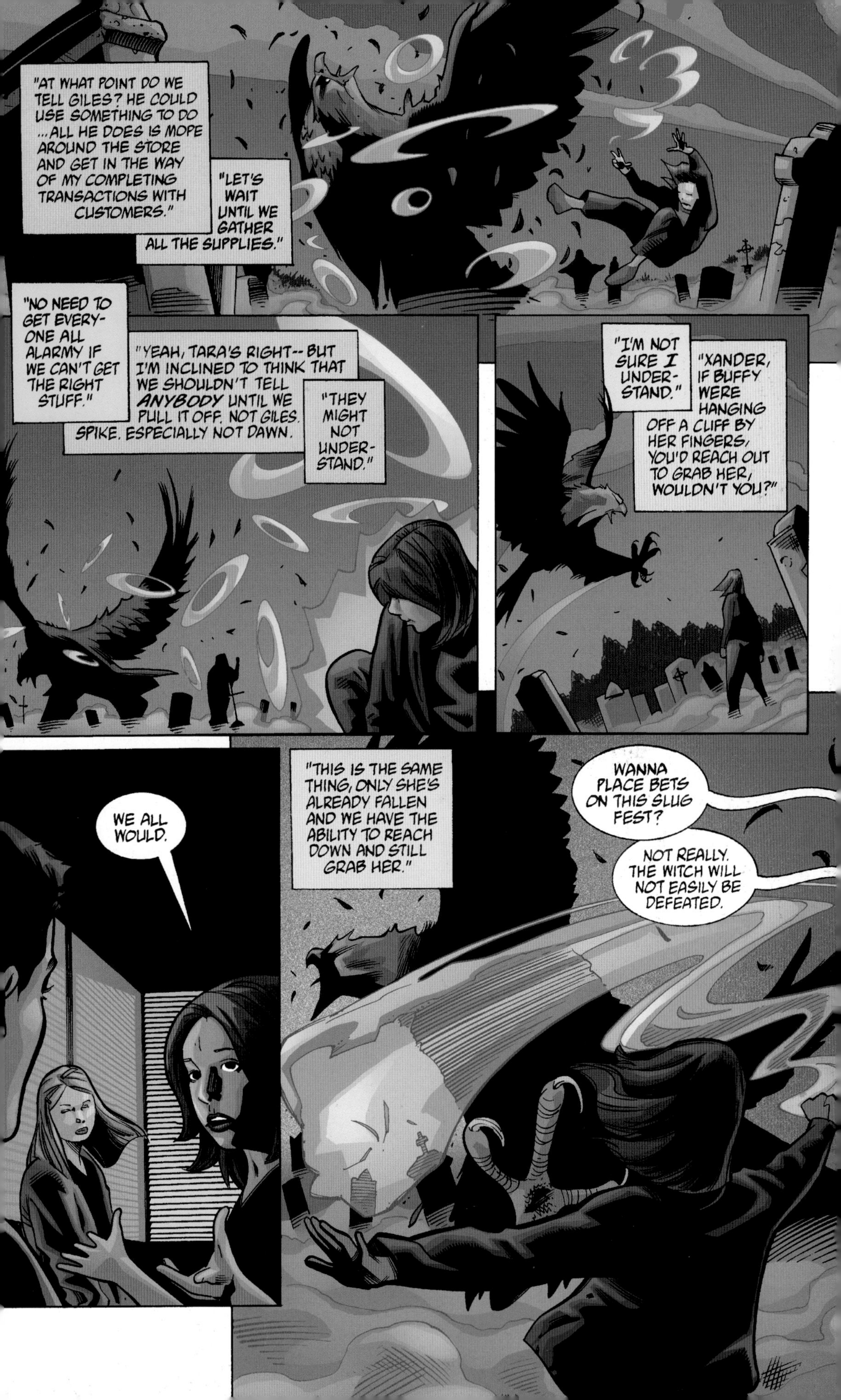
"AT WHAT POINT DO WE TELL GILES? HE COULD USE SOMETHING TO DO ...ALL HE DOES IS MOPE AROUND THE STORE AND GET IN THE WAY OF MY COMPLETING TRANSACTIONS WITH CUSTOMERS."
"LET'S WAIT UNTIL WE GATHER ALL THE SUPPLIES."
"NO NEED TO GET EVERY-ONE ALL ALARMY IF WE CAN'T GET THE RIGHT STUFF."
"YEAH, TARA'S RIGHT-- BUT I'M INCLINED TO THINK THAT WE SHOULDN'T TELL ANYBODY UNTIL WE PULL IT OFF. NOT GILES. SPIKE. ESPECIALLY NOT DAWN.
"THEY MIGHT NOT UNDER-STAND."
"I'M NOT SURE I UNDER-STAND."
"XANDER, IF BUFFY WERE HANGING OFF A CLIFF BY HER FINGERS, YOU'D REACH OUT TO GRAB HER, WOULDN'T YOU?"
WE ALL WOULD.
"THIS IS THE SAME THING, ONLY SHE'S ALREADY FALLEN AND WE HAVE THE ABILITY TO REACH DOWN AND STILL GRAB HER."
WANNA PLACE BETS ON THIS SLUG FEST?
NOT REALLY. THE WITCH WILL NOT EASILY BE DEFEATED.

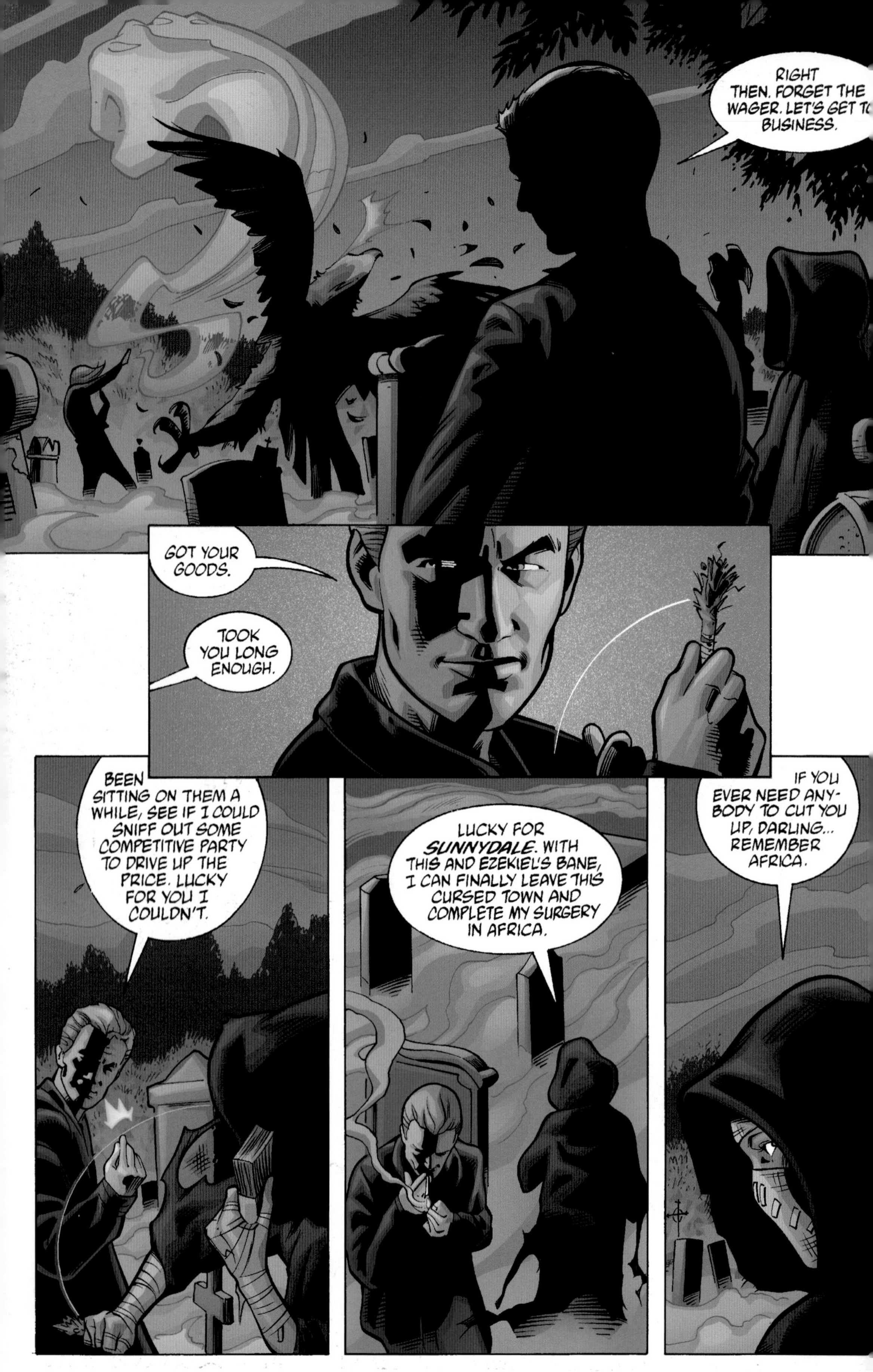
RIGHT THEN. FORGET THE WAGER. LET'S GET TO BUSINESS.
GOT YOUR GOODS.
TOOK YOU LONG ENOUGH.
BEEN SITTING ON THEM A WHILE, SEE IF I COULD SNIFF OUT SOME COMPETITIVE PARTY TO DRIVE UP THE PRICE. LUCKY FOR YOU I COULDN'T.
LUCKY FOR *SUNNYDALE*. WITH THIS AND EZEKIEL'S BANE, I CAN FINALLY LEAVE THIS CURSED TOWN AND COMPLETE MY SURGERY IN AFRICA.
IF YOU EVER NEED ANYBODY TO CUT YOU UP, DARLING... REMEMBER AFRICA.

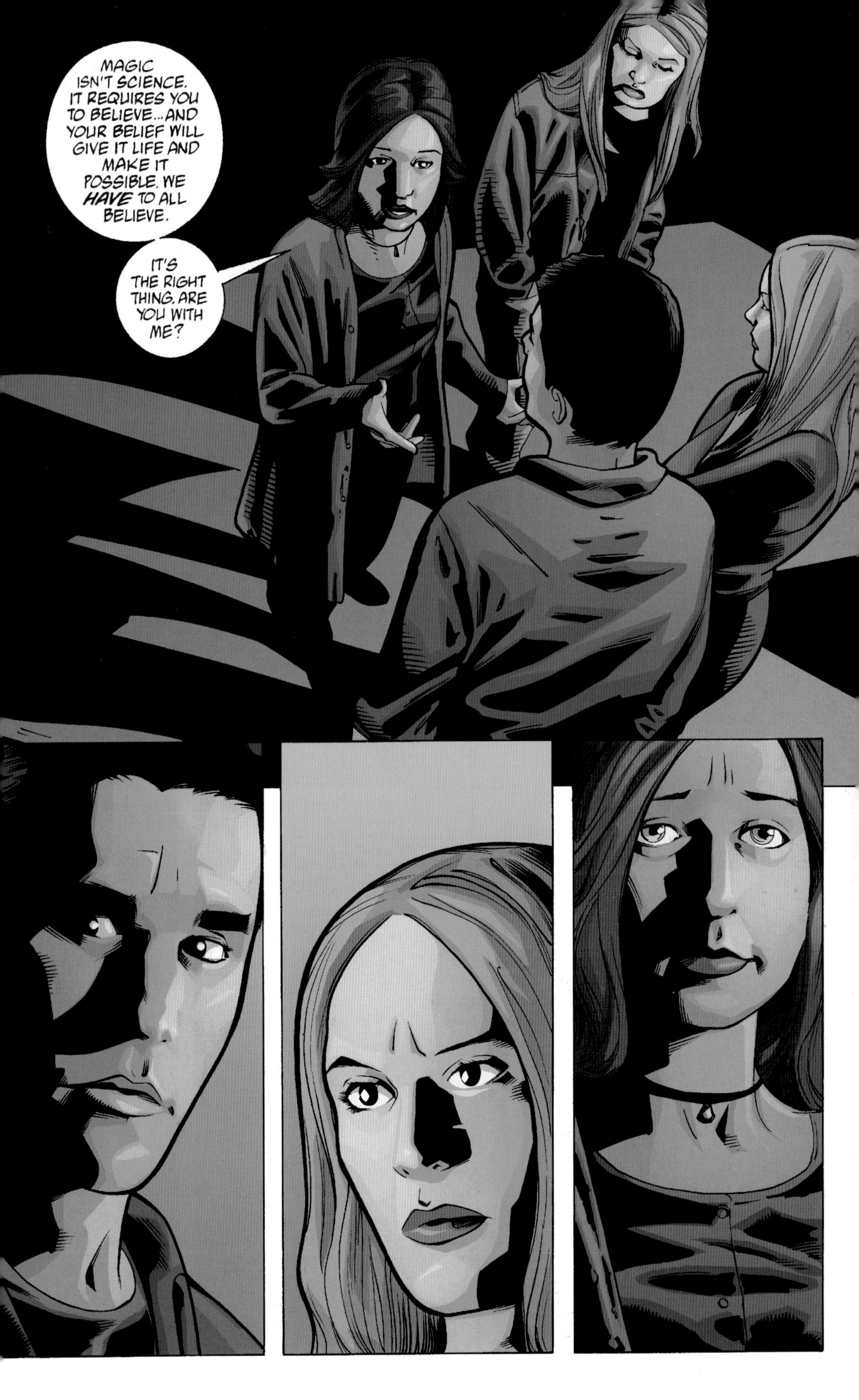
MAGIC ISN'T SCIENCE. IT REQUIRES YOU TO BELIEVE...AND YOUR BELIEF WILL GIVE IT LIFE AND MAKE IT POSSIBLE. WE *HAVE* TO ALL BELIEVE.
IT'S THE RIGHT THING. ARE YOU WITH ME?

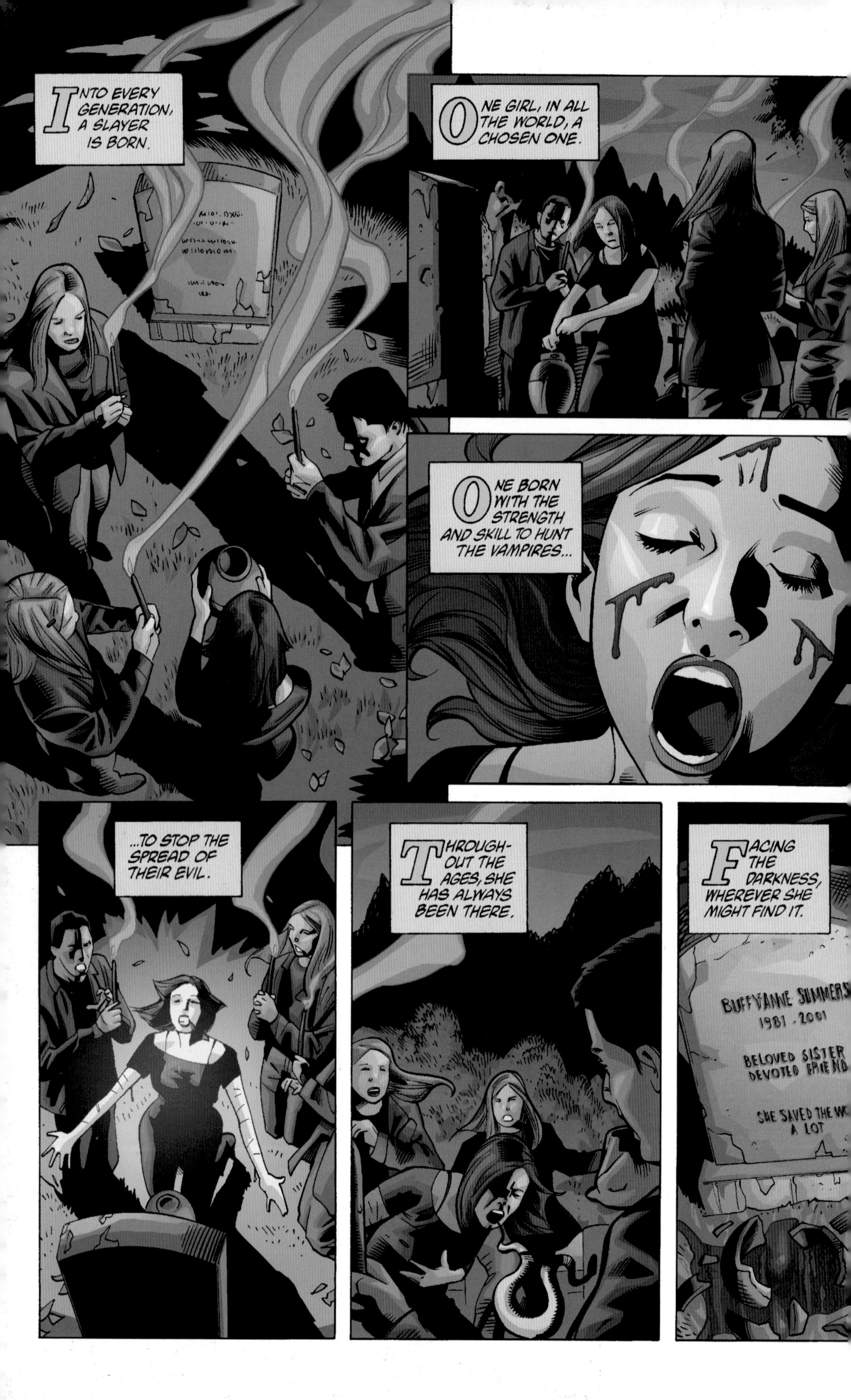
INTO EVERY GENERATION, A SLAYER IS BORN.
ONE GIRL, IN ALL THE WORLD, A CHOSEN ONE.
ONE BORN WITH THE STRENGTH AND SKILL TO HUNT THE VAMPIRES...
...TO STOP THE SPREAD OF THEIR EVIL.
THROUGHOUT THE AGES, SHE HAS ALWAYS BEEN THERE.
FACING THE DARKNESS, WHEREVER SHE MIGHT FIND IT.
BUFFY ANNE SUMMERS
1981 - 2001
BELOVED SISTER
DEVOTED FRIEND
SHE SAVED THE
A LOT

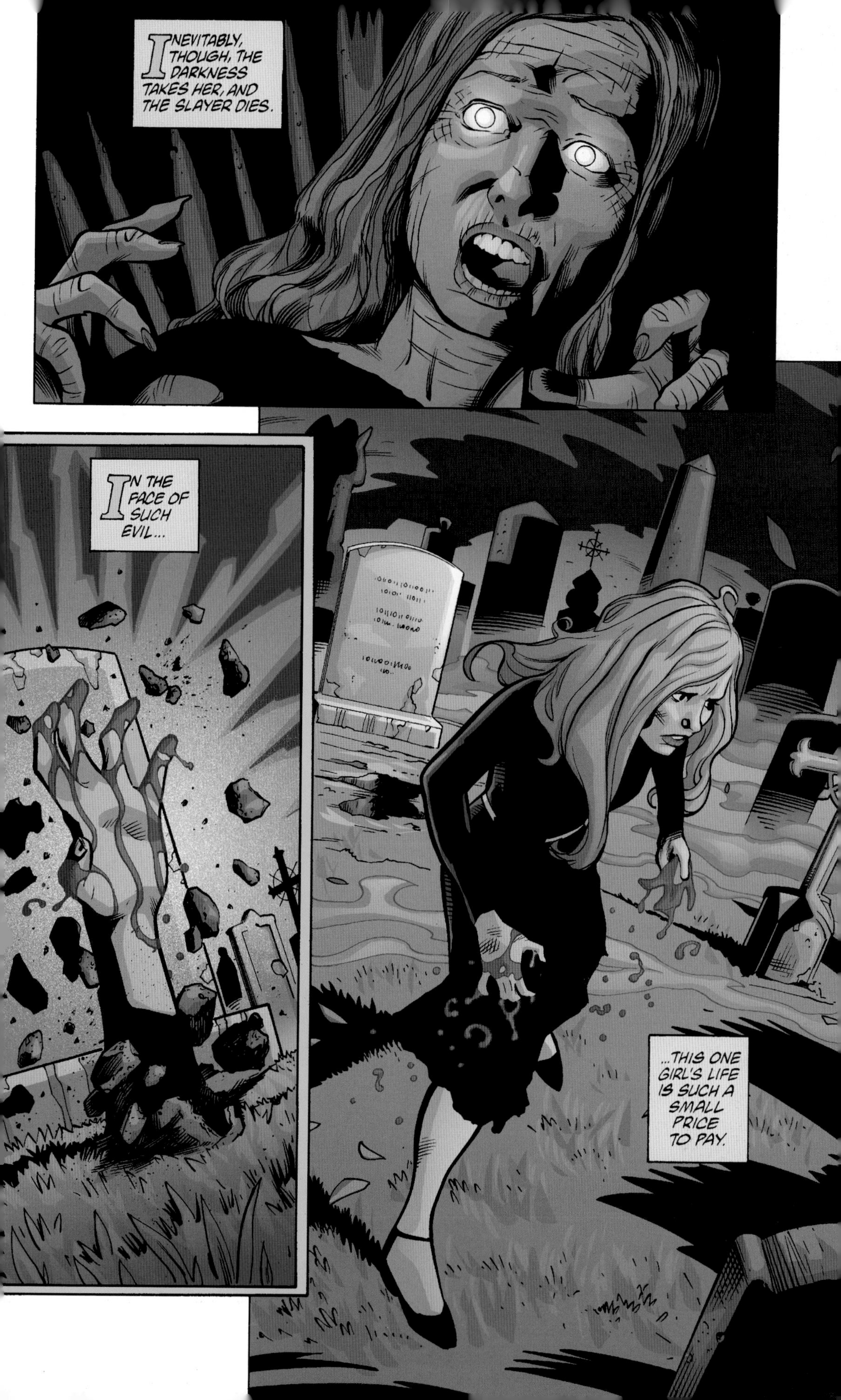
INEVITABLY, THOUGH, THE DARKNESS TAKES HER, AND THE SLAYER DIES.
IN THE FACE OF SUCH EVIL...
...THIS ONE GIRL'S LIFE IS SUCH A SMALL PRICE TO PAY.

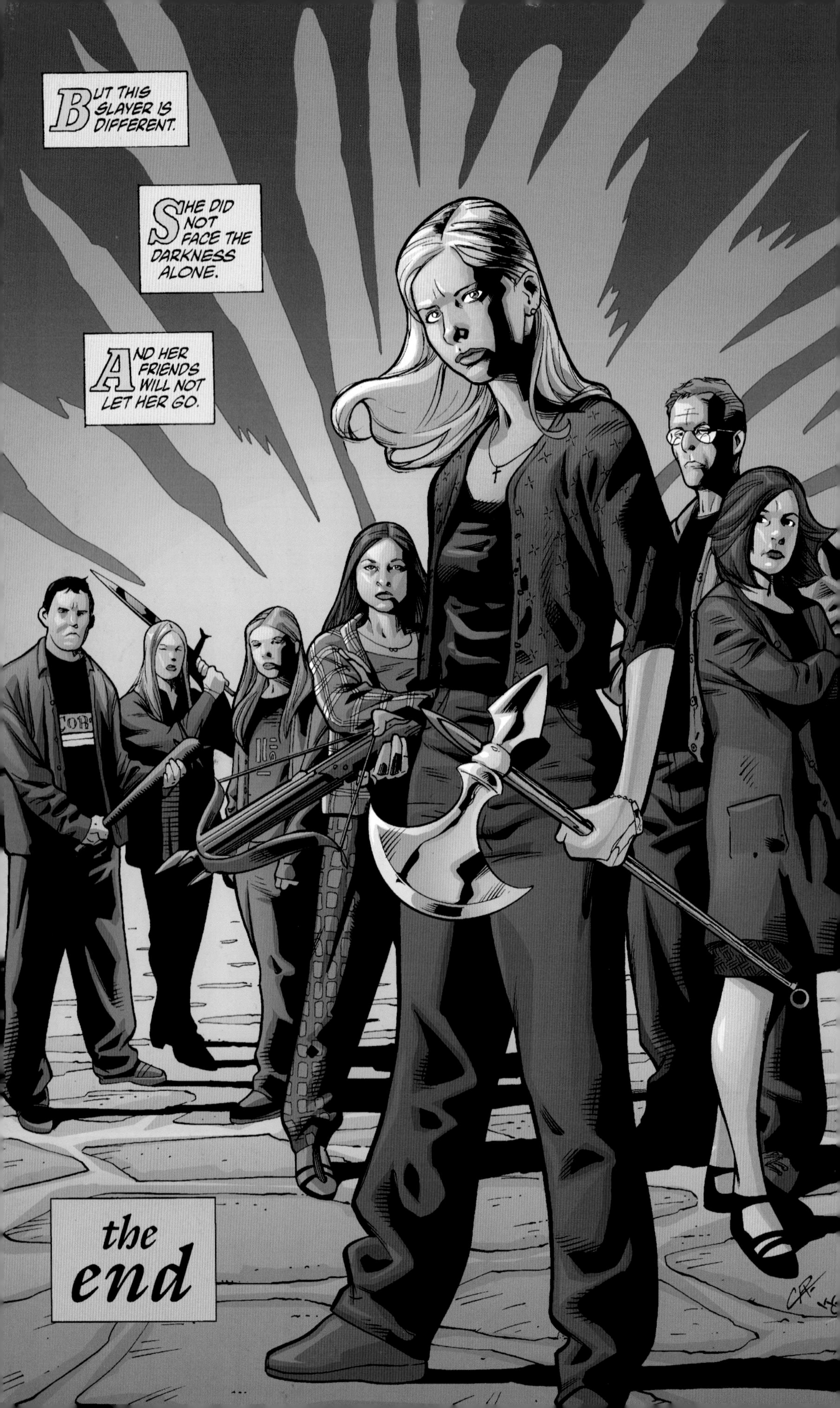
BUT THIS SLAYER IS DIFFERENT.
SHE DID NOT FACE THE DARKNESS ALONE.
AND HER FRIENDS WILL NOT LET HER GO.
the end

Buffy the Vampire Slayer™

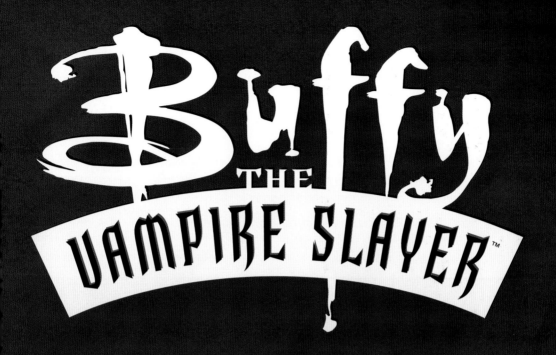

WITHDRAWAL

based on the television series created by
JOSS WHEDON

writers TOM FASSBENDER & JIM PASCOE

artist PAUL LEE

colorist & letterer MICHELLE MADSEN

This story takes place during Buffy the Vampire Slayer's sixth season.

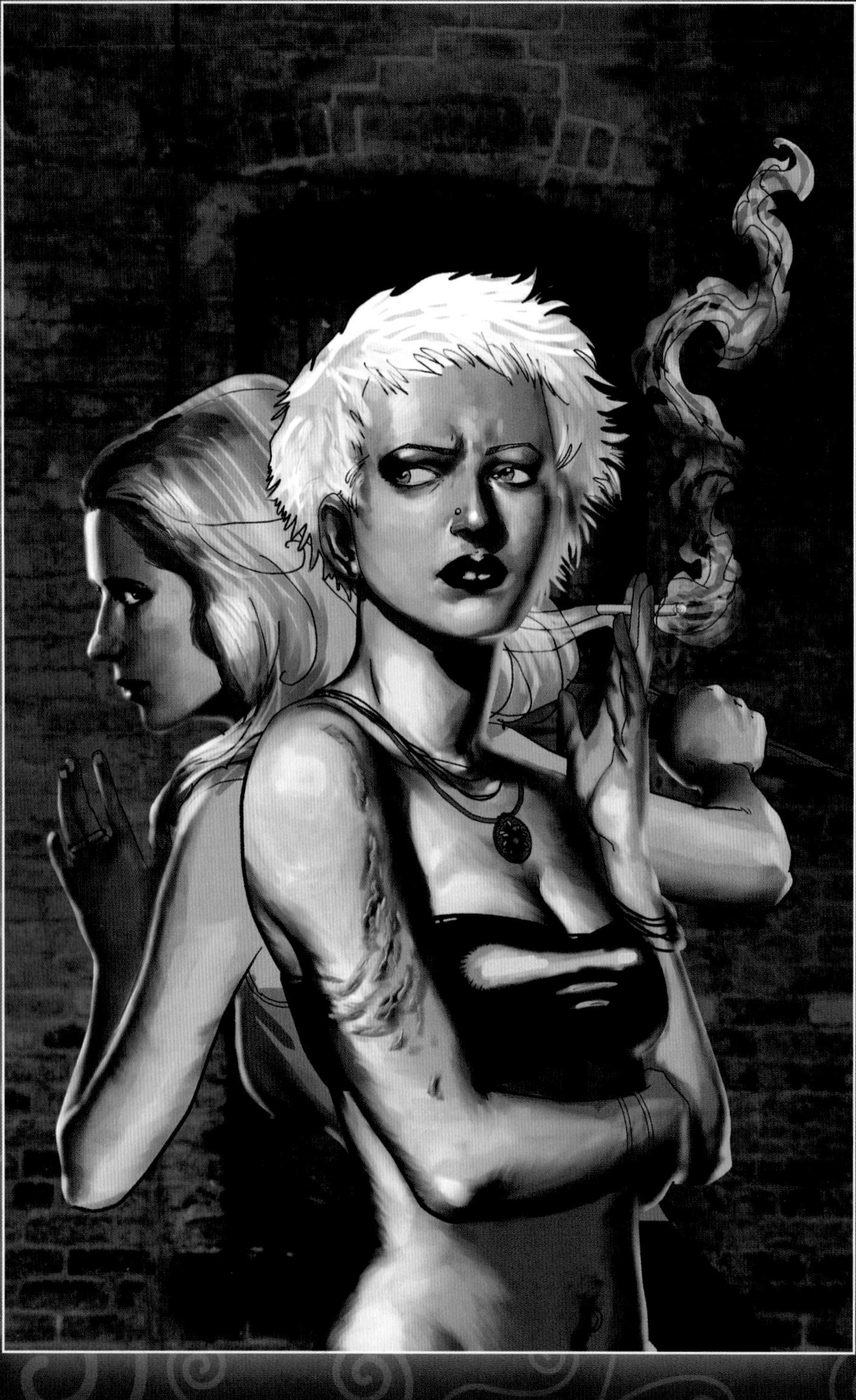

PAUL LEE

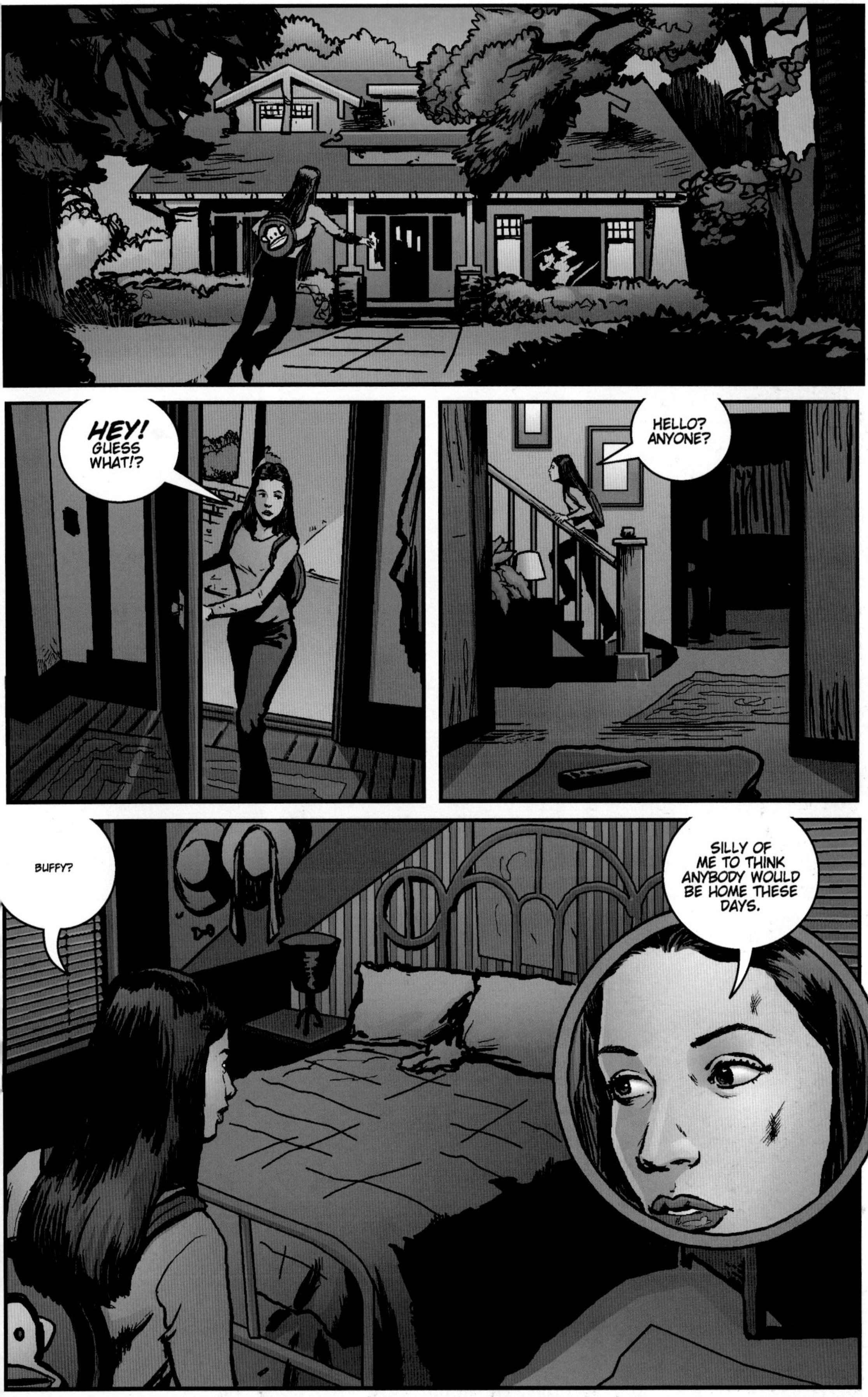
HEY! GUESS WHAT!?
HELLO? ANYONE?
BUFFY?
SILLY OF ME TO THINK ANYBODY WOULD BE HOME THESE DAYS.

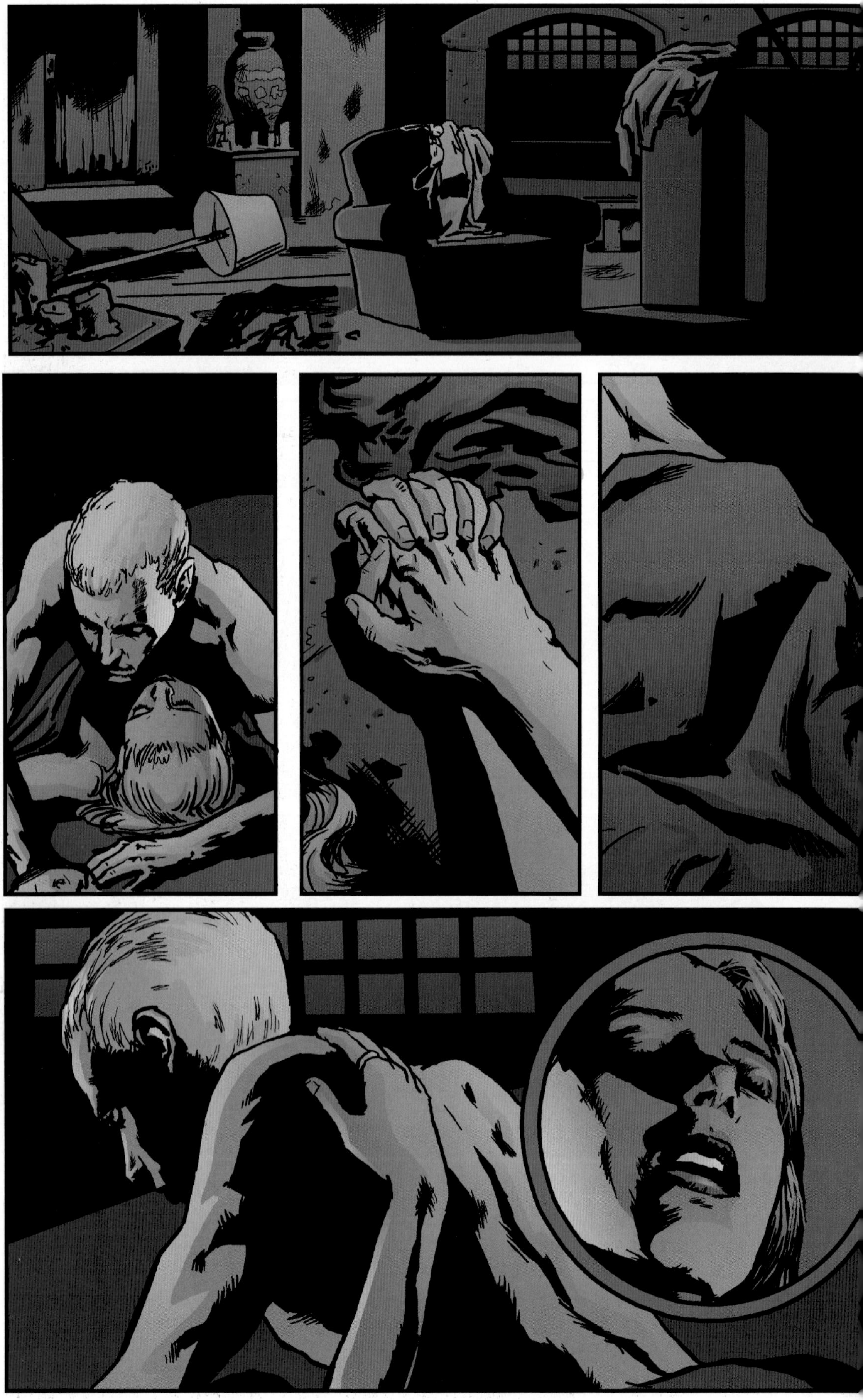

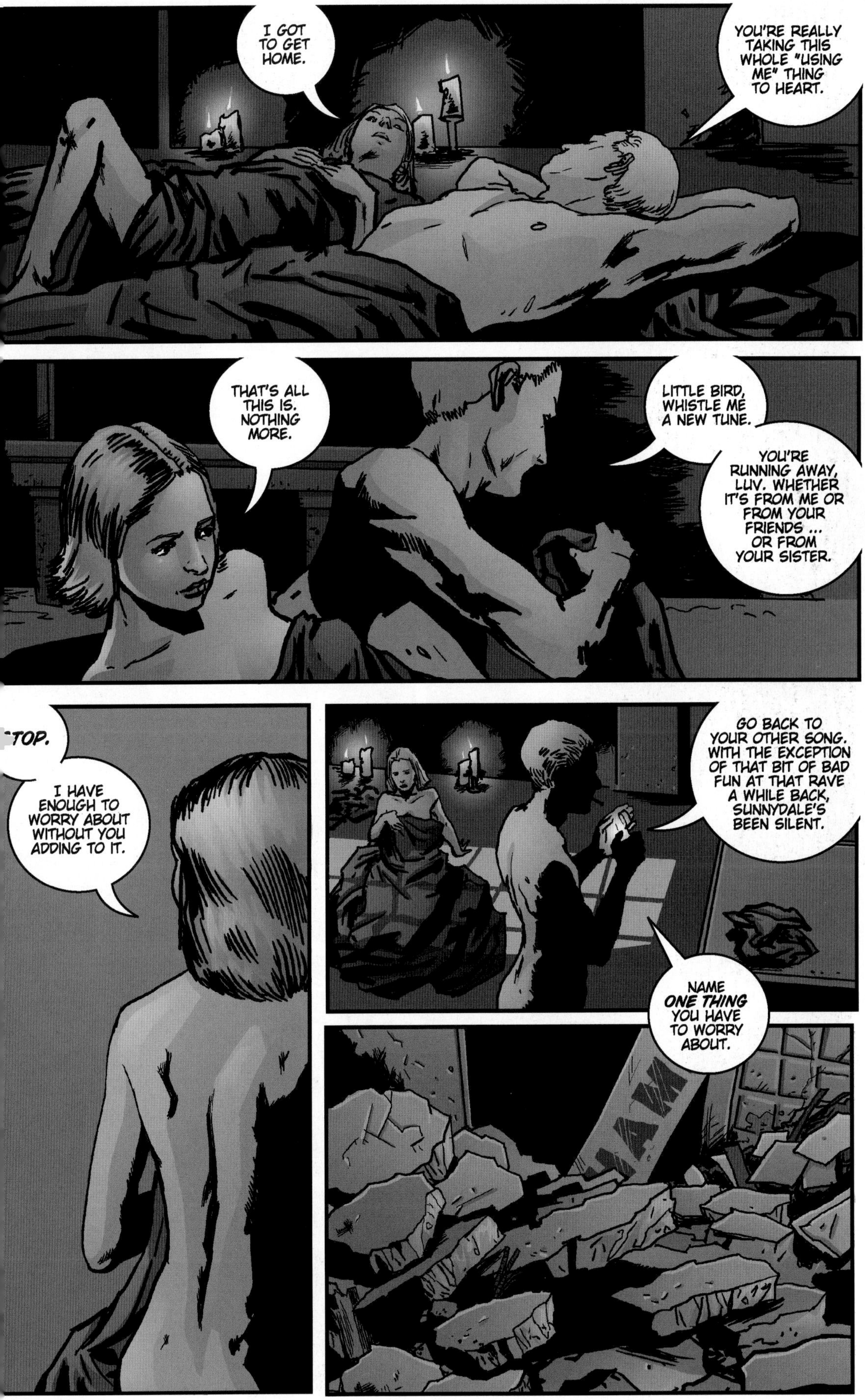
I GOT TO GET HOME.
YOU'RE REALLY TAKING THIS WHOLE "USING ME" THING TO HEART.
THAT'S ALL THIS IS. NOTHING MORE.
LITTLE BIRD, WHISTLE ME A NEW TUNE.
YOU'RE RUNNING AWAY, LUV. WHETHER IT'S FROM ME OR FROM YOUR FRIENDS ... OR FROM YOUR SISTER.
TOP.
I HAVE ENOUGH TO WORRY ABOUT WITHOUT YOU ADDING TO IT.
GO BACK TO YOUR OTHER SONG. WITH THE EXCEPTION OF THAT BIT OF BAD FUN AT THAT RAVE A WHILE BACK, SUNNYDALE'S BEEN SILENT.
NAME ***ONE THING*** YOU HAVE TO WORRY ABOUT.

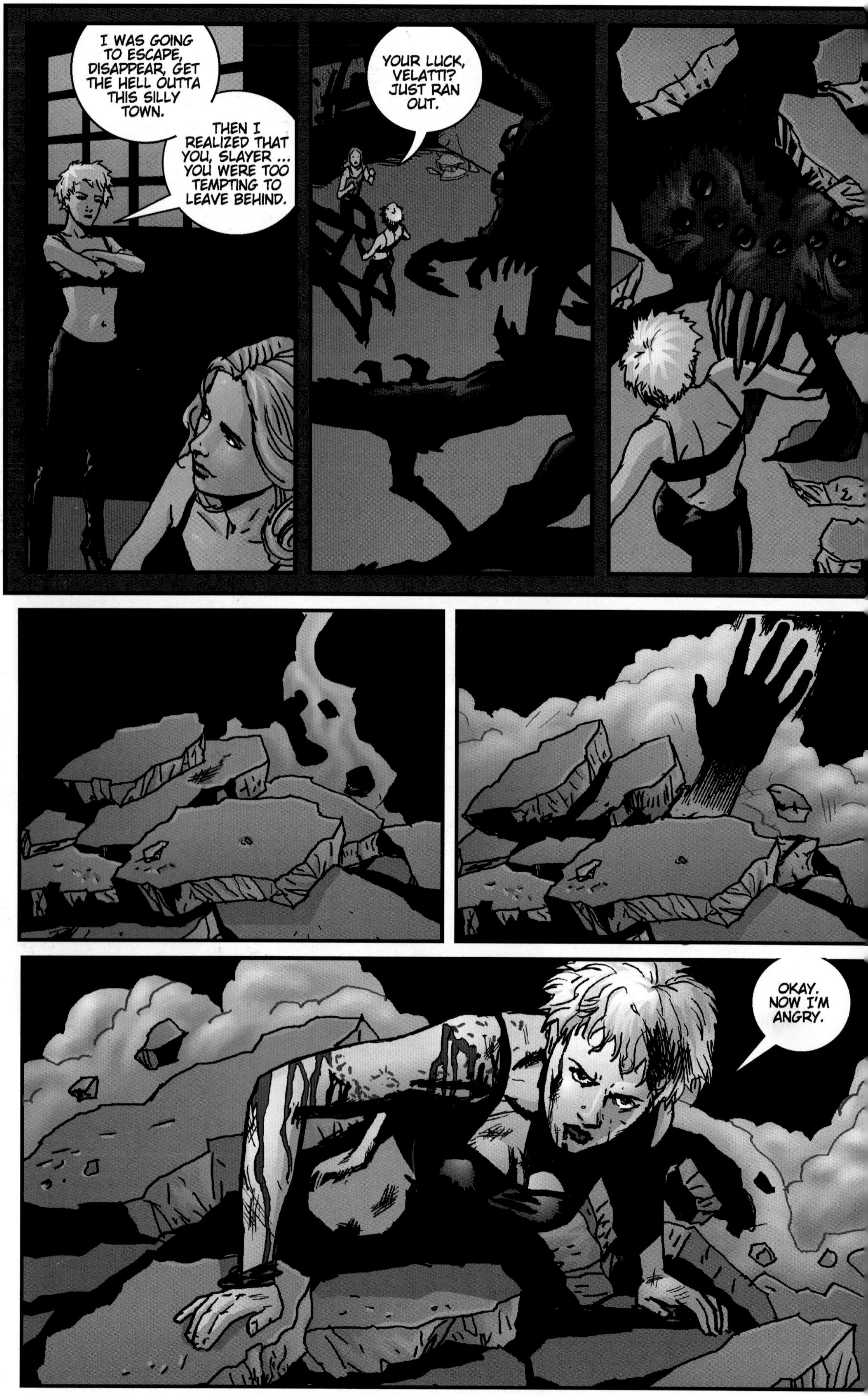
I WAS GOING TO ESCAPE, DISAPPEAR, GET THE HELL OUTTA THIS SILLY TOWN.
THEN I REALIZED THAT YOU, SLAYER ... YOU WERE TOO TEMPTING TO LEAVE BEHIND.
YOUR LUCK, VELATTI? JUST RAN OUT.
OKAY. NOW I'M ANGRY.

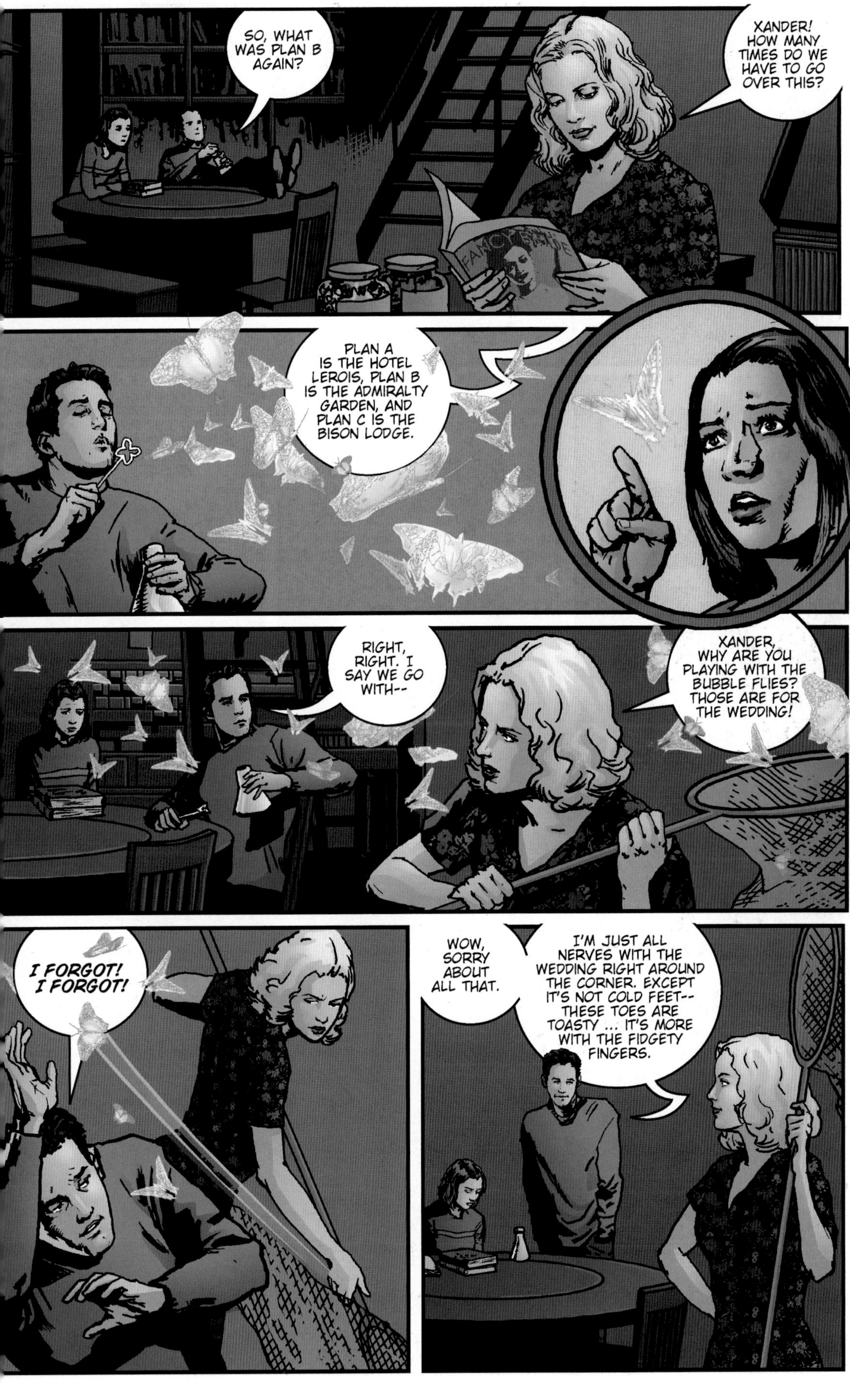
SO, WHAT WAS PLAN B AGAIN?
XANDER! HOW MANY TIMES DO WE HAVE TO GO OVER THIS?
PLAN A IS THE HOTEL LEROIS, PLAN B IS THE ADMIRALTY GARDEN, AND PLAN C IS THE BISON LODGE.
RIGHT, RIGHT. I SAY WE GO WITH--
XANDER, WHY ARE YOU PLAYING WITH THE BUBBLE FLIES? THOSE ARE FOR THE WEDDING!
I FORGOT! I FORGOT!
WOW, SORRY ABOUT ALL THAT.
I'M JUST ALL NERVES WITH THE WEDDING RIGHT AROUND THE CORNER. EXCEPT IT'S NOT COLD FEET-- THESE TOES ARE TOASTY ... IT'S MORE WITH THE FIDGETY FINGERS.

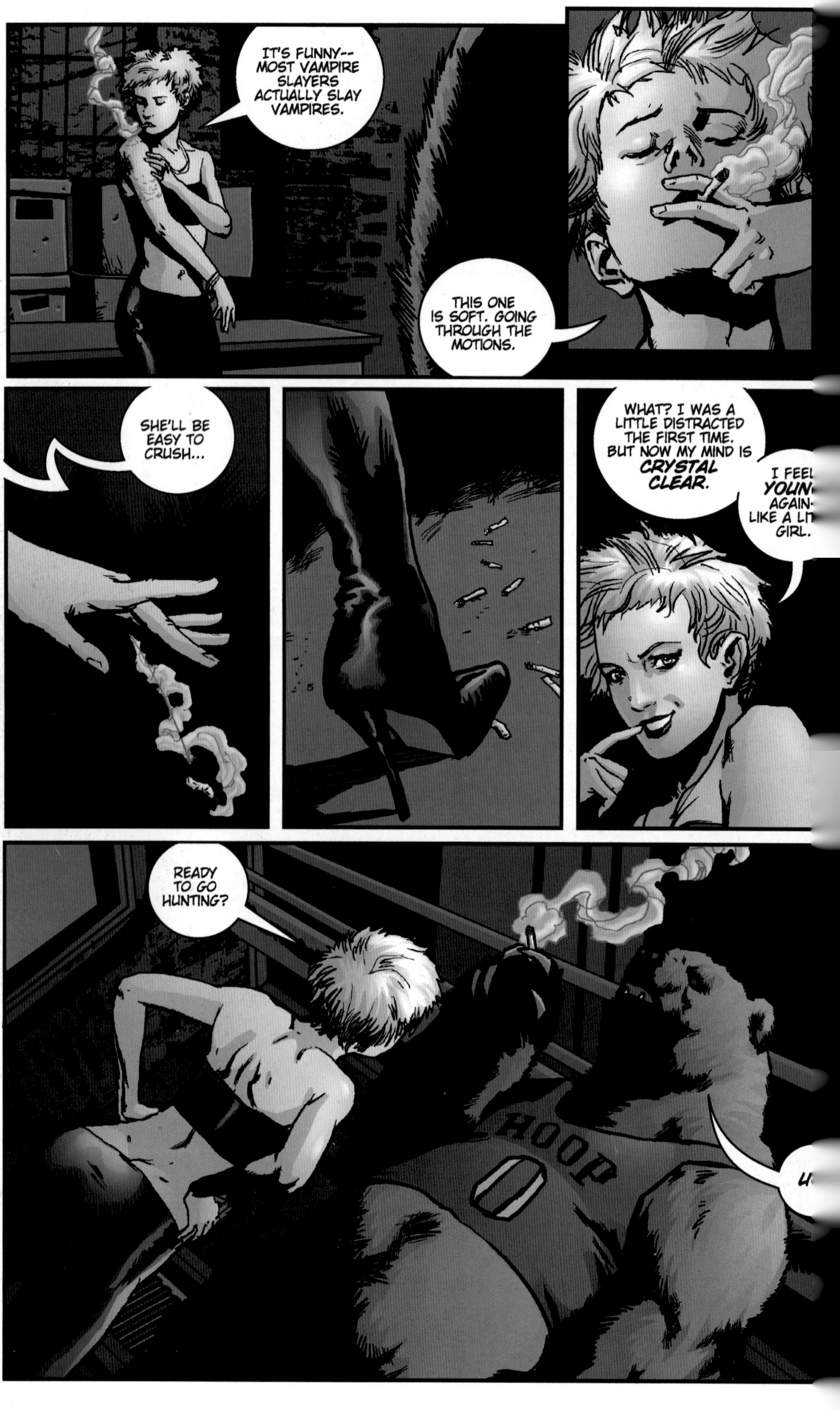
IT'S FUNNY--MOST VAMPIRE SLAYERS ACTUALLY SLAY VAMPIRES.
THIS ONE IS SOFT. GOING THROUGH THE MOTIONS.
SHE'LL BE EASY TO CRUSH...
WHAT? I WAS A LITTLE DISTRACTED THE FIRST TIME. BUT NOW MY MIND IS CRYSTAL CLEAR.
I FEEL YOUN AGAIN LIKE A LI GIRL.
READY TO GO HUNTING?
HOOP
0

STAY A LITTLE LONGER, PET.

DOGS ARE PETS, SPIKE. I'M--

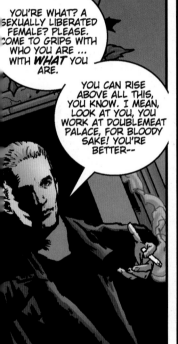

YOU'RE WHAT? A SEXUALLY LIBERATED FEMALE? PLEASE. COME TO GRIPS WITH WHO YOU ARE ... WITH *WHAT* YOU ARE.

YOU CAN RISE ABOVE ALL THIS, YOU KNOW. I MEAN, LOOK AT YOU, YOU WORK AT DOUBLEMEAT PALACE, FOR BLOODY SAKE! YOU'RE BETTER--

I'D KICK YOU, BUT ALL THE STRENGTH HAS GONE OUT OF MY LEGS.

OKAY, GO THEN. YOU BEST LOOK AFTER THE LITTLE BIT AND ALL. GET SOME QUALITY TIME, SIS TO SIS.

DAWN'S FINE, SHE DOESN'T NEED ME CROWDING HER.

I SENSE A PLAN COMING TOGETHER. YOU KNOW WHAT TO DO?

UG.

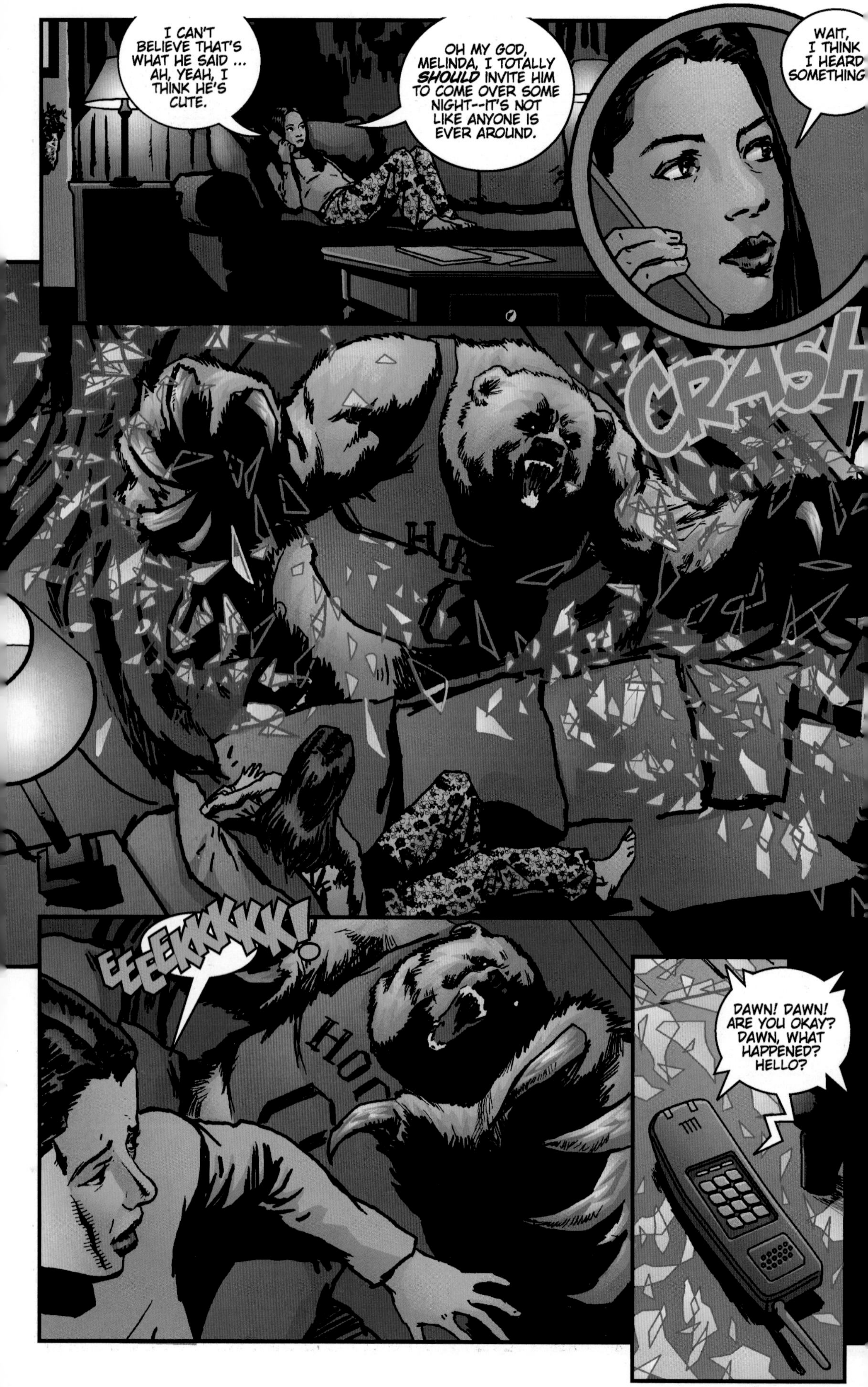
I CAN'T BELIEVE THAT'S WHAT HE SAID ... AH, YEAH, I THINK HE'S CUTE.
OH MY GOD, MELINDA, I TOTALLY SHOULD INVITE HIM TO COME OVER SOME NIGHT--IT'S NOT LIKE ANYONE IS EVER AROUND.
WAIT, I THINK I HEARD SOMETHING
CRASH
EEEEKKKKKK!
DAWN! DAWN! ARE YOU OKAY? DAWN, WHAT HAPPENED? HELLO?

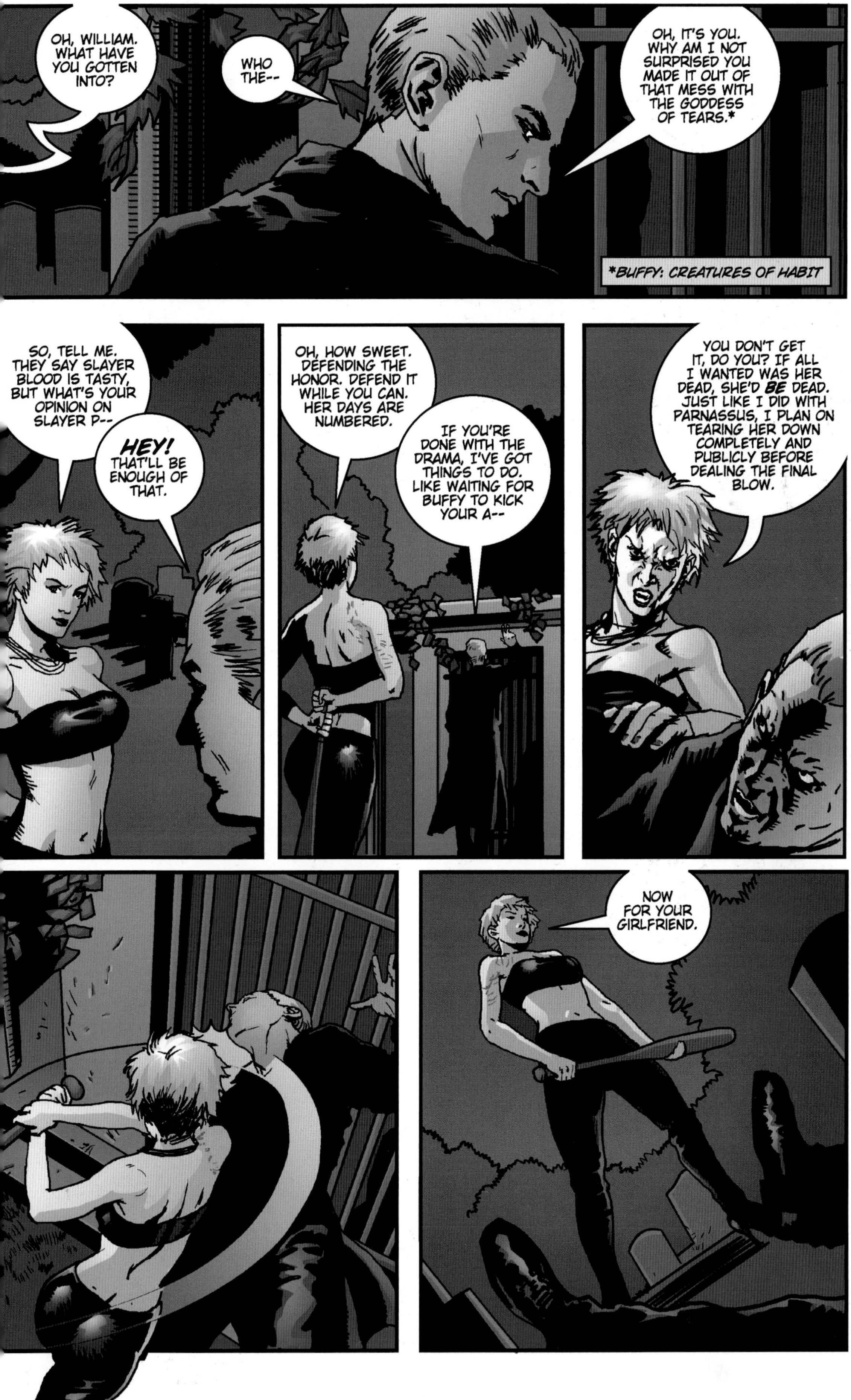
OH, WILLIAM. WHAT HAVE YOU GOTTEN INTO?
WHO THE--
OH, IT'S YOU. WHY AM I NOT SURPRISED YOU MADE IT OUT OF THAT MESS WITH THE GODDESS OF TEARS.*
*BUFFY: CREATURES OF HABIT
SO, TELL ME. THEY SAY SLAYER BLOOD IS TASTY, BUT WHAT'S YOUR OPINION ON SLAYER P--
HEY! THAT'LL BE ENOUGH OF THAT.
OH, HOW SWEET. DEFENDING THE HONOR. DEFEND IT WHILE YOU CAN. HER DAYS ARE NUMBERED.
IF YOU'RE DONE WITH THE DRAMA, I'VE GOT THINGS TO DO. LIKE WAITING FOR BUFFY TO KICK YOUR A--
YOU DON'T GET IT, DO YOU? IF ALL I WANTED WAS HER DEAD, SHE'D BE DEAD. JUST LIKE I DID WITH PARNASSUS, I PLAN ON TEARING HER DOWN COMPLETELY AND PUBLICLY BEFORE DEALING THE FINAL BLOW.
NOW FOR YOUR GIRLFRIEND.

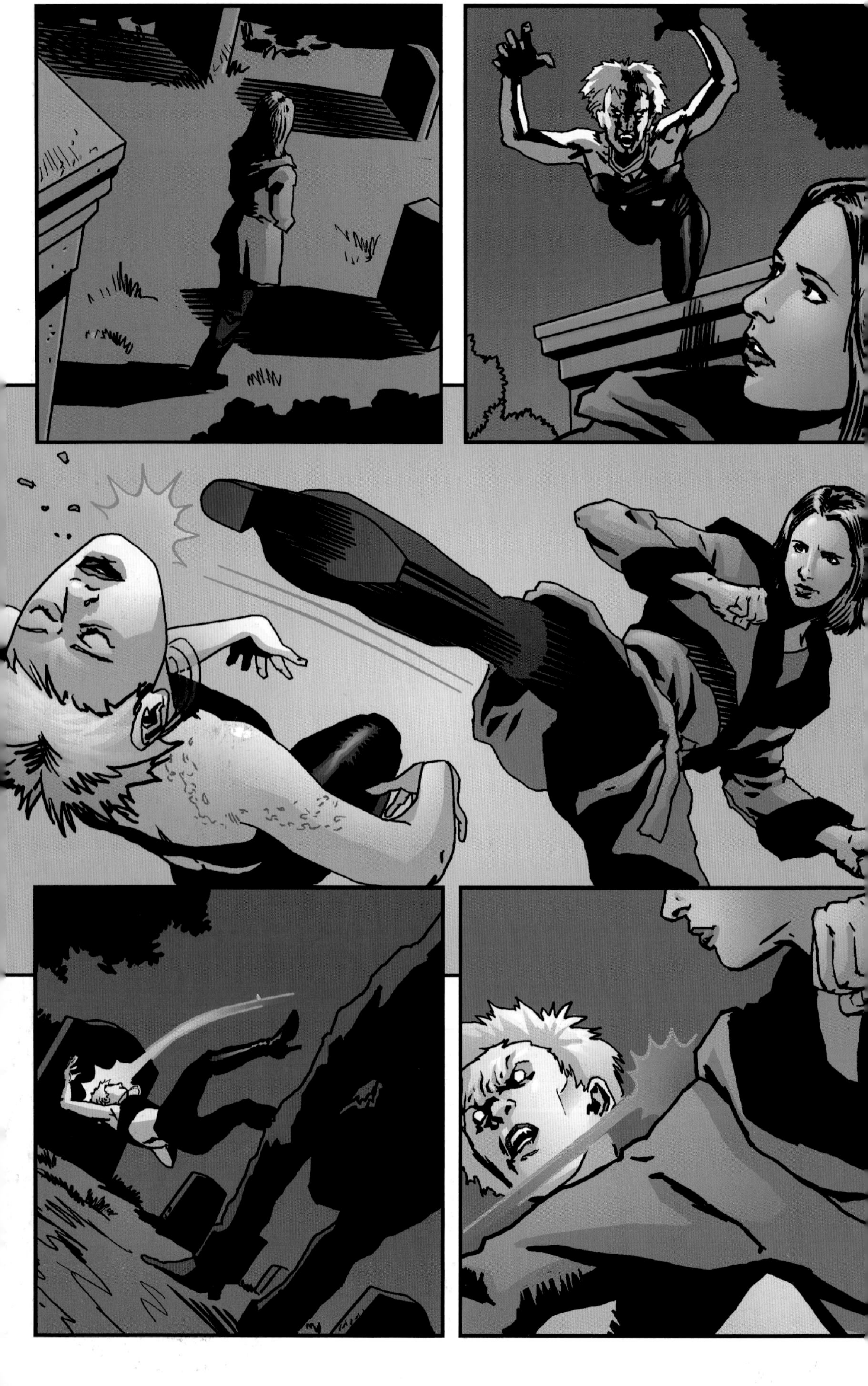

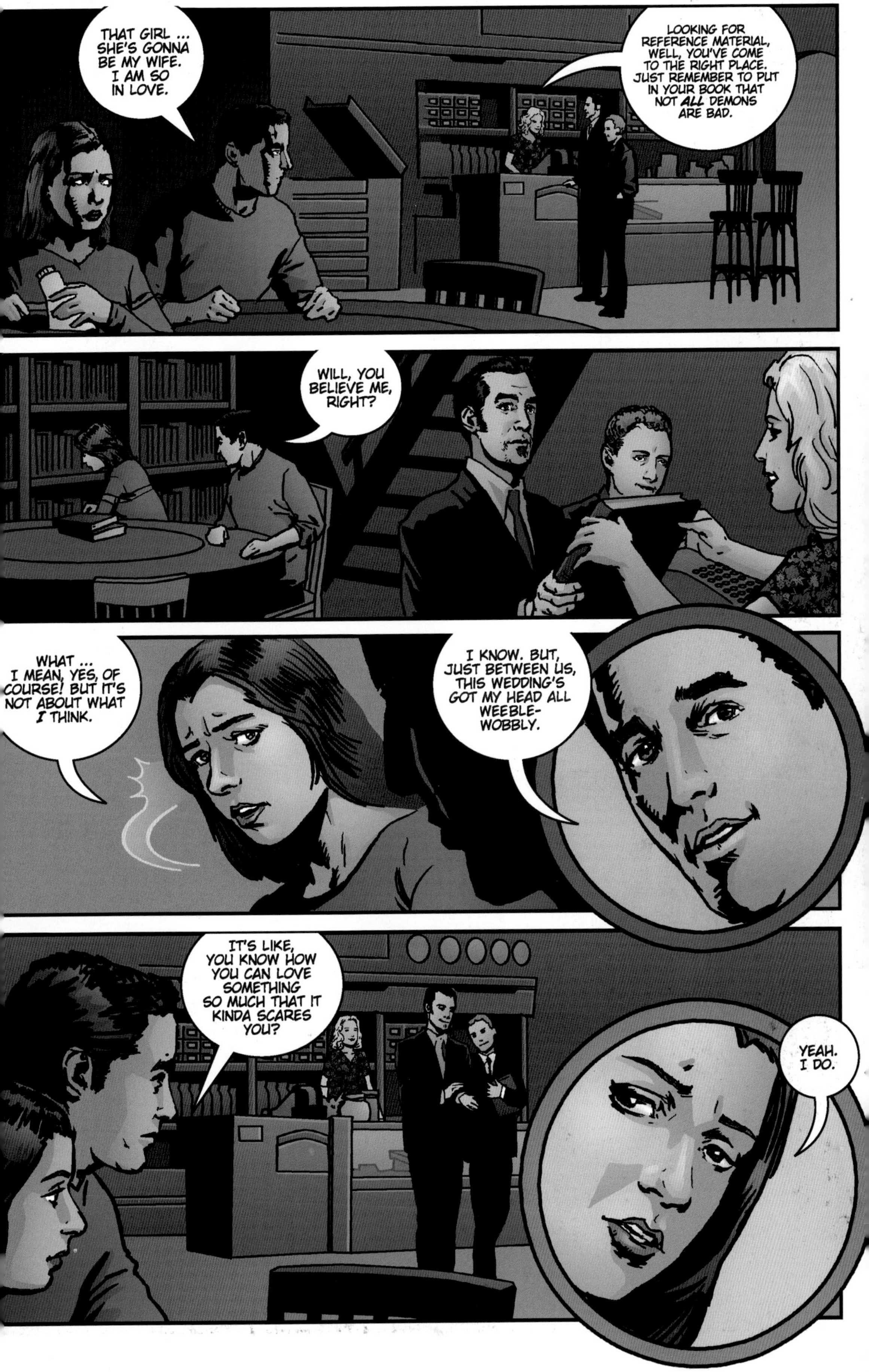
THAT GIRL ... SHE'S GONNA BE MY WIFE. I AM SO IN LOVE.
LOOKING FOR REFERENCE MATERIAL, WELL, YOU'VE COME TO THE RIGHT PLACE. JUST REMEMBER TO PUT IN YOUR BOOK THAT NOT ALL DEMONS ARE BAD.
WILL, YOU BELIEVE ME, RIGHT?
WHAT ... I MEAN, YES, OF COURSE! BUT IT'S NOT ABOUT WHAT I THINK.
I KNOW. BUT, JUST BETWEEN US, THIS WEDDING'S GOT MY HEAD ALL WEEBLE-WOBBLY.
IT'S LIKE, YOU KNOW HOW YOU CAN LOVE SOMETHING SO MUCH THAT IT KINDA SCARES YOU?
YEAH. I DO.

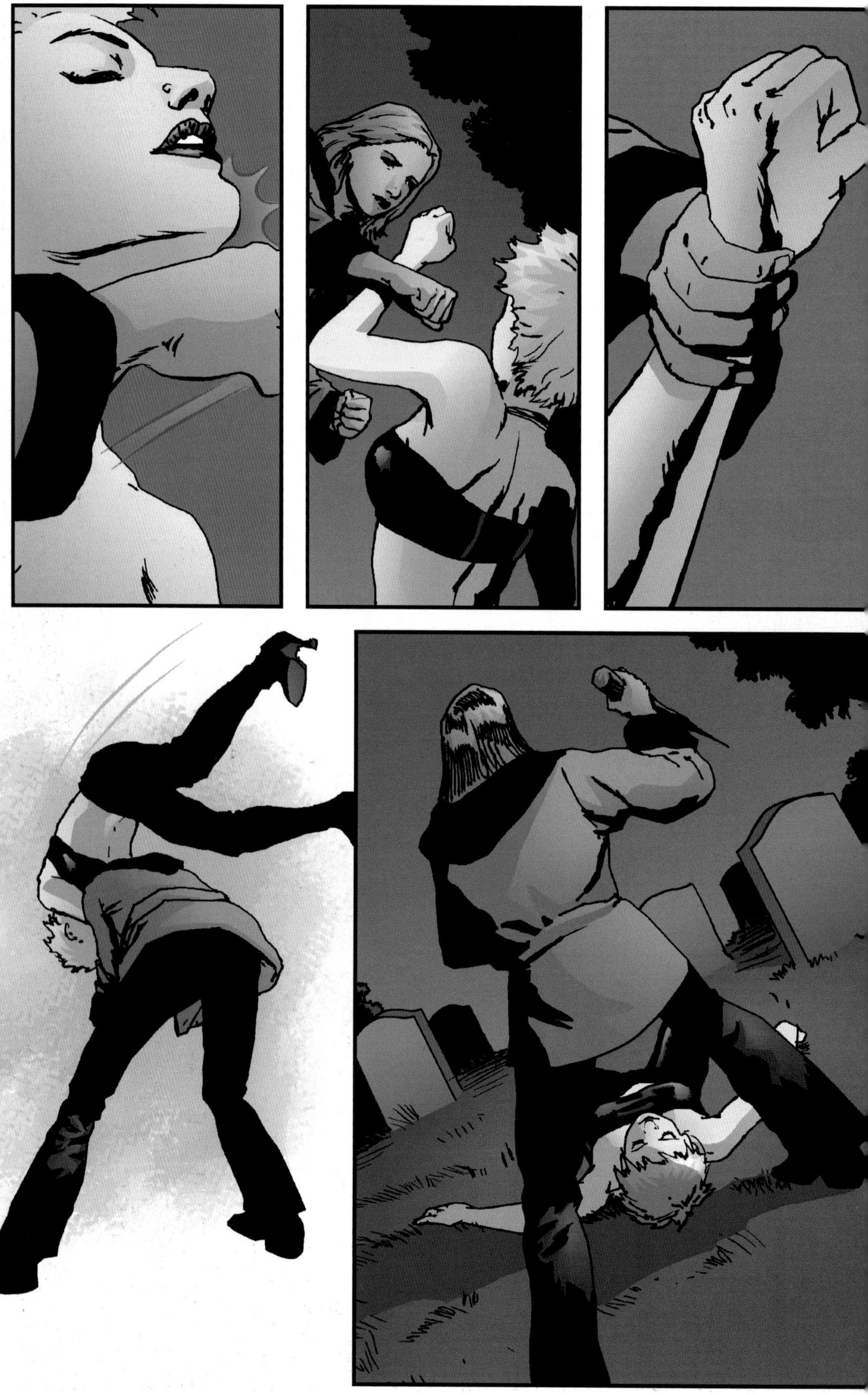

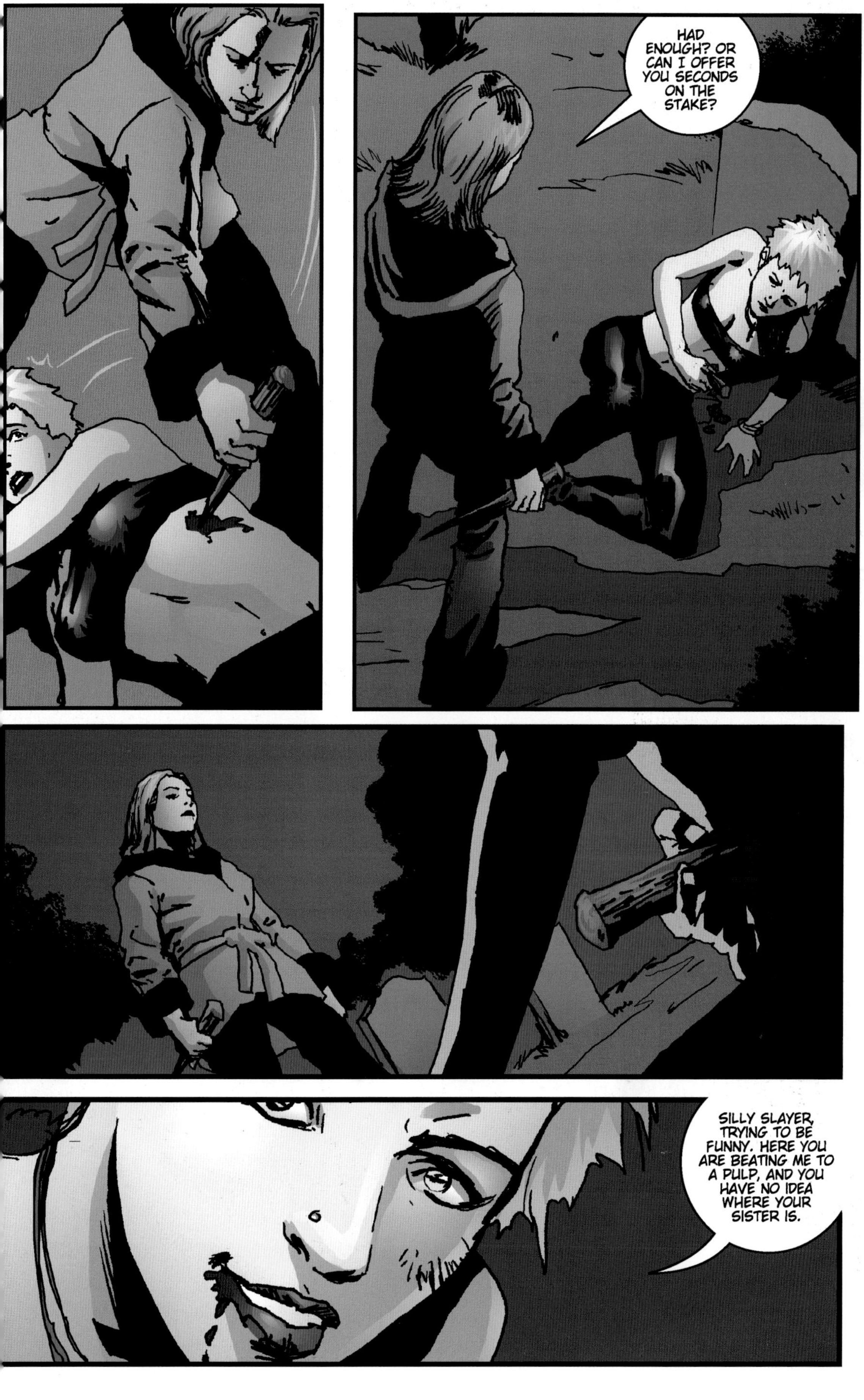
HAD ENOUGH? OR CAN I OFFER YOU SECONDS ON THE STAKE?
SILLY SLAYER, TRYING TO BE FUNNY. HERE YOU ARE BEATING ME TO A PULP, AND YOU HAVE NO IDEA WHERE YOUR SISTER IS.

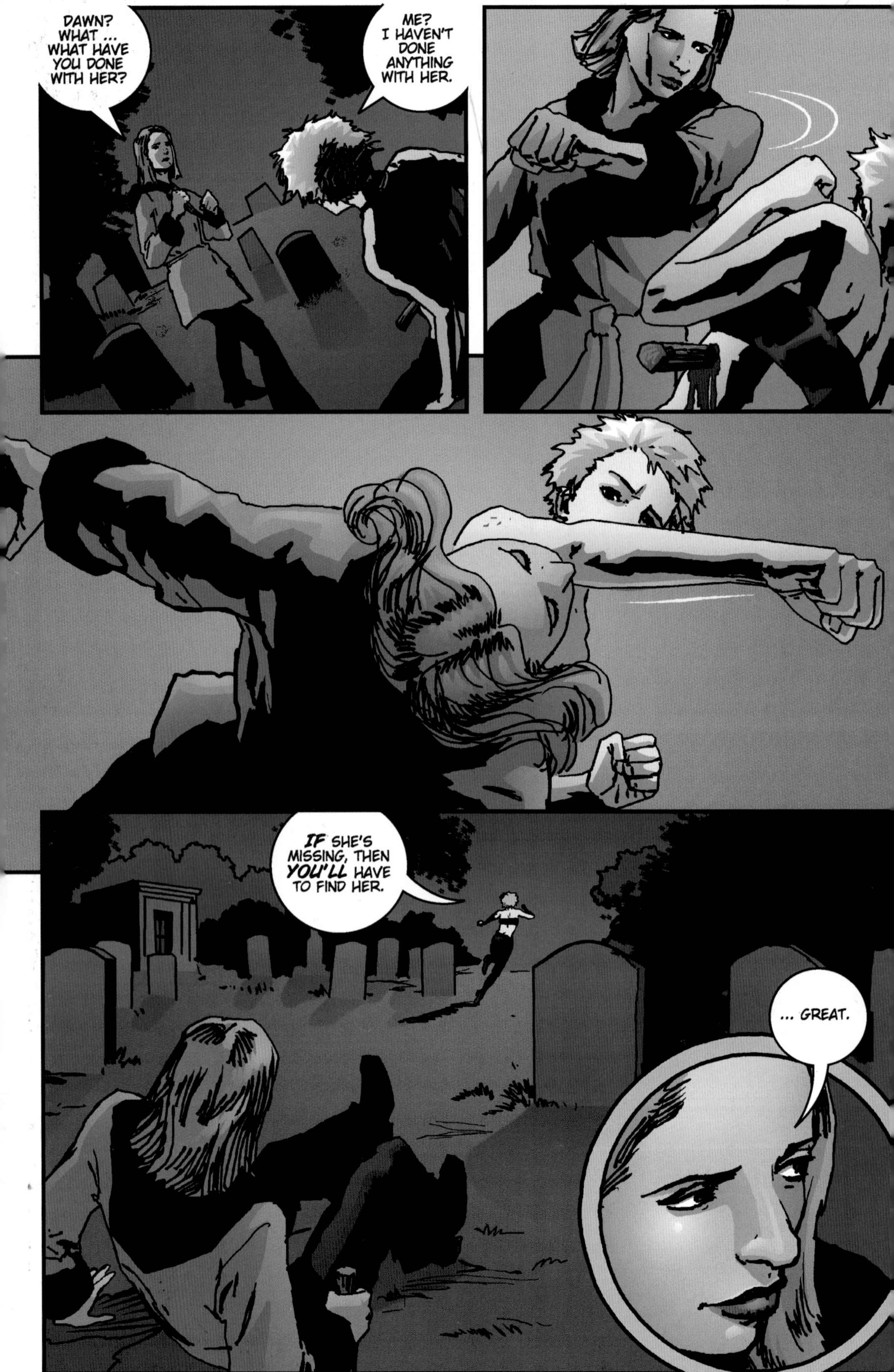
DAWN? WHAT ... WHAT HAVE YOU DONE WITH HER?
ME? I HAVEN'T DONE ANYTHING WITH HER.
IF SHE'S MISSING, THEN YOU'LL HAVE TO FIND HER.
... GREAT.

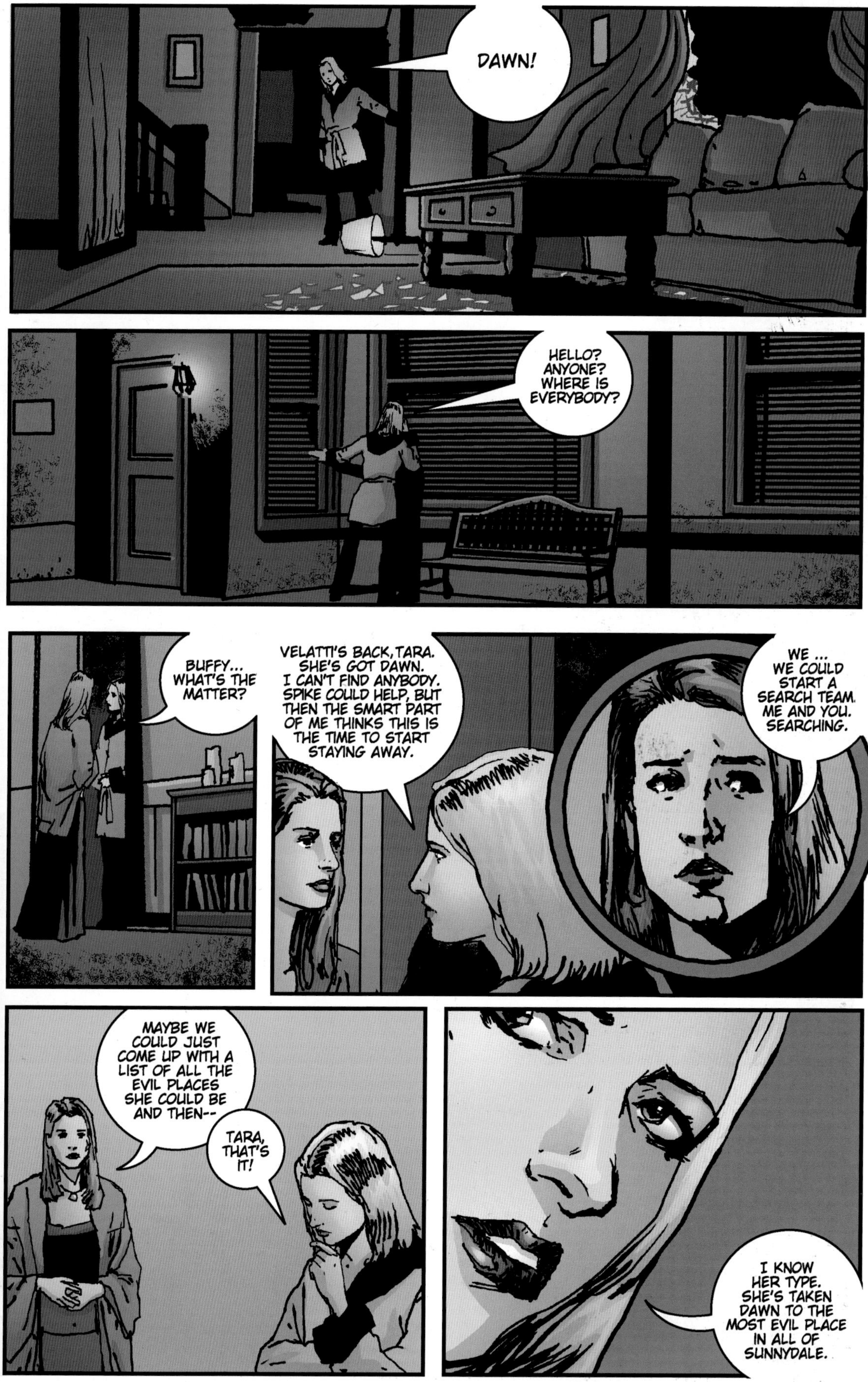
DAWN!
HELLO? ANYONE? WHERE IS EVERYBODY?
BUFFY... WHAT'S THE MATTER?
VELATTI'S BACK, TARA. SHE'S GOT DAWN. I CAN'T FIND ANYBODY. SPIKE COULD HELP, BUT THEN THE SMART PART OF ME THINKS THIS IS THE TIME TO START STAYING AWAY.
WE ... WE COULD START A SEARCH TEAM. ME AND YOU. SEARCHING.
MAYBE WE COULD JUST COME UP WITH A LIST OF ALL THE EVIL PLACES SHE COULD BE AND THEN--
TARA, THAT'S IT!
I KNOW HER TYPE. SHE'S TAKEN DAWN TO THE MOST EVIL PLACE IN ALL OF SUNNYDALE.

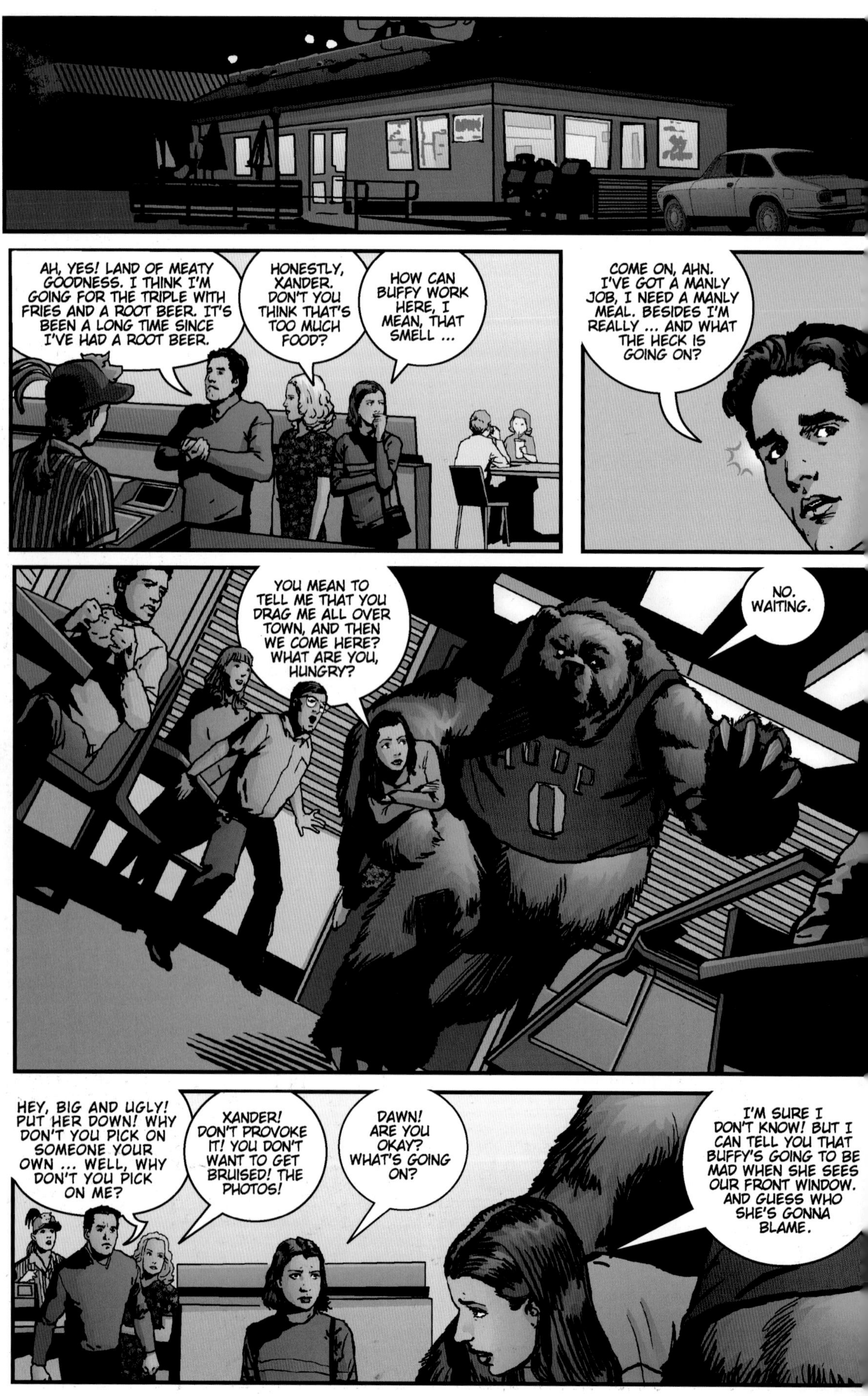
AH, YES! LAND OF MEATY GOODNESS. I THINK I'M GOING FOR THE TRIPLE WITH FRIES AND A ROOT BEER. IT'S BEEN A LONG TIME SINCE I'VE HAD A ROOT BEER.
HONESTLY, XANDER. DON'T YOU THINK THAT'S TOO MUCH FOOD?
HOW CAN BUFFY WORK HERE, I MEAN, THAT SMELL ...
COME ON, AHN. I'VE GOT A MANLY JOB, I NEED A MANLY MEAL. BESIDES I'M REALLY ... AND WHAT THE HECK IS GOING ON?
YOU MEAN TO TELL ME THAT YOU DRAG ME ALL OVER TOWN, AND THEN WE COME HERE? WHAT ARE YOU, HUNGRY?
NO. WAITING.
HOOP
0
HEY, BIG AND UGLY! PUT HER DOWN! WHY DON'T YOU PICK ON SOMEONE YOUR OWN ... WELL, WHY DON'T YOU PICK ON ME?
XANDER! DON'T PROVOKE IT! YOU DON'T WANT TO GET BRUISED! THE PHOTOS!
DAWN! ARE YOU OKAY? WHAT'S GOING ON?
I'M SURE I DON'T KNOW! BUT I CAN TELL YOU THAT BUFFY'S GOING TO BE MAD WHEN SHE SEES OUR FRONT WINDOW. AND GUESS WHO SHE'S GONNA BLAME.

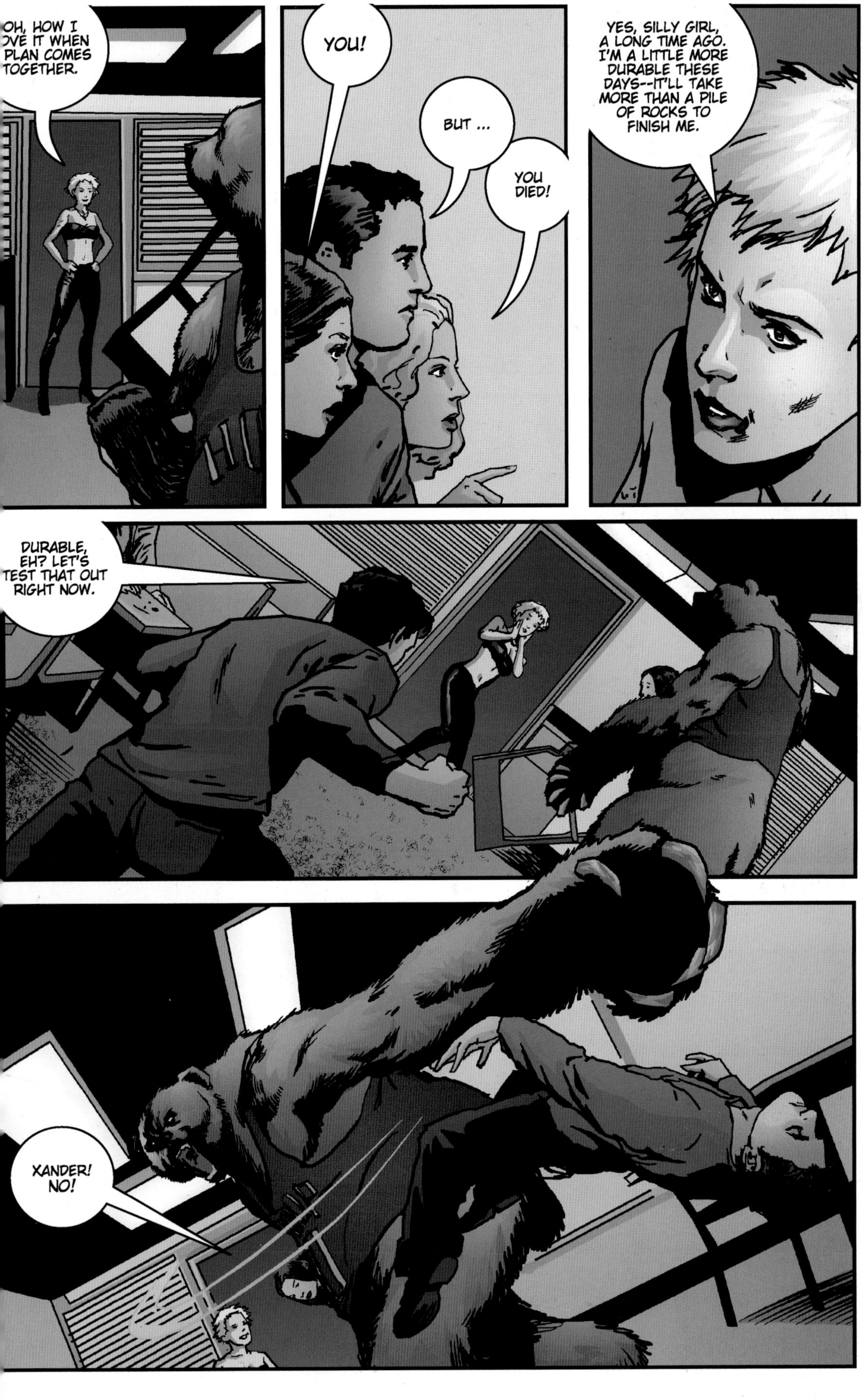
OH, HOW I OVE IT WHEN PLAN COMES TOGETHER.
YOU!
BUT ...
YOU DIED!
YES, SILLY GIRL, A LONG TIME AGO. I'M A LITTLE MORE DURABLE THESE DAYS--IT'LL TAKE MORE THAN A PILE OF ROCKS TO FINISH ME.
DURABLE, EH? LET'S TEST THAT OUT RIGHT NOW.
XANDER! NO!

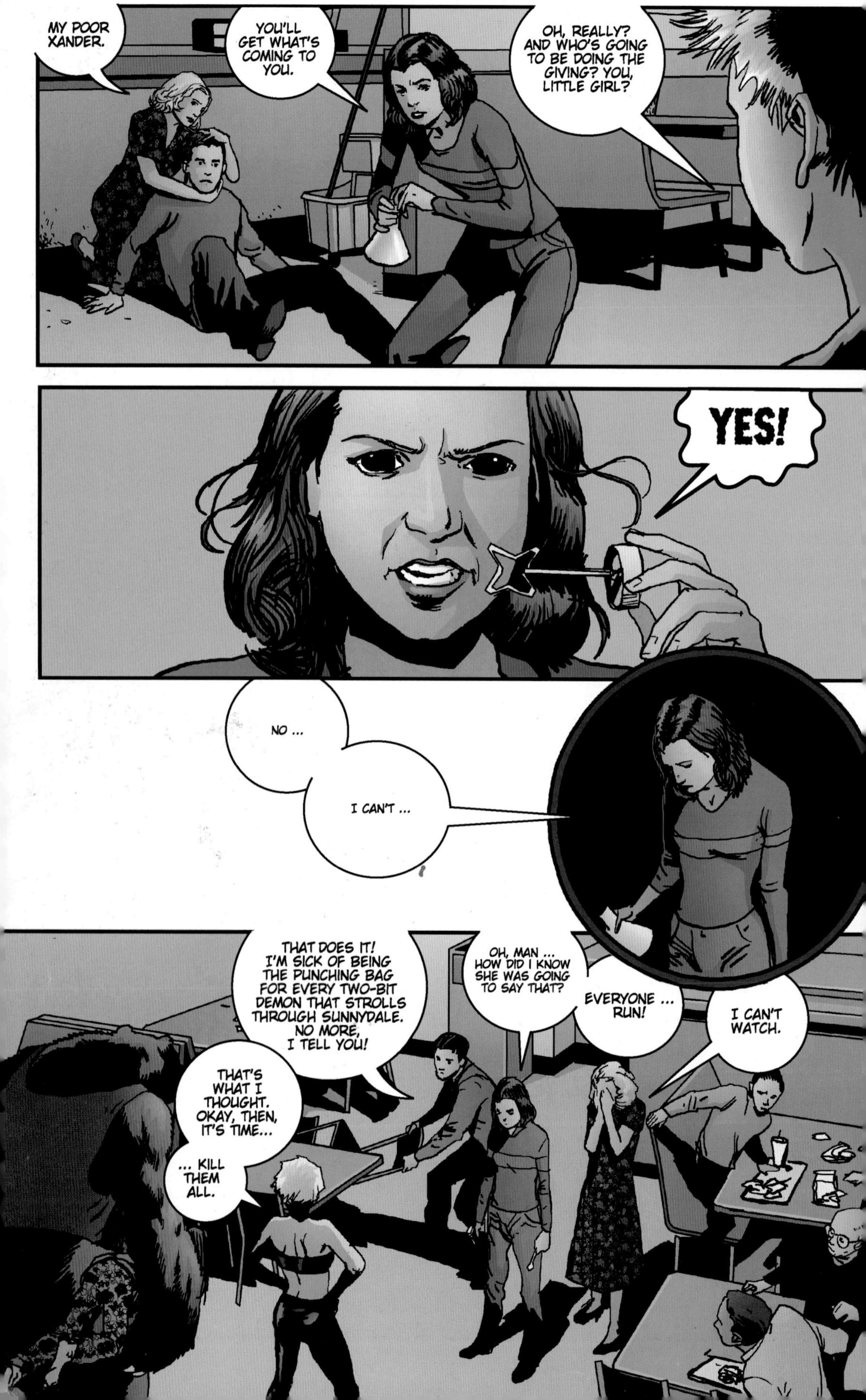
MY POOR XANDER.
YOU'LL GET WHAT'S COMING TO YOU.
OH, REALLY? AND WHO'S GOING TO BE DOING THE GIVING? YOU, LITTLE GIRL?
YES!
NO ...
I CAN'T ...
THAT DOES IT! I'M SICK OF BEING THE PUNCHING BAG FOR EVERY TWO-BIT DEMON THAT STROLLS THROUGH SUNNYDALE. NO MORE, I TELL YOU!
OH, MAN ... HOW DID I KNOW SHE WAS GOING TO SAY THAT?
EVERYONE ... RUN!
I CAN'T WATCH.
THAT'S WHAT I THOUGHT. OKAY, THEN, IT'S TIME...
... KILL THEM ALL.

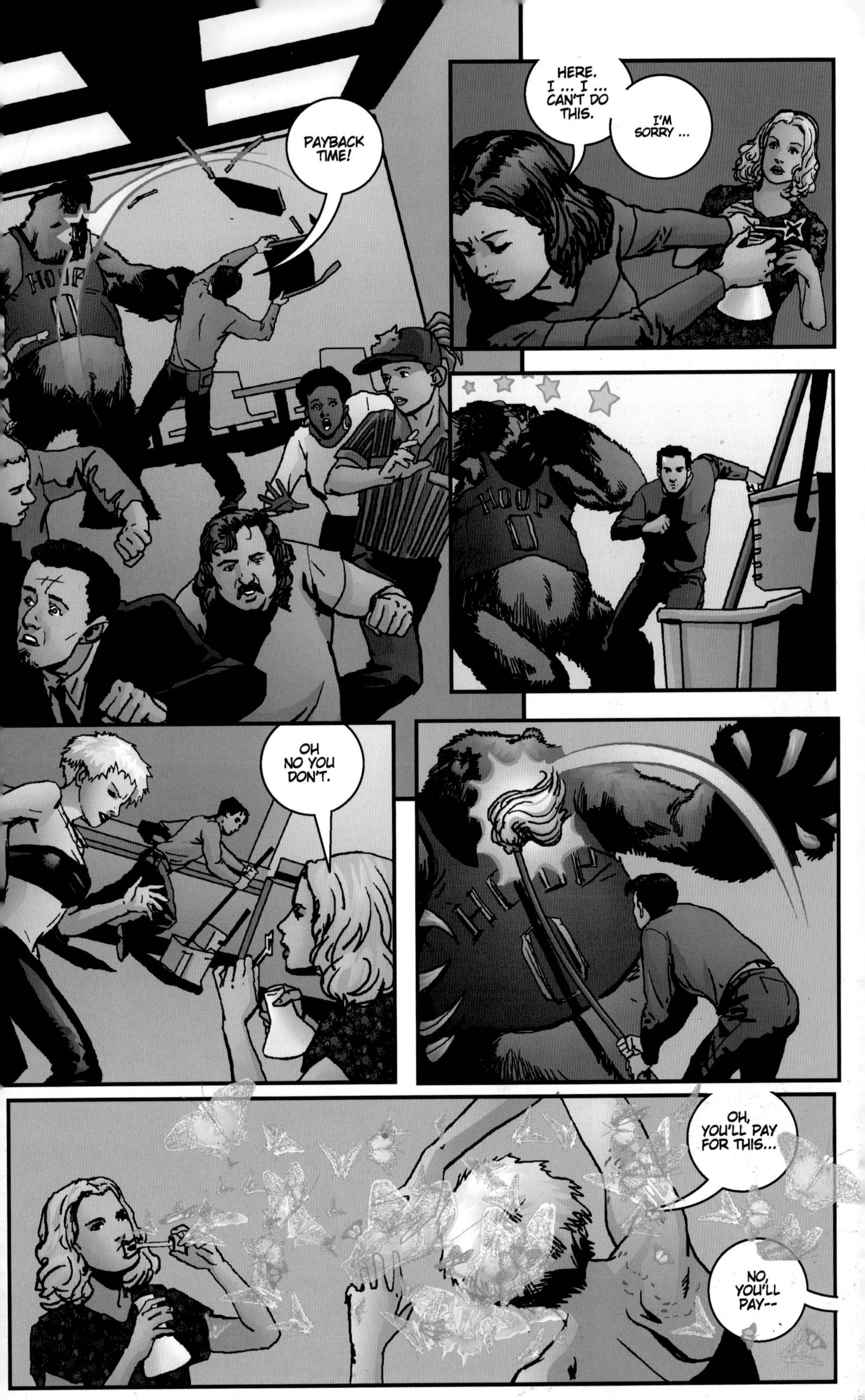
PAYBACK TIME!
HERE. I ... I ... CAN'T DO THIS.
I'M SORRY ...
HOOP
HOOP
OH NO YOU DON'T.
OH, YOU'LL PAY FOR THIS...
NO, YOU'LL PAY--

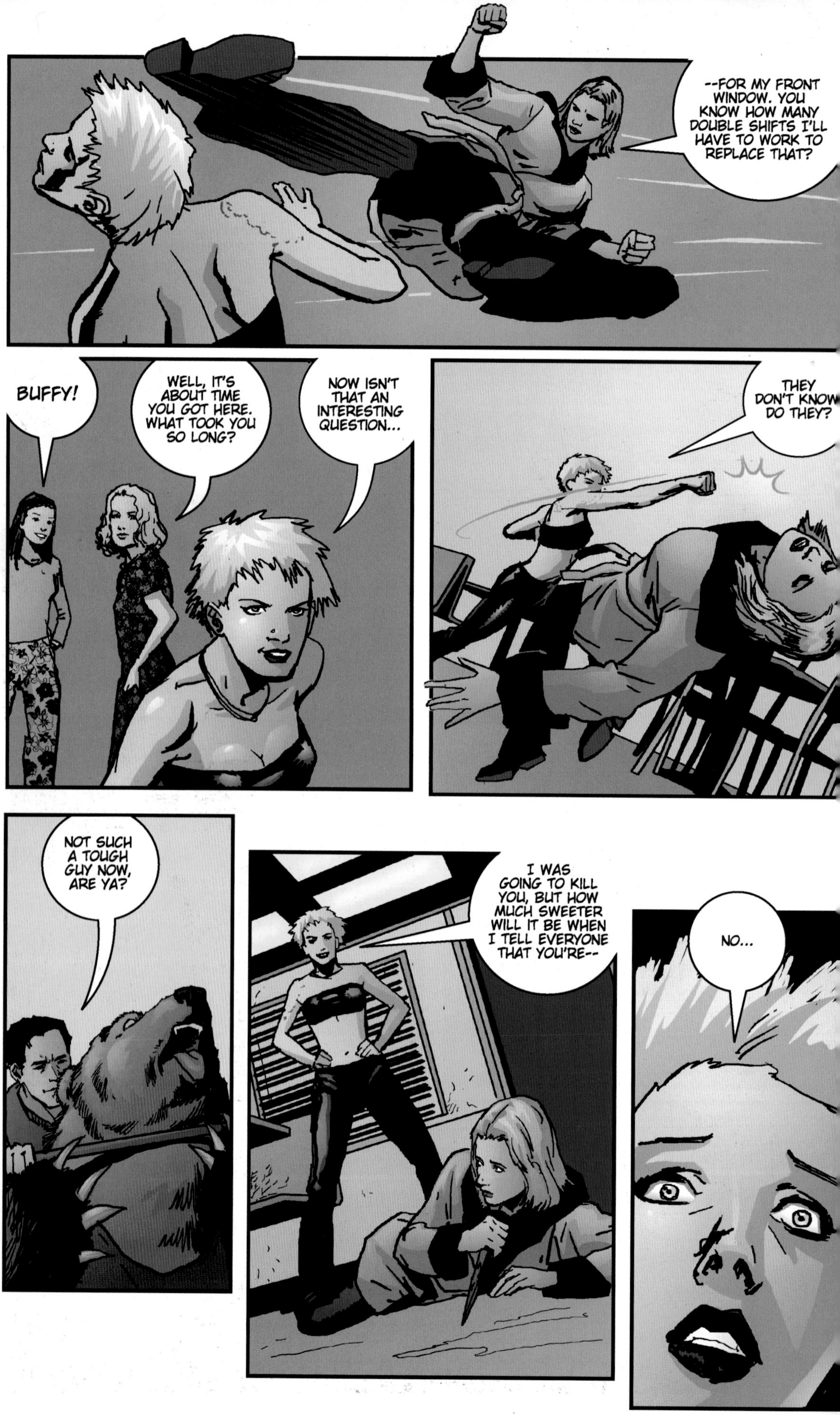
--FOR MY FRONT WINDOW. YOU KNOW HOW MANY DOUBLE SHIFTS I'LL HAVE TO WORK TO REPLACE THAT?
BUFFY!
WELL, IT'S ABOUT TIME YOU GOT HERE. WHAT TOOK YOU SO LONG?
NOW ISN'T THAT AN INTERESTING QUESTION...
THEY DON'T KNOW DO THEY?
NOT SUCH A TOUGH GUY NOW, ARE YA?
I WAS GOING TO KILL YOU, BUT HOW MUCH SWEETER WILL IT BE WHEN I TELL EVERYONE THAT YOU'RE--
NO...

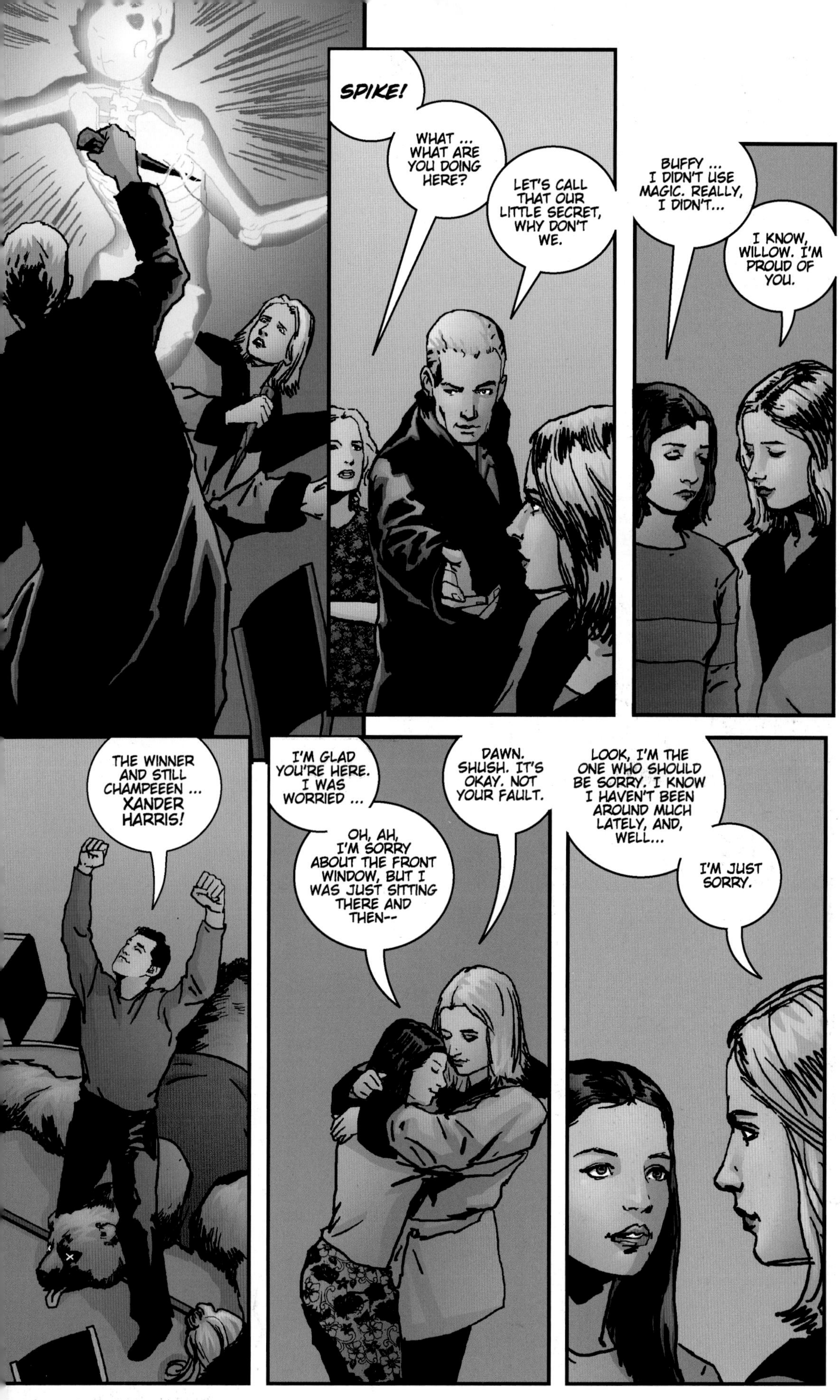

SPIKE!
WHAT ... WHAT ARE YOU DOING HERE?
LET'S CALL THAT OUR LITTLE SECRET, WHY DON'T WE.
BUFFY ... I DIDN'T USE MAGIC. REALLY, I DIDN'T...
I KNOW, WILLOW. I'M PROUD OF YOU.
THE WINNER AND STILL CHAMPEEEN ... XANDER HARRIS!
I'M GLAD YOU'RE HERE. I WAS WORRIED ...
OH, AH, I'M SORRY ABOUT THE FRONT WINDOW, BUT I WAS JUST SITTING THERE AND THEN--
DAWN. SHUSH. IT'S OKAY. NOT YOUR FAULT.
LOOK, I'M THE ONE WHO SHOULD BE SORRY. I KNOW I HAVEN'T BEEN AROUND MUCH LATELY, AND, WELL...
I'M JUST SORRY.

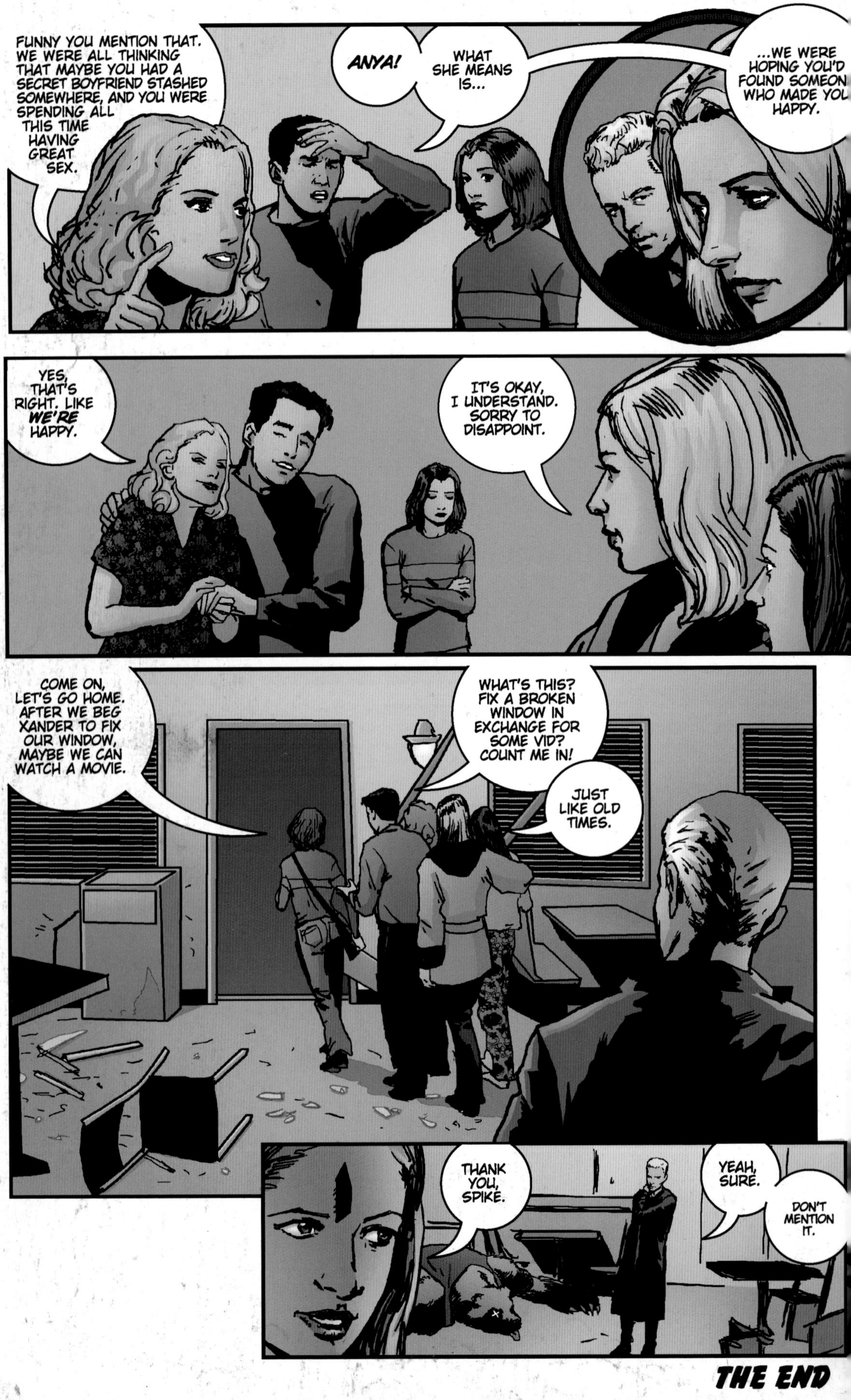
FUNNY YOU MENTION THAT. WE WERE ALL THINKING THAT MAYBE YOU HAD A SECRET BOYFRIEND STASHED SOMEWHERE, AND YOU WERE SPENDING ALL THIS TIME HAVING GREAT SEX.
ANYA!
WHAT SHE MEANS IS...
...WE WERE HOPING YOU'D FOUND SOMEONE WHO MADE YOU HAPPY.
YES, THAT'S RIGHT. LIKE *WE'RE* HAPPY.
IT'S OKAY, I UNDERSTAND. SORRY TO DISAPPOINT.
COME ON, LET'S GO HOME. AFTER WE BEG XANDER TO FIX OUR WINDOW, MAYBE WE CAN WATCH A MOVIE.
WHAT'S THIS? FIX A BROKEN WINDOW IN EXCHANGE FOR SOME VID? COUNT ME IN!
JUST LIKE OLD TIMES.
THANK YOU, SPIKE.
YEAH, SURE.
DON'T MENTION IT.
THE END

Stake out these Angel and Buffy the Vampire Slayer trade paperbacks

ANGEL
The Hollower

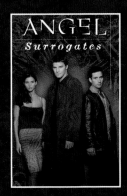

ANGEL
Surrogates

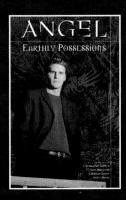

ANGEL
Earthly Possessions

ANGEL
Hunting Ground

the blood of Carthage

Out of the Woodwork

the ORIGIN

false Memories

Ring of Fire

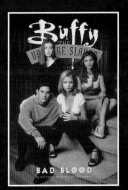

BAD BLOOD

CRASH TEST DEMONS

PALE REFLECTIONS

Spike and Dru

FOOD CHAIN

AUTUMNAL

ANGEL
PAST LIVES

Angel™ & © 2002 Twentieth Century Fox Film Corporation. Buffy the Vampire Slayer™ & ©2002 Twentieth Century Fox Film Corporation. TM designates a trademark of Twentieth Century Fox Film Corporation. Dark Horse Comics® and the Dark Horse logo are trademarks of Dark Horse Comics, Inc., registered in various categories and countries. All rights reserved. www.buffy.com

CHECK OUT THESE *BUFFY THE VAMPIRE SLAYER*™ GRAPHIC NOVELS AVAILABLE FROM COMICS SHOPS AND BOOKSTORES!

    Ring of Fire

BUFFY THE VAMPIRE SLAYER

THE DUST WALTZ
Brereton • Gomez • Florea
color paperback
ISBN: 1-56971-342-1 $9.95

THE REMAINING SUNLIGHT
Watson • Bennett • Ketcham
color paperback
ISBN: 1-56971-354-5 $9.95

THE ORIGIN
From the original screenplay!
Golden • Brereton • Bennett • Ketcham
color paperback
ISBN: 1-56971-429-0 $9.95

UNINVITED GUESTS
Watson • Gomez • Florea
color paperback
ISBN: 1-56971-436-3 $10.95

SUPERNATURAL DEFENSE KIT
Watson • Richards • Pimentel
color hardcover w/slipcase
comes with golden-colored cross,
"claddagh" ring, and vial of "holy water"
ISBN: 1-56971-486-X $19.95

BAD BLOOD
Watson • Bennett • Ketcham
color paperback
ISBN: 1-56971-445-2 $9.95

CRASH TEST DEMONS
Watson • Richards • Pimentel
color paperback
ISBN: 1-56971-461-4 $9.95

RING OF FIRE
Petrie • Sook
color paperback
Written by *Buffy the Vampire Slayer*
TV show writer Doug Petrie!
ISBN: 1-56971-482-7 $9.95

PALE REFLECTIONS
Watson • Richards • Pimentel
color paperback
ISBN: 1-56971-475-4 $9.95

THE BLOOD OF CARTHAGE
Golden • Richards • Pimentel
color paperback
ISBN: 1-56971-534-3 $12.95

FOOD CHAIN
Petrie • Golden • Richards • Others
color paperback
ISBN: 1-56971-602-1 $17.95

AUTUMNAL
Boal • Fassbender • Pascoe • Richards
color paperback
ISBN: 1-56971-554-8 $9.95

SPIKE AND DRU
Marsters • Golden • Sook • Powell
color paperback
ISBN: 1-56971-541-6 $11.95

BUFFY/ANGEL: PAST LIVES
Golden • Sniegoski • Richards• Zanier
color paperback
ISBN: 1-56971-552-1 $9.95

TALES OF THE SLAYERS
Whedon • Petrie • Benson • Others
color paperback
Written by *Buffy the Vampire Slayer*
creator Joss Whedon, TV show writer
Doug Petrie, Buffy's "Tara" Amber Benson,
and others!
ISBN: 1-56971-605-6 $14.95

OUT OF THE WOODWORK
Fassbender • Pascoe • Richards • Pimentel
color paperback
ISBN: 1-56971-738-9 $12.95

FALSE MEMORIES
Fassbender • Pascoe • Richards • Pimentel
color paperback
ISBN: 1-56971-736-2 $12.95

CREATURES OF HABIT
Illustrated novel
Fassbender • Pascoe • Horton • Lee
color paperback
ISBN: 1-56971-563-7 $17.95

UGLY LITTLE MONSTERS
Fassbender • Pascoe • Richards
color paperback
ISBN: 1-56971-750-8 $12.95

HAUNTED
Espenson • Richards
color paperback
ISBN: 1-56971-737-0 $12.95

THE DEATH OF BUFFY
Fassbender • Pascoe • Nicieza •
Richards
color paperback
ISBN: 1-56971-748-6 $12.95

And don't miss these *Angel* grap
novels available at comics shop
& bookstores!

ANGEL

THE HOLLOWER
Golden • Gomez • Florea
color paperback
ISBN: 1-56971-450-9 $9.95

SURROGATES
Golden • Zanier • Owens
color paperback
ISBN: 1-56971-491-6 $9.95

HUNTING GROUND
Golden • Sniegoski • Horton • Lee
Powell
color paperback
ISBN: 1-56971-547-5 $9.95

AUTUMNAL
Golden • Sniegoski • Zanier • Pov
color paperback
ISBN: 1-56971-559-9 $9.95

STRANGE BEDFELLOWS
Golden • Sniegoski • Zanier • Pov
color paperback
ISBN: 1-56971-753-2 $12.95

Don't miss the ongoing adventures from *Buffy the Vampire Slayer*
and *Angel* comics every month! Available at your local comics shop.
To locate a comics shop in your area, call 1-888-266-4226.
www.darkhorse.com • www.buffy.com

Available from your local comics shop or bookstore!

To find a comics shop in your area, call 1-888-266-4226
For more information or to order direct:
•On the web: www.darkhorse.com •E-mail: mailorder@darkhorse.com
•Phone: 1-800-862-0052 or (503) 652-9701 Mon.-Sat. 9 A.M. to 5 P.M. Pacific Time
*Prices and availability subject to change without notice

Angel™, *Buffy the Vampire Slayer*™ & © 2002 Twentieth Century Fox Film Corporation. All rights reserved.
TM designates a trademark of Twentieth Century Fox Film Corporation. Dark Horse Comics® and the Dark Horse
logo are trademarks of Dark Horse Comics, Inc., registered in various categories and countries. All rights reserved.